Apple Training Series

GarageBand

Mary Plummer

Apple
Certified

Apple Training Series: GarageBand
Mary Plummer
Copyright © 2004 by Mary Plummer

Published by Peachpit Press. For information on Peachpit Press books, contact:

Peachpit Press
1249 Eighth Street
Berkeley, CA 94710
(510) 524-2178
Fax: (510) 524-2221
http://www.peachpit.com
To report errors, please send a note to errata@peachpit.com
Peachpit Press is a division of Pearson Education

Editor: Serena Herr
Production Coordinator: Hilal Sala
Project Editor: Geta Carlson
Technical Editor: Stephen Kanter
Technical Reviewer: Robert Brock
Copy Editor: Darren Meiss
Compositor: David Van Ness
Indexer: Jack Lewis
Interior Design: Frances Baca
Cover Design: Frances Baca Design and Tolleson Design
Cover Illustration: Tolleson Design; images © Getty Images, Inc;
keyboard photo provide by D&W Images

ISBN 0-321-26876-8
9 8 7 6 5 4 3 2 1

Printed and bound in the United States of America

Dedicated to the universal language of music, and GarageBand
for bringing the world a little closer one song at a time.

Acknowledgments

First and foremost, deepest thanks to my partner in business and life, Klark Perez, for your incredible devotion and strength in carrying the weight for both of us and our company InVision Digital and Media Arts while I was writing.

Thanks to Patty Montesion for a career I adore as an Apple Certified Trainer, and the extraordinary opportunity to write this book.

Thanks to Serena Herr and the amazing Peachpit Press team for making this book a reality: William Rodarmor, Darren Meiss, Hilal Sala, David Van Ness, Jack Lewis and Jay Payne. Special thanks to Geta Carlson, who led this writing marathon like a coach, air traffic controller, and friend. Thanks also Steve Kanter for great notes and Robert Brock for your audio recording experience.

Thanks to our friends at Universal Studios Florida for the opportunity to have a production company and training center on the lot, and for providing the ultimate creative environment.

Thank you William L. Whitacre for your guitar recordings and advice.

I also want to acknowledge the piano teachers from my youth, Marla Knox and Katherine Knucklles. Also, Guy Marshall of Tutt & Babe music for producing my first album and inspiring songwriters and musicians with your time and talent.

Extra special thanks to my family for their unconditional love throughout my freelance career. Thanks "Meem," Lee, Dad, Ginny, Chris, Sessely, Jorin, Kim, Guy, Emily, Chris, Jackson, Peg, Jim, Sergio, Virginia, Kent, Klark, and my dog Niki. Finally, my mother Jane Ann, her mother Betty K. and her mother Kathryn for the musical gift and heirloom—your piano.

Contents at a Glance

Table of Contents

Introduction
Getting Started

Welcome to the official training course for GarageBand, Apple's dynamic and powerful music arrangement software. This book is a detailed guide to recording, arranging, and mixing music using GarageBand, instrument recordings, and the library of more than 1,000 royalty-free Apple Loops that is included with the software. It is based on the premise that a training book should go beyond a basic tour of the application by providing you with practical techniques that you will use on a daily basis to add professional-quality music and sound effects to your projects.

Whether you are a seasoned composer or have never written a piece of music before, you will learn how to use GarageBand for a variety of real world scenarios, including recording, arranging, and mixing music from scratch. You'll work with Real Instruments, MIDI Software Instruments, and prerecorded Apple Loops to edit music and add effects that sweeten your finished songs. Finally, you'll export your finished music to iTunes, where you'll learn to share it with the other iLife applications.

The Methodology

This book emphasizes hands-on training. Each exercise is designed to help you learn the application inside and out, starting with the basic interface and moving on to advanced music editing, arranging, and mixing techniques. The book assumes a basic level of familiarity with the Apple OS X operating system. If you are new to GarageBand, it would be helpful for you to start at the beginning and progress through each lesson in order, since each lesson builds on information learned in previous ones. If you are already familiar with GarageBand, you can start with any section and focus on that topic.

Course Structure

Each of the nine lessons in this book focuses on a different aspect of creating music with GarageBand. Each lesson expands on the basic concepts of the program, giving you the tools to use GarageBand for your own projects.

The lessons in this book are informally divided into four groups or sections:

- Lessons 1–2: Learning the interface and working in the Timeline
- Lessons 3–5: Using the different types of GarageBand musical regions, including Software Instruments, Real Instruments, and Apple Loops
- Lessons 6–8: Arranging, mixing, and exporting a finished song
- Lesson 9–Appendix A: Advanced GarageBand tips and techniques and the Jam Pack expansion kit

System Requirements

Before beginning to use *Apple Training Series: GarageBand*, you should have a working knowledge of your computer and its operating system. Make sure that you know how to use the mouse and the standard menus and commands and also how to open, save, and close files. If you need to review these techniques, see the printed or online documentation included with your system.

Basic system requirements for GarageBand are as follows:

- Mac OS X version 10.2.6 or later.

- GarageBand can be installed on a Macintosh computer with at least a 600 MHz G3 processor.

- At least 256 megabytes (MB) of memory.

- For use of Software Instruments, a Macintosh G4 or better is strongly recommended.

- In order to make full use of all features of GarageBand, a screen resolution of 1024 x 768 pixels or more is recommended.

- Approximately 2.5 GB of free disk space to install the GarageBand application and media.

System Requirements for Software Instruments

Software Instruments require a Macintosh G4 or faster and at least 256 MB of physical RAM. If you are working on a G3, you will not be able to play or record Software Instruments in GarageBand. You will be able to open the song; you just won't be able to play it without overloading your processor.

If you are working with a slower computer, follow along with the exercises in the book using the actual lessons to learn how to work with Software Instruments. Then, open the alternative version of the projects in the G3 folder included with the book. The G3 versions of the songs are re-creations of the songs using Real Instrument regions instead of Software Instrument regions. You will be able to play the songs in the G3 project to hear the different tracks and the finished songs.

If you are working with a slower computer, you will find some useful tips and techniques for dealing with slower computers in the first part of Lesson 9.

Hardware Compatibility

GarageBand can operate with any Core Audio- and Core MIDI-compliant audio interface, USB MIDI interface, or even a microphone, keyboard or guitar with the correct adapter. You may need to install additional drivers from the manufacturer of the audio interface in order to provide full Mac OS X support.

For a list of supported audio and MIDI interfaces that work with GarageBand, see the GarageBand Web site at www.apple.com/ilife/garageband/accessories.

Installing GarageBand

To install GarageBand, double-click the GarageBand installer and follow the instructions that appear.

If you see a message that you do not have sufficient privileges to install this software, click the lock icon in the installer window and enter an administrator name and password. The administrator users for your computer are shown in the Accounts pane of System Preferences.

The installer places the Instrument Library, the Apple Loops Library, and the index for the Apple Loops Library in the /Library/Application Support/GarageBand folder on your computer's hard drive. Do not move them from this location.

Copying the Lesson Files

This book includes an *ATS_GarageBand* CD-ROM containing all the files you'll need to complete the lessons. For each chapter of the book, there is a Lessons folder containing the applicable lessons, projects, and media. Inside each Lessons folder are Lesson subfolders organized by lesson number. Within each Lesson subfolder, you will find numbered projects for each exercise.

When you install these files on your computer, it's important to keep all of the numbered Lessons subfolders together in the main Lessons folder on your hard drive. If you copy the Lessons folder directly from the CD-ROM to your hard drive, you should not need to reconnect any media files or have problems opening projects.

Installing the Lesson Files

1   Put the *ATS_GarageBand* CD-ROM into your computer's CD-ROM drive.

2   Create a folder on your hard drive called *GarageBand_Book_Files*. Drag the Lessons folder from the CD to the GarageBand_Book_Files folder.

3   To begin each lesson, launch GarageBand. Then follow the instructions in the exercises to open the project files for that lesson.

About the Apple Training Series

GarageBand is part of the official training series for Apple iLife applications developed by experts in the field and certified by Apple Computer. The lessons are designed to let you learn at your own pace. Although each lesson provides step-by-step instructions for creating specific projects, there's room for exploration and experimentation. You can progress through the book from beginning to end, or dive right into the lessons that interest you most. It's up to you.

For those who prefer to learn in an instructor-led setting, Apple also offers training courses at Apple Authorized Training Centers worldwide. These courses, which use the Apple Training Series books as their curriculum, are taught by Apple Certified Trainers and balance concepts and lectures with hands-on labs and exercises. Apple Authorized Training Centers have been carefully selected and have met Apple's highest standards in all areas, including facilities, instructors, course delivery, and infrastructure. The goal of the program is to offer Apple customers, from beginners to the most seasoned professionals, the highest quality training experience.

To find an Authorized Training Center near you, go to www.apple.com/software/pro/training.

Resources

Apple Training Series: GarageBand is not intended to be a comprehensive reference manual, nor does it replace the documentation that comes with the application. For comprehensive information about program features, refer to these resources:

- The Reference Guide. Accessed through the GarageBand Help menu, the Reference Guide contains a complete description of all features.
- Apple's Web site: www.apple.com.

1

Lesson Files	Lessons > Lesson_01 > 1-1 Eyewitness
Time	This lesson takes approximately 60 minutes to complete.
Goals	Launch GarageBand
	Explore the GarageBand window
	Navigate in the Timeline
	Work with the transport controls
	Start and stop playback in the Timeline
	Open the Track Editor
	Compare Real Instruments and Software Instruments
	Open the Loop Browser
	Work with the Button and Column View buttons

Lesson **1**

Working with the Interface

GarageBand is powerful enough to record and mix a professional-sounding music demo, yet simple enough that anyone can use it right out of the box.

Over the years, I've worked with many frustrated musicians who bought their first computers and software specifically to try recording their own music. Unfortunately, instead of finding inspiration and a new creative tool, they got more frustrated because the software was way too complicated.

That was before GarageBand. This software is different. You don't have to be a computer major or audio engineer to record music. You don't even have to be a musician. If you can click a mouse, you can turn your Mac into a basic recording studio—it's really that simple.

In this lesson, you'll work with the GarageBand interface and learn how to use the transport controls and navigate in the Timeline. Along the way, you'll learn some useful keyboard shortcuts as you get to know the program.

Before You Start

Before you start, you need to load the GarageBand program onto your hard drive. You also need to copy the lesson files from the CD in the back of the book to your computer.

The instructions for loading the software and files are in "Getting Started," the introduction to this book. Once those two steps are complete, you can move forward with this lesson.

Now that you have the GarageBand program and lesson files loaded onto your hard drive, you're ready to begin this lesson.

Launching GarageBand

There are three ways to launch GarageBand:

- Double-click the GarageBand application icon in your hard drive.

- Click once on the GarageBand icon in the Dock.

- Double-click any GarageBand project file.

For this exercise, you'll launch GarageBand by opening a project file.

1   Locate the Lessons folder on your computer.

    NOTE ▶ If you haven't copied the Lessons folder for this book to your
    hard drive, do so at this time.

2   Select the Lesson_01 folder, then double-click the **1-1 Eyewitness** project
    file to open the song and launch the program.

An initializing progress window appears, showing that GarageBand is
opening the selected project. When GarageBand opens, you will see a
large window containing all the elements for the song **1-1 Eyewitness**.

Exploring the GarageBand Window

One of the many advantages of GarageBand is the simplicity of the interface.
As with all the iLife applications, GarageBand uses one window as the base of
operations. This window is your recording studio.

Let's take a quick tour of the GarageBand window.

*   Track headers—Show the instrument icon and name to the left of each
    instrument track. The track headers also include a Mute button to silence
    a track and a Solo button to silence all other tracks.

    Track Mixer—Includes a Volume slider to adjust the track volume and a
    Pan wheel to adjust the position of the track in the left-to-right stereo field.

*   Timeline—Acts as your music recording and arranging workspace.
    The Timeline is made up of horizontal tracks for each individual instru-
    ment. The Timeline graphically represents linear time from left to right

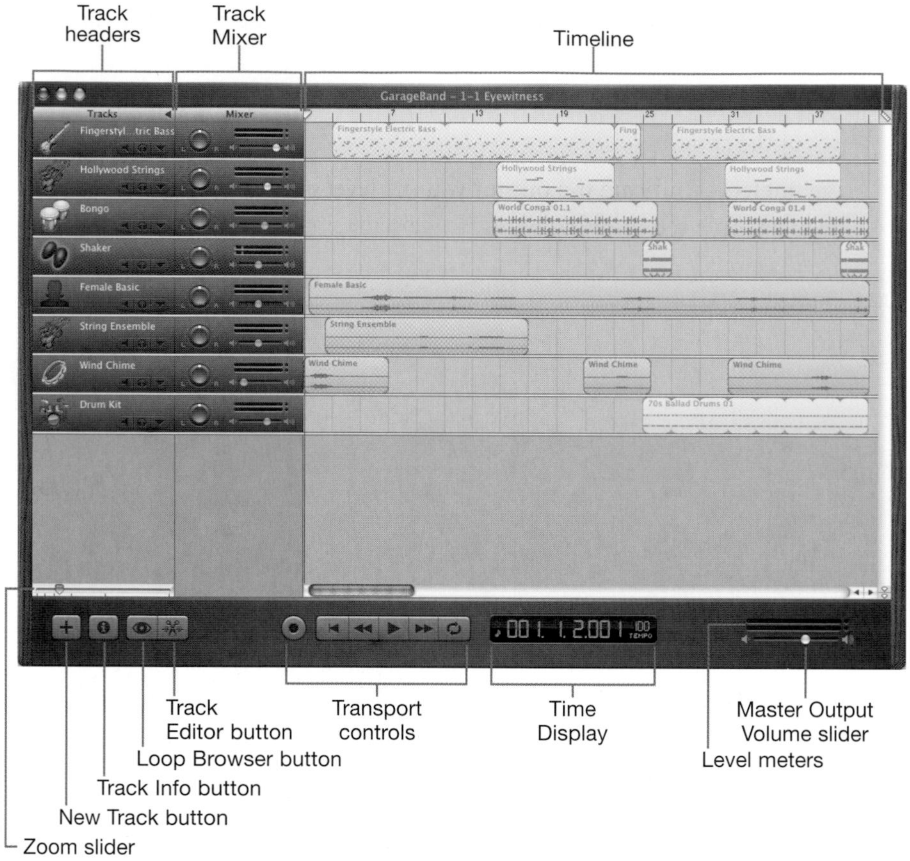

Track headers   Track Mixer   Timeline

Track
Editor button   Transport
controls   Time
Display   Master Output
Volume slider
Loop Browser button   Level meters
Track Info button
New Track button
Zoom slider

using a Beat Ruler at the top of the window. The far-left edge of the
Timeline represents the beginning of a song.

- Zoom slider—Can be used to zoom in to or out of the Timeline.

- New Track button—Adds a new track in the Timeline.

- Track Info button—Opens the Track Info window.

- Loop Browser button—Opens the Loop Browser.

- Track Editor button—Opens the Track Editor.

- Transport controls—Provide the standard recording and playback buttons
  to navigate in the Timeline, including Record, Go To Beginning, Rewind,
  Fast Forward, and Cycle.

- Time Display—Shows the song's tempo and current playhead position in musical time or absolute time.

- Master Output Volume slider—Can be used to adjust the output volume level of the song.

- Level meters—Indicate the output volume level of a song. The Level meters include red warning lights if levels are clipping (too loud).

Window Basics

GarageBand was designed for Macintosh OS X, and the GarageBand window works the same as other OS X windows. If you're new to the Mac or to OS X, follow these steps to get some practice zooming, moving, and minimizing the GarageBand window.

There are three buttons in the upper-left corner of the window: Close window (red X), Minimize (yellow –), and Zoom (green +).

1   Click the green Zoom button (+) to zoom the window so it fills your computer screen.

The GarageBand window will resize to fill your screen.

NOTE ▶ Make sure your screen resolution is set to 1027 x 768 or higher in the display preferences for your computer. If your resolution is below 1027 x 768, you won't be able to see the entire GarageBand window on your screen.

You can also adjust the window by clicking and dragging the size control in the lower-right corner of the window.

2   Click the diagonal lines in the lower-right corner of the window and drag upward to make the window smaller.

To move the GarageBand window, you can click and drag anywhere in the gray header bar at the top of the window, or on the wooden side panels.

3   Click the top of the window near the name of the project. Don't release your mouse.

4   Drag the window to the lower-right corner of your screen. Release the mouse.

5   Click the wooden side panel at the left of the window. Then drag the window to the left side of the screen.

6   Click the green Zoom button again to zoom the window back to full-screen size.

If your window is already full-screen, clicking the Zoom button will make your window revert to its previous size and position.

TIP ▶ If you're using a laptop or a large studio display, the Zoom button is a very useful tool to maximize the size of your workspace. Also, any time you can't see the entire window because part of it is offscreen, you can click the Zoom button to bring the entire window into view.

You can also minimize or hide your GarageBand window without quitting the program. When you minimize the window, it moves to the Dock near the Trash. To reopen the window, simply click the GarageBand icon in your Dock.

7   Click the yellow Minimize button (–) to hide your GarageBand window in the Dock.

8   Locate the GarageBand window in your Dock and click it to unhide (show) the window.

NOTE ▶ You can also double-click the header at the top of the GarageBand window to minimize and hide the window.

Now that you know how to adjust the full GarageBand window, let's take a closer look at some other features, starting with the Timeline.

Exploring the Timeline

The Timeline is the largest portion of the GarageBand window. It contains tracks where you can record both Software Instruments and Real Instruments. You can also add loops of prerecorded musical parts and arrange the different regions to create a finished song.

The Timeline includes the following controls:

- Playhead—Shows exactly what part of the song is currently playing. The playhead is a white triangle (with a red vertical line underneath) on the Beat Ruler. You also use the playhead to determine where to cut, copy, and paste music regions within the Timeline.

- Beat Ruler—Shows musical time in beats and measures. Click anywhere in the Beat Ruler to move the playhead to that position.

- Tracks—Contain recordings of the Real Instrument or Software Instrument parts. They can also contain loops of prerecorded musical parts from the Loop Browser called Apple Loops. Each track separates the individual instruments to arrange a song.

- Timeline Grid button—Lets you choose the note value of the Timeline grid, or you can choose Automatic so the value will change as you zoom in and out of the Timeline.

- Regions—Display the individual musical parts that are either prerecorded loops or parts that you record using Real Instruments and Software Instruments. Each prerecorded loop, Software Instrument, or Real Instrument part you record is represented in the Timeline as a differently colored region. Regions can be moved, copied, cut, and pasted, as well as extended or looped, in the Timeline. Software Instruments and Apple Loops can be edited and transposed in the Track Editor.

- Volume curves—Graphically represent the volume within a track. You can dynamically change the volume of a track for different parts of a song using control points along the Volume curve.

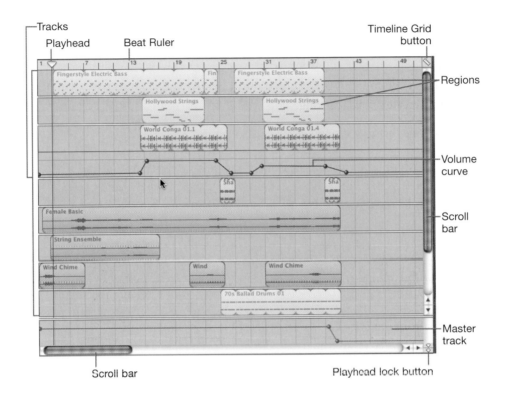

• **Master track**—Lets you change the volume and effects for the overall song. You can dynamically adjust the Volume curve in the Master track just as you can for individual tracks, but adjustments to the Master track affect all of the tracks in the Timeline.

• **Playhead Lock button**—Locks (gangs) the playheads in the Timeline and Track Editor together, or unlocks them to show different sections of the song at the same time.

• **Scroll bars**—Let you see a different part of the song in the Timeline. Click and drag the horizontal scroll bar to move horizontally in the Timeline. Use the vertical scroll bar to move vertically.

Using the Mouse and Keyboard

There are at least two ways to do almost everything in GarageBand. You can
either use the mouse, or you can use the keyboard. Since everyone has a
preference, I'll show you different methods throughout this book. Choose
whichever method works best for you.

Practicing Mouse Maneuvers

You use the mouse for many functions in GarageBand, including pointing,
selecting, grabbing, clicking, dragging, dropping, and stretching. It's a good
idea to practice using the mouse if this is your first time at the computer.

We'll start with the mouse as a pointer, and use it to move the playhead in
the Timeline.

1   Locate your pointer (it looks like an arrow).

2   Move your mouse to move the pointer anywhere on the GarageBand
window.

3   Locate the playhead on the Timeline.

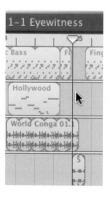

The playhead is a vertical red line with a white
triangular head at the top in the Beat Ruler. You
can use the playhead to play all tracks in the
Timeline simultaneously. The playhead moves
from left to right in the Timeline and plays
whatever regions (music parts) it scrubs across
as it moves.

4   Click the top of the playhead and drag it along the Beat Ruler.

The top of the playhead turns blue when you click and drag it to a new position. The blue color shows that it has been selected.

You can also move the playhead by simply clicking anywhere in the Beat Ruler. The numbers in the Beat Ruler represent each measure of the song.

5   Click the vertical line just to the left of the number 3 in the Beat Ruler.

The playhead jumps to the first beat in the 3rd measure of the song.

Using the Keyboard

Now let's look at how to use the keyboard to move the playhead in the Timeline.

1   Press the left arrow key to move the playhead one measure to the left.

2   Press the right arrow key twice to move the playhead two measures to the right.

3   Press the Home key to move the playhead to the beginning of the Timeline.

4   Press the right arrow several times to move the playhead to the right.

5   Press the Z key to move the playhead back to the beginning of the Timeline.

As you can see, the Home key and the Z key do the same thing. Choose whichever key is easier for you to find and remember.

TIP ► If you're working on a laptop, it may be easier to press the Z key to get to the beginning of the Timeline. On a laptop, the Home key is also the left arrow, so you need to hold down the function key first. The function key for Mac PowerBooks is located in the lower-left corner of the keyboard and is labeled "fn."

Playing a Song in the Timeline

It's time to actually play the song that is in the Timeline. There are several ways to do that. You can click the Play button in the transport controls (the mouse method), or you can use the keyboard.

1   Press the Home or Z key to move the playhead to the beginning of the song (if it is not already there).

2   Press the spacebar to begin playback. Listen to the song **1-1 Eyewitness**.

NOTE ► If you get a warning message that your computer is too slow, your computer may not meet the system requirements to play this song. Click the Mute button (speaker) in the track controls on the String Ensemble track and on the Wind Chime track. If you still have problems, your computer probably doesn't have the required processing speed. Open the alternative G3 version of this song located in the G3 Lessons folder.

For more information on system requirements and performance, see the introduction to this book, "Getting Started."

3   Press the spacebar again to stop the playhead.

Now let's try the transport control buttons located at the bottom of the GarageBand window, below the Timeline.

4 Click the Go To Beginning button to move the playhead to the beginning of the Timeline.

The Go To Beginning button is the first button on the left of the transport controls. It looks like a line with an arrow pointing to the left.

The playhead moves to the beginning of the Timeline.

5 Click the Play button, located in the middle of the transport controls, to play the song.

6 Click the Play button again to stop playback.

7 Click and hold the Fast Forward or Rewind buttons to move the playhead through the song. Release the mouse to stop rewinding or fast forwarding.

8 Click the Go To Beginning button again to move the playhead back to the beginning of the song.

I composed and recorded the original version of the **1-1 Eyewitness** song back in 1994 for a documentary I edited and scored about the Northridge earthquake called "Live from the Epicenter." That was a decade ago, using what now seems like ancient recording technology, an audio engineer, and a studio full of equipment. If someone told me back then that I would be able to record and mix music with a simple program on my home computer, I probably would have said something skeptical like, "We'll put a rover on Mars before that ever happens!" Of course, that was before GarageBand.

Exploring Tracks and Regions

As you can see, playing a song in the Timeline is easy. Let's take a moment to examine what makes up the song in the Timeline.

The song **1-1 Eyewitness** contains eight tracks.

Each track, in turn, contains individual musical parts—regions—from a particular instrument. An instrument track may contain only one region, or it may contain many smaller regions—individual takes and retakes, often called *overdubs*—which, when arranged in a track, are the basic building blocks of an entire instrument's part for a song

Regions come in a variety of colors and sizes. A track may have one region that lasts the entire duration of the song, or different regions representing different musical parts played by the same instrument at different times in the song.

Take a look at your Timeline. The Female Basic region is one long region that lasts for the entire duration of the song. This indicates that the performance was recorded all in one take from start to finish. The Wind Chime track has three separate wind chime regions located at the beginning, middle, and end of the song. These regions were recorded one at a time with the same instrument. The 70s Ballad Drums 01 region is only at the end of the song because that's the only place where the musical part was needed. Also, that particular region has notches (rounded corners), to show that it was created by extending a single loop to repeat multiple times. The notches indicate the ending of one repetition and the beginning of another.

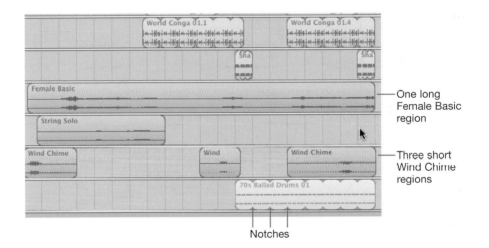

Real Instruments

Purple regions are the Real Instrument parts. They are exactly what the name suggests—parts recorded from real instruments.

Real Instrument parts can be recorded into GarageBand through a microphone, guitar, or keyboard that is plugged into the microphone jack on your computer. You can also record Real Instrument parts through other input devices that you connect to your computer. You will learn more about recording Real Instruments later in this book.

For the **1-1 Eyewitness** song, I recorded three Real Instrument parts using a synthesizer as the instrument (Female Basic, String Ensemble, and Wind Chime).

Real Instrument regions are placed in the Timeline as is. In contrast to Software Instruments, you can't change the timing, notation, or tempo of a Real Instrument region once it is recorded.

Software Instruments

Software Instruments are recorded performances that are more flexible than Real Instruments because they use professional MIDI samples. Software Instruments utilize some of the same powerful music editing tools found in Apple's professional recording software, Logic.

> **NOTE** ▶ MIDI stands for Musical Instrument Digital Interface. It's an industry standard that allows all devices, such as synthesizers and computers, to communicate with each other.

Software Instrument regions are green and are recorded using a USB music keyboard, a MIDI synthesizer–type keyboard, or the GarageBand onscreen keyboard. Once the notes for the Software Instrument region are recorded, you can change the sound of the instrument that plays the notes, fix the timing and velocity, or transpose the note to a different key.

For this song, I recorded two Software Instruments located in the top two tracks in the Timeline.

Apple Loops

GarageBand also comes with over 1,000 prerecorded Apple Loops. These loops are regions that contain either digital recordings of real instruments or editable MIDI notes. Just like Real Instrument or Software Instrument parts you record yourself, Real Instrument Apple Loops are colored blue, and Software Instrument Apple Loops are green. Prerecorded loops can be used to accompany the other instrument tracks and are incredibly useful for adding tracks with instruments you can't play and record yourself. These loops are like your backup band.

For the **Eyewitness** song, I used prerecorded Apple Loops for the percussion section. The Bongo and Shaker regions are blue, which means they are a digital recording with notes that can't be edited.

I also included an Apple Loop on the last track. This loop shows up as a green region, which means it is editable, like a Software Instrument.

Zooming In and Out of the Timeline

Now that you have identified the different regions and tracks, let's zoom in for a closer look.

You can zoom in and out of the Timeline using the Zoom slider, located in the lower-left corner of the window, or by using a keyboard shortcut.

GarageBand zooms in to your current playhead position in the Timeline. For this exercise, let's start by zooming in to the beginning of the song.

1   Press the Z key to move the playhead to the beginning of the Timeline (if it is not there already).

2   Press and hold the Ctrl key, located on the far left and far right of the spacebar.

NOTE ▶ The shorthand for the Control key is Ctrl. In this book, if you read instructions that ask you to press Ctrl–right arrow, that indicates that you need to press the Control and right arrow keys together.

3   While you hold down the Ctrl key, press the right arrow key several times to zoom in to the Timeline.

As you zoom in, the tracks in the Timeline get longer, and you can see more detail within a track.

Notice that you can see the waveform (recorded audio that is graphically displayed) in the Wind Chime track.

Wind Chime region before zooming in to the Timeline

Wind Chime region after zooming in to the Timeline

4   Press Ctrl–right arrow several more times to zoom further into the Timeline.

5   Press Ctrl–left arrow several times to zoom out of the Timeline until you can see the entire song again.

6 Click the Beat Ruler around the 20th measure to move the playhead.

You may need to zoom in or out of the Timeline to clearly see the 20th measure in the Beat Ruler.

Now let's zoom in to the 20th measure of the song using the Zoom slider. The Zoom slider works the same as pressing the Ctrl key and tapping the left and right arrows.

7 Locate the Zoom slider in the lower-left corner of the window.

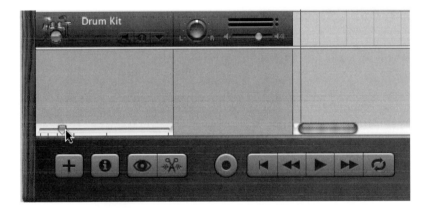

8 Click and drag the blue arrow on the slider toward the left to zoom out of the Timeline.

9 Click and drag the blue arrow on the slider toward the right to zoom in to the Timeline at the playhead position.

10 Click and drag the blue arrow to the middle position on the slider.

Exploring the Track Editor

Now that you're zoomed in to the Timeline, look at the regions on the top three tracks of the Timeline.

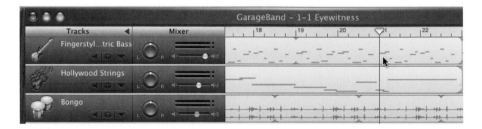

Notice that the green regions have a series of dashes and lines to represent the musical note events. The blue regions, on the other hand, show a waveform that illustrates the digital recording.

The Track Editor is a tool that lets you magnify and edit a particular region or track.

Let's start by opening the Track Editor for a Software Instrument region.

Opening the Track Editor

The Track Editor can be used to edit an entire track or a specific region within that track.

The Track Editor differs depending on the type of region that you open. If you're working with a Software Instrument, you will use the Track Editor for Software Instruments. If you're working with a Real Instrument, you will use the Track Editor for Real Instruments. You can have only one Track Editor open at a time because they occupy the same space in the lower third of the GarageBand window.

Let's start with the Track Editor for Software Instruments. Remember that the green regions are created by Software Instruments and can be edited in the Track Editor.

There are four ways to open the Track Editor:

* Double-click the region you wish to edit in the Track Editor.
* Click the Track Editor button located in the lower-left corner of the window.

* Go to the Control menu at the top of the screen and choose Show Editor.
* Press Cmd-E (the Command key and the E key at the same time).

Since we haven't used any of the menus in this lesson, this is a good time to try out the menus at the top of the screen.

1   Locate the Control menu.

2   Choose the Control menu by clicking and holding it with your mouse.

3   Continue holding your mouse on the Control menu and scroll down to choose Show Editor.

NOTE ▸ The shorthand for steps that involve menus will be written as "Choose Control > Show Editor." In other words, Control is the title of the menu, and Show Editor is the selection within that menu.

The Track Editor appears in the lower third of the GarageBand window. Its appearance varies depending on the type of region you open.

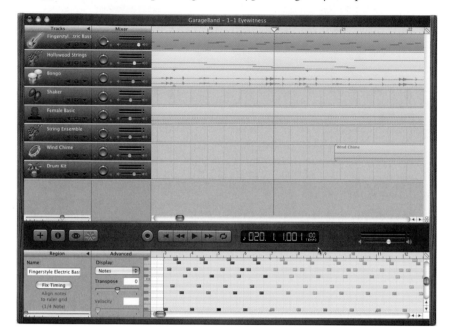

Software Instruments allow you to record input from a MIDI input device, like a MIDI keyboard, as a Software Intrument region. Software Instrument regions don't contain sounds from actual musical instruments, nor do they display the sounds, or notes, as waveforms, as do Real Instrument regions (purple or blue). Green Software Intrument regions represent individual notes as "note events" that look like a series of bars, lines, or dashes, which can be assigned to any Software Instrument, before or after it is recorded.

MIDI note events in Software Instrument regions can have their pitch, timing, and duration edited in the Track Editor, whereas Real Instrument regions can't be transposed or edited in any way. The only reason to load a Real Instrument track or region into the Track Editor is to change its name.

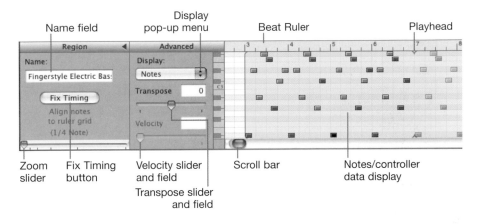

Here's a quick tour of the Track Editor controls:

- Name field—Shows the name of a selected track or region, and can be used to change the names of both tracks and regions.

- Fix Timing button—Allows you to fix the timing of all the notes in a selected region. This works by moving each note to the nearest grid line.

- Zoom slider—Enables you to zoom in or out of the region in the Track Editor.

- Display pop-up menu—Allows you to choose whether to show notes or controller data in the Track Editor.

- Velocity slider and field—Lets you change the velocity of a note to make it play harder or softer, which translates to louder or quieter.

- Beat Ruler—Corresponds to the Beat Ruler in the Timeline, and can be used to navigate to specific locations within the selected track.

- Notes/controller data display—Can be used to change a note's size, pitch, and length of play.

- Playhead—Plays the track or region in the Track Editor and corresponds to the playhead position in the Timeline.

- Scroll bar—Allows you to move left or right to view a different portion of the track in the editor.

Using the Track Editor for Software Instruments

Let's take the Track Editor out for a test drive. In this exercise, you'll change the velocity of one note in the Hollywood Strings track.

1   Click the Hollywood Strings track header to select that track in the Timeline.

The track header turns green to indicate it has been selected. Note that the green color of the track header also shows that the regions within that track are Software Instrument regions.

NOTE ▶ Selecting a track also selects all of the regions within that track.

2   Click and drag the Timeline Zoom slider to the left so that you can view the entire song in the Timeline.

3   Locate the first Hollywood Strings region on the Hollywood Strings track.

4   Double-click the first Hollywood Strings region in the Timeline to open it in the Track Editor.

Notice that the Track Editor has a Region section showing Hollywood Strings in the Name field. This means that you have opened that region in the Track Editor. There is also a Track Editor Zoom slider located at the bottom of the Region section so you can zoom in or out of the selected region in the Track Editor.

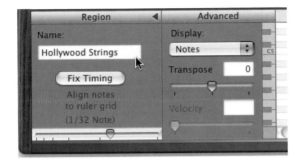

5   Click and drag the arrow in the Track Editor Zoom slider all the way to the left to see the entire selected region in the Track Editor.

The gray bars in the Track Editor represent the individual note events. You can listen to a note by clicking it with your pointer.

If you Cmd-click a note, your pointer turns into a pencil in the Track Editor. The pencil means you're in an editing mode. When you select a note, it turns green.

6   Cmd-click the first note (bar) in the Track Editor to hear the note.

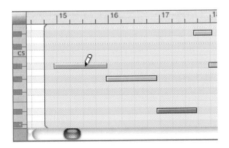

Notice that the Velocity field shows a velocity of 11 for the note you selected.

Velocity is indicated by a number between 1 and 127, with 1 being the lightest, and 127 being the hardest. You can also see a visual representation of velocity in the shades of gray used for the notes, from lightest to darkest. The darker the shade, the higher the velocity or louder the note.

TIP ▶ Keep in mind that a little variation in velocity is a good thing. Most people play instruments with passion and feeling that includes emphasis on certain notes. Some notes may be passing notes that are played delicately (low velocity), while others are strong notes—they carry the melody and are played more heavily or with higher velocity.

7 Press the spacebar to play the region along with that portion of the song in the Timeline.

Watch the playhead move across the different note events in the Track Editor and listen to the volume for the Hollywood Strings change with the different velocities.

8 Press the spacebar again to stop playback.

9 Click and drag the scroll bar at the bottom of the Track Editor to move back to the beginning of the region.

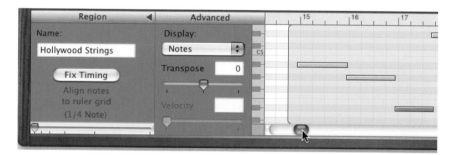

10 Click the Beat Ruler at the beginning of the region to move the playhead.

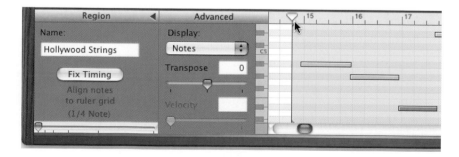

11 Locate the 6th note event in the region.

Note 6 is the darkest gray line. It starts at the beginning of the 19th measure.

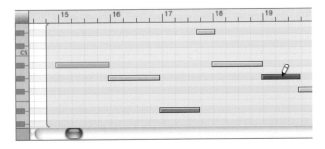

12 Cmd click the 6th note to hear it.

The velocity for this note is 70.

The difference between 11 and 70 is quite dramatic, and in this case a mistake. Before you lower the velocity, it's a good idea to check the velocity of the notes just before and after it.

13 Click the note just before the 6th note and check the velocity in the Velocity field.

14 Click both of the notes directly to the right of the 6th note and check their velocities.

Chances are this note was meant to be louder than the others—just not as loud as it was actually played. Let's lower the velocity to 50.

There are two ways to change the velocity. You can type a new number in the Velocity field, or you can click and drag the Velocity slider.

15   Click the 6th note to select it in the Track Editor and drag the Velocity slider until you see 50 in the Velocity field.

If you have trouble dragging the slider to 50, type *50* in the Velocity field to change the velocity. As you can see, there are advantages to both methods. Drag for a general velocity change; type a number for a specific velocity.

16   Click anywhere in the green space near the notes to deselect the note and see the new shade of gray.

17   Move the playhead back to the beginning of the region and play the section again to hear the new velocity.

Project Tasks

Now it's your turn to put together everything you have learned so far and try the same velocity change again. It just so happens that when I built this song, I copied and pasted the Hollywood Strings region so I would only have to record it once. When you're building music, reusing parts can be a real time-saver. However, it also means that the same velocity mistake is in both regions.

1   Double-click the second Hollywood Strings region in the Hollywood Strings track to load it in the Track Editor.

2   Locate the 6th note event.

3   Change the velocity to 50.

4   Listen to the change to make sure it is correct.

5   Click the Track Editor button or press Cmd-E to close the Track Editor.

Using the Track Editor for Real Instruments

The Track Editor is different when you're working with Real Instrument
tracks. Let's look at the Real Instrument track that was used at the beginning
of the **Eyewitness** song to record the same part as the Hollywood Strings.

1 Locate the String Ensemble track in the Timeline.

2 Double-click the String Ensemble region in the Timeline.

The String Ensemble Region opens in the Track Editor.

Once again, the purple color of the track means this track is a digital recording of a Real Instrument through either a microphone or other input device. The good news is that you have the ability to record live musicians and their instruments directly into the Timeline. The bad news is that this recording method maintains the integrity of the recorded performance. In other words, you can't edit the notes or velocity.

3 Locate the Name field that reads String Ensemble.

Regions don't have to be named after the track and vice versa. Let's change the name of this region.

4 Type *String Solo* in the Name field and press Return.

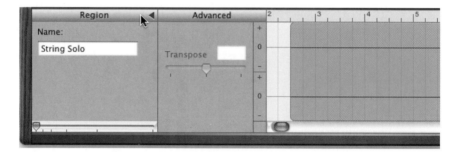

The name of the region in the Timeline changes, yet the name of the track stays the same.

To change the name of the track, you first need to deselect the region by clicking the empty track space next to the selected region.

5 Click the empty gray track space to the right of the String Solo region.

The Track Editor now shows that you're working on the full track instead of just a region. Notice that the header in the left column of the Track Editor now reads Track instead of Region.

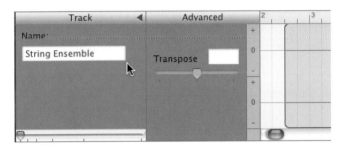

6   Type *Synth Strings* in the name field to change the name of the track. Press Return.

7   Double-click the String Solo region to reopen it in the Track Editor.

8   Press the spacebar to play the selected region in the Track Editor.

    Watch the playhead as it moves over the waveform of the recording.

9   Press the spacebar again to stop playback when you get to the end of the region.

    Locate the Advanced section of the Track Editor. Notice that the only advanced option for a Real Instrument is Transpose, and it is disabled. Once again, this is because you can't transpose (change the key) of a recorded Real Instrument.

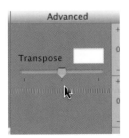

Using the Track Editor for Apple Loops

There are two types of Apple Loops that come with GarageBand: Software
Instrument loops (green) and Real Instrument loops (blue). The Software
Instrument loops can be edited in the Track Editor in the same way as any
Software Instrument region. Real Instrument loops, on the other hand, have
the same limitations as Real Instrument regions that you record into the
Timeline.

Let's quickly examine how the Track Editor looks when you use it for
Apple Loops.

1   Locate the Bongo track in the Timeline.

2   Double-click the first World Conga region to load it in the Track Editor.

Notice the waveform of the conga drums in the Track Editor. These look
different from the note events you worked with previously for the
Software Instruments.

Also notice that this region is blue, indicating that it is a Real Instrument
Apple Loop. You can use the Track Editor to zoom in and edit these loops
as needed when you're arranging a song. You'll learn more about editing
loops later in this book.

3   Move the Zoom slider to the right to zoom in to the track for a more
detailed view of the waveform.

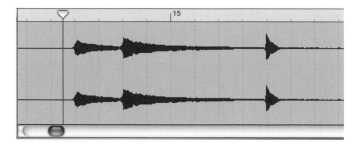

Exploring the Loop Browser

The World Conga region in your Track Editor came from a library of over 1,000 prerecorded Apple Loops that are included with the GarageBand software. Loops are musical parts that can be repeated (looped) over and over seamlessly. These loops can be accessed through the Loop Browser. The Loop Browser organizes the loops by categories and helps you search for loops using either the Button or Column view.

There are three ways to open the Loop Browser:

• Click the Loop Browser button.

• Choose Control > Show Loop Browser.

• Press Cmd-L.

Let's open the Loop Browser now.

1 Click the Loop Browser button to open the Loop Browser.

The Loop Browser opens. The Loop Browser and the Track Editor occupy the same space in the GarageBand window. You can either have the Loop Browser open, or the Track Editor open, but not both at once.

The Loop Browser helps you search through all of your loops to make it easier to find the right loops for your song. Imagine if you had to listen to hundreds of loops just to find the sound you want. Luckily, the Loop Browser sorts and organizes the loops for you. All you need to do is narrow the search.

View buttons | Scale type pop-up menu | Search text field | Preview Volume slider | Results list

The Loop Browser has the following controls:

- Keyword buttons or columns—Click the keywords to display the matching loops. Click additional keywords to narrow the search.

- View buttons—Use these buttons to change the layout of the Loop Browser to Column view or Button view.

- Scale type pop-up menu—Use this menu to narrow your search to a specific scale.

- Search text field—Type the name of the loop or the kind of loops you want to find.

- Preview Volume slider—Adjust the volume of the loops as you preview them.

- Results list—Shows the results that match whatever keywords you have selected or loop you search for. Once you have used keywords or buttons to narrow or refine your search, the results are listed in this pane. You can sort the results by columns, including by name, tempo, and key.

  NOTE ▶ GarageBand comes with over 1,000 prerecorded Apple Loops. You can add 2,000 additional loops with the Jam Pack expansion package for GarageBand. You can also add Apple Loops from the Soundtrack application.

There are two different ways you can view the Loop Browser: Button view and Column view.

Using the Loop Browser in Button View

Let's locate a prerecorded cowbell loop that might work with this song. To use the Loop Browser in Button view, you need to click the Button View button in the lower-left corner of the window.

1   Click the Button View button, if you're not already in Button view.

2   Locate and click the Percussion button to narrow the search to percussion instrument loops.

The search results appear in the results list on the right side of the Loop Browser.

	Name	Tempo	Key	Beats
	Bongo Groove 01	95	–	2
	Bongo Groove 02	96	–	4
	Bongo Groove 03	95	–	4
	Bongo Groove 04	94	–	4
	Bongo Groove 05	96	–	4
	Ceramic Drum 03	121	–	8
	Ceramic Drum 04	120	–	8

TIP ▶ If you can't read the full names of the loops in the Name column of the search results, click and drag the top-right edge of the Name column header to the right to extend the width of the column.

There are 105 results from your initial search of percussion instrument loops. The number of items is listed at the bottom of the Loop Browser.

Let's see if you can narrow the search again. Since the cowbell is usually played as an acoustic (non-electronic) instrument, let's also add another keyword to our search.

3 Click the Acoustic button.

A cowbell is also a single item or instrument. Use this information to further refine your search.

4   Click the Single button.

There are now 81 items in the search results.

5   Click the scroller on the right side of the results list and scroll to the loop named Cowbell Groove 01.

Name	▲	Tempo	Key	Beats
Conga Groove 08		90	C	8
Conga Groove 09		131	–	8
Conga Groove 10		130	–	8
Conga Groove 11		100	–	8
Cowbell Groove 01		96	C	8
Dumbek Beat 01		120	–	8
Dumbek Beat 02		120	–	8
Ethnic Shake Loop 01		96	–	8

6   Click the name Cowbell Groove 01 in the search results to preview (listen to) the loop.

The icon to the left of the filename turns to a speaker when you preview a loop.

7   Click the Cowbell Groove 01 name again to stop the preview.

8   Click the Reset button in the upper-left corner of the keyword buttons to clear the search results and reset the buttons so no buttons are selected.

You found the cowbell loop, along with many other percussion loops. Searching for loops is a great method if you're not sure exactly what you want to use, and you'd like to preview different sounds.

In this case, we know specifically what we are looking for—a cowbell sound. When you know exactly what you want, the easiest way to find it is to type the name, or part of the name, in the Search text field.

9 Type *cow* in the Search field located at the bottom center of the Loop Browser. Press Return.

The Cowbell Groove 01 is the only loop in the search results.

Name	▲	Tempo
Cowbell Groove 01		96

Again, this method works great if you're looking for something specific, but it might not be very helpful for a broad search—for instance, for drum loops.

Using the Loop Browser in Column View

You can also search for loops using columns instead of buttons. To change the view to columns, all you need to do is click the Column View button in the lower-left corner of the Loop Browser.

1 Click the Column View button to change the Loop Browser to Column view.

The buttons disappear and are replaced by empty columns.

Let's try to find the cowbell loop again, this time using the Column view.

2   Click By Instruments in the first column.

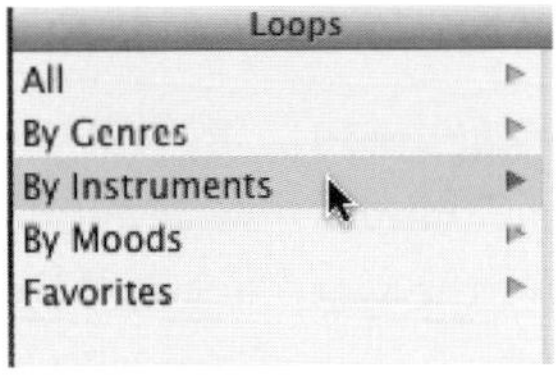

The Instruments column appears with many instrument choices.

3   Scroll down through the Instruments column until you see Cowbell.

4   Select Cowbell from the Instruments column.

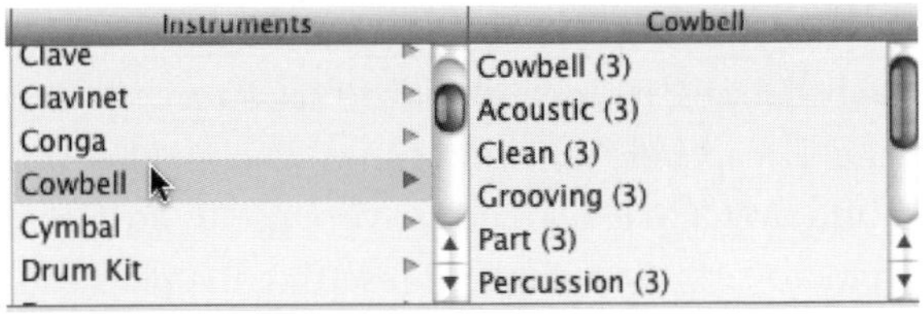

A Cowbell column appears to the right, listing different cowbell sounds sorted by descriptors.

Each descriptor in the Cowbell column lists three different cowbell loops. Based on the consistency of the number three, I would guess there are a total of three different cowbell loops that are all grouped together under each different descriptor.

5 Select any of the descriptors in the Cowbell column to reveal the cowbell loops in the results column.

Cowbell		Name ▲	Tempo
Cowbell (3)		♪ Cowbell Groove 01	96
Acoustic (3)		♪ World Agogo 01	105
Clean (3)		♪ World Agogo 02	105
Grooving (3)			
Part (3)			
Percussion (3)			

Interesting. When you went searching for cowbell loops using the buttons and then refined your search, you found only one cowbell loop. However, when you searched using the Column view, you found three.

The moral of this cowbell search story is that sometimes the results will vary depending on which method you use to search. The Column view allowed you to find loops that sound like a cowbell but don't have the word "cowbell" in the name. Using the Button view, you had no idea which loops sounded like a cowbell without listening to them all.

Feel free to experiment with the Loop Browser on your own time. Meanwhile, let's audition the cowbell loops to find one that might work with this song.

Creating a Cycle Region in the Timeline

Before you audition the cowbell loops, it's a good idea to set up a cycle region in the Timeline. A *cycle region* is a specific portion of the Timeline that you wish to repeat (cycle) over and over. Cycle regions are very useful for tasks like auditioning, so you don't have to keep stopping and resetting the playhead every time the song ends.

1 Click the Cycle button in the transport controls.

The Beat Ruler extends to reveal the Cycle Region Ruler.

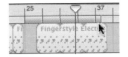

To select a specific part of the Timeline to cycle, click and drag in the Cycle Region Ruler below the Beat Ruler. The cycle region appears as a yellow bar. You can move a cycle region by clicking in the middle of the yellow bar and dragging forward or backward in the Cycle Region Ruler. You can extend or shorten the cycle region by dragging the left or right edge of the yellow bar.

2   Click the cycle area below the Beat Ruler at the beginning of the 25th measure.

This is the beginning of the break in the Bass part of the song.

3   Click and drag through the Cycle Region Ruler toward the end of the song.

4   Release the mouse once you have created a cycle region.

5   Click the Play button in the transport controls to hear the cycle region.

The playhead will play only the portion of the song marked by the yellow cycle region. The cycle region is played over and over until you stop playback.

Auditioning Loops with a Song

Now that you have found three different cowbell loops and set up a cycle region, we can audition the cowbell loops to see which, if any, sounds best with the song in the Timeline.

1   Click the Play button to start playing the cycle region in the Timeline.

2   Select the first cowbell loop in the search results to hear it with the song.

3   Press the down arrow key to move down to the next cowbell sound in the search results.

4   Press the down arrow again to audition the last sound.

5   Use the up and down arrow keys to move between the different cowbell sounds and find your favorite.

6   Press the spacebar to stop playback of both the loops and the song.

Once you have auditioned your loops and selected one that works, you can add it to the Timeline and make it part of the song. That will be the first thing we do in the next lesson.

To finish off this lesson, let's take a moment to close up the cycle region and the Loop Browser.

7   Click the Cycle button in the transport controls to hide and close the cycle region.

8   Click the Loop Browser button to close the Loop Browser.

9   Press Cmd-S to save your project.

Congratulations! You now have a basic working knowledge of the GarageBand interface and are ready to start working with tracks in the Timeline.

What You've Learned

- There are three ways to launch GarageBand: double-clicking the application icon in the Finder; clicking once on the GarageBand icon in the Dock; and double-clicking any GarageBand song file.

- You can use the green Zoom button (+) in the upper-left corner of the GarageBand window to fit the window to your entire screen. You can click and drag the lower-right corner to resize the window.

- To move the GarageBand window, click and drag on the top, right, or left edges of the window.

- Musical time is in measures and beats and is marked in the Timeline by the Beat Ruler.

- You can move the playhead by clicking in the Beat Ruler, click-dragging the top of the playhead, or pressing the right or left arrow keys to move a measure at a time right or left.

- You use the transport control buttons to play, fast forward, rewind, move to the beginning of the Timeline, and turn on the cycle region.

- There are three different types of musical regions used in GarageBand: Software Instruments, Real Instruments, and prerecorded Apple Loops.

- Software Instruments record editable note events. Real Instrument recordings make digital recordings of waveforms.

- You can find loops in the Loop Browser using either the Button view or the Column view.

- You can use the Track Editor to edit pitch, velocity, and the type of note for Software Instruments.

- Velocity refers to the hardness or softness with which a note was played, and the volume of that note as a result. Velocity is measured on a scale from 0 to 127, with 0 being the softest and 127 the hardest.

- To listen to only part of the Timeline over and over, you can create a cycle region.

- Auditioning loops means you listen to a loop in the Loop Browser while playing a song in the Timeline.

2

Lesson Files   Lessons > Lesson_02 > 2-1 Eyewitness Starting; 2-2 Eyewitness Finished; 2-3 Homecoming Starting; 2-4 Homecoming Finished

Time   This lesson takes approximately 60 minutes to complete.

Goals   Understand tracks

Use the Time Display as a reference

Select prerecorded loops

Extend a loop region in the Timeline

Add and delete tracks in the Timeline

Add a Software Instrument track

Use the onscreen keyboard

Record a basic Software Instrument part

Undo a recording

Delete a region from the Timeline

Change a track's icon and instrument

Mute and solo tracks

Save a project and open a new song

Working with Tracks in the Timeline

In this lesson, you'll learn how to work with tracks. Sure, that doesn't sound like much fun—until you get a better perspective on the power of tracks. Have you ever heard of a 4-track recorder? In its time, the 4-track revolutionized the music industry as much as the mouse revolutionized computers. The 4-track recorder made it possible to record four different instrument tracks one at a time, and play them back all mixed together. Eventually, 4-track recorders were replaced by 8-track recorders, and finally by digital recording.

What does that mean to you? For one thing, you don't have to limit your songs to four tracks. In fact, you can have up to 255 Real Instrument tracks or 64 Software Instrument tracks, depending on the speed of your computer. Chances are, most of your songs can be arranged in 10 or fewer tracks, but it's nice to know that if you need more tracks, they're there for you.

This lesson will focus on the different types of tracks. You'll learn to add, delete, and change tracks, as well as evaluate tracks using mute and solo to determine how well they fit with the song.

Understanding Tracks

Think of the tracks in your Timeline as the different musicians in your band. Each musician plays a different instrument and is represented by a separate track. As the leader of your band, you can decide which instruments are used in a song and how you want to record them. If you don't like an instrument part, you can always fire the musician—or in this case, just delete the track. If you really like the way a part sounds, you can clone the musician, or just double that track in the Timeline.

The best way to understand tracks is to work with them, so let's get started.

Preparing the Project

Open project **2-1 Eyewitness Starting** from the Lesson_02 folder. This is the same project that you were working on in the previous lesson. You may continue working with **1-1 Eyewitness** if you still have that project open. We'll open a new project later on in this lesson.

Selecting Prerecorded Loops

Remember the cowbell loops you auditioned in the last lesson? Well, it's time to select the cowbell track to use in the song **2-1 Eyewitness**.

1   Click the Loop Browser button or press Cmd-L to open the Loop Browser.

2   Click the Column View button in the lower-left corner to list the loops in Column view. (If you haven't changed anything since the previous lesson, your Loop Browser will already be in Column view.)

3   Select By Instruments > Cowbell > Cowbell to see the three cowbell loops in the results list.

Loops	Instruments	Cowbell	Name ▲
All ▶	Clave ▶	Cowbell (3)	Cowbell Groove 01
By Genres ▶	Clavinet ▶	Acoustic (3)	World Agogo 01
By Instruments ▶	Conga ▶	Clean (3)	World Agogo 02
By Moods ▶	Cowbell ▶	Grooving (3)	
Favorites ▶	Cymbal ▶	▲ Part (3) ▲	
	Drum Kit ▼	▼ Percussion (3) ▼	

Scale: Any   Q   3 items

In the last lesson, you auditioned all three cowbell loops with the end of
the song. Now that we are ready to add the loop, it's a good idea to audition them again. Consider this the callback audition—it's time to narrow
it down to one.

How do you decide which one works best? Trust your instincts. Our
rhythmic instincts go way back to the original rock music—when cavemen pounded rocks and sticks together to communicate.

4   Click the Cycle button in your transport controls to open the cycle region.

Your yellow cycle region should still be set for the end of the song. If you
happened to erase it, click in the Cycle Region Ruler and drag your mouse
to create a new cycle region.

5   Press the spacebar to start playback of your cycle region in the Timeline.

6   Click the first cowbell loop—Cowbell Groove 01—to audition it with
the song.

7   Press the spacebar to stop all playback.

What do your instincts tell you? Mine say it's a little busy. It overpowers the bass track, and gets annoying after a few measures. Next!

8   Press the spacebar again to play the cycle region.

9   Click the World Agogo 01 cowbell loop to audition it with the song.

10   Press the spacebar to stop playback.

Well? What do you think? I think this one has a nice groove that fits well with the rest of the tracks. I'd say it's a keeper, but to be fair, you should listen to the last one, just in case.

11   Repeat the previous steps to audition the World Agogo 02 loop. Stop playback when you finish.

So, what's your verdict on this loop? It's not bad, but it doesn't fit the groove of the song. You could use it and it wouldn't sound awful (neither would cavemen banging rocks), but that doesn't mean you should settle for mediocre and put it in *this* song.

Remember, just because something doesn't sound bad doesn't mean it sounds good. Trust your instincts to figure out what to use and what not to use. If you're undecided, that may mean it isn't really helping the song, so leave it out.

One last thing about selecting loops. If a loop doesn't fit a particular song, it might still be perfect for another song. That's why you have at least a thousand loops from which to choose.

There you have it. Let's add the World Agogo 01 loop to the Timeline.

Adding a Loop Track

Since you're working with prerecorded Apple Loops, you don't have to add a track to the Timeline first. A track will be created automatically when you add the loop to the Timeline.

The easiest way to add a prerecorded loop to the Timeline is to click and drag it there. First, it's a good idea to decide where to put it.

1 Drag the scroller on the right side of the Timeline all the way to the bottom to view the lowest tracks in the Timeline.

> **NOTE ▶** If you're working on a PowerBook or iMac and you used the Zoom (+) button to fit the GarageBand window to the display, you may see all tracks without seeing the scroller. If you resize the window so you can't see all tracks, the scroller will appear so you can see any tracks that are out of view.

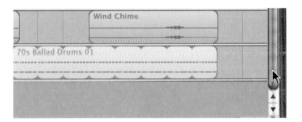

2 Click the Beat Ruler on the measure line for the 25th measure to move the playhead to the first beat in measure 25.

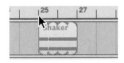

> **TIP ▶** If you don't see the number 25 in the Beat Ruler, zoom in to the Timeline (Ctrl–right arrow). More numbered measures will appear in the Beat Ruler.

A quick way to tell exactly where your playhead actually is in the Timeline is to look at the Time Display at the bottom of the Timeline.

The Time Display is currently set to show musical time—in measures, beats, ticks (counts within a beat), and thousandths of a beat. You can also set the Time Display to show actual time—in hours, minutes, seconds, and hundredths of a second.

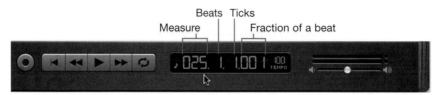

Notice the Time Display shows 025.1.1.001. If you read it from right to left, it would be the first tick in the first beat of the 25th measure. In other words, you're at the beginning of the 25th measure.

NOTE ▶ If your Time Display doesn't show that you're at the beginning of the 25th measure, click the playhead in the Beat Ruler and drag it to the beginning of the 25th measure. You'll know you're in the right place by reading the Time Display.

Now that your playhead is in position, you know where to put the World Agogo 01 loop in the Timeline.

You don't have to make a track for the loop in the Timeline. Simply dragging a loop from the browser to the space below the bottom track will automatically create a new track for the selected loop. The loop will appear in the new track wherever you release the mouse. It's a good idea to use the playhead as a guide when dragging and dropping loops in the Timeline.

3   Click and drag the World Agogo 01 loop from the results list in the Loop Browser to the Timeline and release it at the playhead position below the bottom track.

The green circle with the plus sign in it shows that you're adding a loop to the Timeline.

A new track appears at the bottom of the Timeline with the World Agogo 01 loop region at the playhead position.

The new track is named after the instrument category, Cowbell, and the loop maintains its original name, World Agogo 01.

As you can see, adding a prerecorded loop to the Timeline is as easy as select, drag, and release.

4 Press Cmd-L to close the Loop Browser.

5 Click the Cycle button to turn off the cycle region.

6 Press the spacebar to listen to the Cowbell track with the rest of the song. Press the spacebar again to stop playback.

Project Tasks

Now that you know how to add a loop to the Timeline and create a new track, it's your turn to try these skills on your own. Your mission is to reopen the Loop Browser, find the Claypot Percussion 01 loop, and add it to the Timeline in a new track starting at the beginning of the 27th measure. The next picture shows how it should look when you're finished.

1   Open the Loop Browser and find the Claypot Percussion 01 loop.

    Hint: You can easily locate the Claypot using the Search text field.

2   Move the playhead to the beginning of the 27th measure in the Timeline.

3   Click and drag the loop from the search results to the playhead below the lowest track and release.

4   Listen to the new Claypot Percussion track to hear how it sounds with the other tracks.

Extending a Loop Region

So, what did you think of the Claypot Percussion 01 loop? I feel it really complements the song's organic-feeling acoustic groove.

Now let's extend the claypot sound so it will last until the Hollywood Strings section kicks in around the 31st measure. The whole process is incredibly easy. Loop regions are designed to repeat (loop) over and over seamlessly. To extend a loop region, all you have to do is click the upper-right corner and pull.

First, let's move the playhead so we can use it as a guide for extending the loop region.

1   Click and drag the playhead through the Beat Ruler to the beginning of the 31st measure.

Check the Time Display to make sure your playhead is in the right location.

2   Move your pointer over the upper-right corner of the Claypot Percussion 01 loop region.

The pointer becomes a loop pointer, a vertical line next to a curved arrow, which indicates the cursor is in the correct position to drag the loop to repeat.

3   Click-drag the upper-right corner of the Claypot Percussion 01 loop region and extend it to the playhead position (the beginning of the 31st measure).

You don't have to extend a loop for the full length of the original region. If you make the looped section shorter than the original, you will only hear the notes included in the new loop segment.

Notice that as the loop repeats, you can see notches that show the beginning and end of the original loop within the new region.

4   Move the playhead back to the beginning of the 24th measure and play the song through the end of the 31st measure.

The song is really coming together. I like the way the Claypot Percussion stops just as the World Conga takes over. It's as if one instrument passes the percussive baton to the other.

There's just one problem. In retrospect, I'm not crazy about the Cowbell track. After all that work, it really doesn't fit in as well as I hoped.

Muting a Track

Before you retire the cowbell and delete the track, it would be a good idea to hear how the song sounds with and without the cowbell. That way you can make an informed decision.

To mute a track, all you need to do is click the Mute button in the track header. The mute button looks like a speaker.

1   Locate the track header for the Cowbell track.

2   Click the Mute button in the Cowbell track header to silence the track.

The Mute button turns blue when it is on.

The regions within the muted track turn light gray to indicate that they have been muted.

3   Click the Cycle button in the transport controls to turn on the cycle region.

To change a cycle region, simply click-drag a new location on the Cycle Region Ruler.

4   Create a cycle region that starts about a measure before the cowbell, and ends about a measure after. (It does not have to be exact.)

5   Press the spacebar to start playback of the cycle region.

6 Listen to the section of the song without the cowbell.

7 Click the Mute button again during playback to unmute the track and hear the cowbell.

8 Continue playback, and click the Mute button on and off to compare the section with and without cowbell.

9 Press the spacebar to stop playback.

10 Click the Cycle button to turn off the cycle region.

The song could work with or without the cowbell, but I'm going to go with my instincts here and delete the Cowbell track. Why, after all that work to audition the cowbells, would I want you to cut it out of the song? Because sometimes a musical part seems like a good idea until you put it in perspective and hear it with the entire song. The cowbell cuts through the feel of the song too much. It's as if it jumps out at you and screams—"Hey listen to me, I'm a cowbell!" This isn't a song about a cowbell. For this song, the percussion is supposed to feel organic and subtle, like a percussive heartbeat. The cowbell breaks the flow of the piece.

Of course, that's just my opinion. Music is incredibly subjective, and if any of you really want the cowbell, you can put it back after this lesson.

Deleting a Track in the Timeline

Fortunately, GarageBand makes it really easy to change your mind—all you have to do is delete the track. It's not like the real world, where you have to tell the poor musician with the cowbell to sit this one out.

Once you've decided to delete a track, the process is incredibly simple. After you select the track, there are two ways to delete it from the Timeline:

- Choose Track > Delete Track.

- Press Cmd-Delete (Command plus the Delete key).

Let's try it.

1   Click the Cowbell track header to select it (if it's not already selected).

The track header is green if it is selected.

2   Choose Track > Delete Track.

That's it—the cowbell is gone. The song still needs one more thing—a better wind chime sound at the end. The wind chime that I recorded originally is OK, but why settle for OK when you have GarageBand to help you make it great?

Recording a Basic Software Instrument

You can record Software Instruments in GarageBand using a USB music keyboard or a MIDI synthesizer-type keyboard. You can also use the handy built-in onscreen keyboard that comes with GarageBand.

For this exercise, you'll work with the onscreen keyboard. You'll learn more about recording with external devices in a later chapter.

Using the Onscreen Keyboard

There are two ways to open the built-in onscreen keyboard:

- Press Cmd-K.

- Choose Window > Keyboard.

Let's use the menu method so you'll know where to find the keyboard in the future.

1   Choose Window > Keyboard to open the keyboard window.

A small window opens that looks like a music keyboard.

For some of you, this may be your first fully functional MIDI keyboard controller. What is a MIDI keyboard controller? MIDI is an acronym that stands for *Musical Instrument Digital Interface*. MIDI is a standard protocol that is used for computers to communicate with electronic musical instruments and vice versa.

The instruments you play using a MIDI keyboard come from professional samples. Each note you press on the keyboard triggers a digitally sampled sound.

What's a sample? A *sample* is a digital re-creation of an instrument sound. Have you ever tasted one of those little half-moon shaped apple pies that come in a wrapper from a vending machine? It says apple pie, tastes like apple, but it actually contains no apple. None! The apple is a sampled flavor that was re-created in a lab, just as sampled instruments are re-creations that sound almost exactly—if not exactly—like the real thing.

Selecting a Software Instrument Track

Now that you have your onscreen keyboard open, let's test it out. Remember, the onscreen keyboard works only with Software Instruments, so you will need to select a Software Instrument track.

1   Select the Fingerstyle Electric Bass track in the Timeline.

The instrument name changes at the top of the onscreen keyboard to match the selected Software Instrument track.

2   Click any of the keys with your mouse to trigger the sampled Fingerstyle Electric Bass notes.

The keys turn blue as you select them.

There are only 12 different musical notes (white and black keys on the keyboard) before the same note repeats either higher or lower. If you move 12 notes to the right, you will be moving an octave higher. If you move 12 notes to the left, you will be moving an octave lower.

3   Click the small arrow at the left of the keyboard to move an octave lower.

4   Click several keys on the keyboard to hear the change in octave.

5   Click-drag your pointer across several keys to play them one after another.

6   Select the Hollywood Strings track header to switch to a different Software Instrument.

7   Click several notes to trigger the Hollywood Strings sampled notes.

8 Click and hold one note.

The note will keep playing (sustain) until you release the mouse.

9 Release the mouse to stop the note.

10 Select the Bongo track.

The onscreen keyboard becomes disabled because the Bongo track is a Real Instrument track instead of a Software Instrument track.

Remember, the onscreen keyboard works only for Software Instrument tracks. Real Instrument tracks (blue and purple) are recorded instrument tracks.

11 Select the Drum Kit track to trigger the drum samples.

12 Play several notes using the drum samples.

Each white or black key represents a different sampled drum or percussion instrument. The drum samples are packaged with additional percussion instruments that usually accompany a drum kit.

MIDI drum and percussion samples are assigned to the same notes, so the cymbals, bass drum, kick, snare, whistle, and even cowbell sounds are always the same key on any MIDI keyboard.

Project Tasks

Take a moment to familiarize yourself with the various percussion samples. Click each of the onscreen keyboard keys to hear the different drum and percussion sounds.

Be sure to change octaves by clicking the right and left arrows on either side of the onscreen keyboard. When the octaves get too high or too low, you will no longer hear percussion samples. That's because MIDI samples are only assigned to keys within a certain range of the keyboard.

- Try to locate the key that triggers the wind chime sound.
- See if you can find the cowbell sound (if you're feeling sentimental).

Adding a New Software Instrument Track

To record the new wind chime part, you'll need to create a new Software Instrument track in the Timeline.

There are three ways to add a new Software Instrument track:

- Choose Track > New Track.

- Press Option-Cmd-N.
- Click the Add New Track button.

For this exercise, you'll use the Add New Track button.

1   Click the Add New Track Button located in the lower-left corner of the window. It looks like a plus sign (+).

The New Track window appears in the middle of your screen.

The New Track window lets you choose either a Real Instrument track or a Software Instrument track.

2 Click Software Instrument, if it is not already selected.

The next step is to assign the type of Software Instrument you would like to use. The drum kits include percussion instruments like cowbells, shakers, and wind chimes. Since your goal is to record a wind chime sound, the drum kits would be a good place to start.

3 Select Drum Kits from the list of Software Instruments.

A list of different drum kits appears in the column on the right.

4   Select Jazz Kit from the list.

Dance Kit
Hip Hop Kit
Jazz Kit
Pop Kit
Rock Kit
Techno Kit

5   Click OK to finish the selection and create the Jazz Kit Software
Instrument track.

A new Jazz Kit track appears at the bottom of the Timeline, and the
onscreen keyboard name changes to Jazz Kit.

6   Click the Octave Change arrows on the keyboard until you see the key
labeled C5.

7   Click the C5 key to play the wind chime sample on the keyboard.

C5 is the note that triggers the wind chime sound.

Next, to record the wind chime sound, you need to move the playhead to
the position on the Timeline where you want to start recording. This is not
always where you want the first recorded note to appear in the Timeline.

8 Move the playhead to the beginning of the 34th measure in the Beat Ruler. Check your playhead position in the Time Display.

Why the 34th measure if we actually want the wind chime to start later in the song? Because the final recorded region will start whenever you click the first note. If you back your playhead up a few measures and then click Record, it's like giving yourself time to count in and prepare—one, two, three, go. If you click Record exactly where you need to record the first note, you start on go!

It's always a good idea to start your recording a measure or two before the point at which you actually need to record a part. That gives you a chance to follow along with the music and get into the groove of the song before you have to perform.

9 Click the C5 note again to practice clicking and holding the wind chime sound.

Practice is always a good idea, even if it is only a wind chime.

10 Mute the Wind Chime track that is already in the Timeline so you won't hear it while you're recording.

11 Select the Jazz Kit track, if it is not already selected.

TIP ▶ Move the onscreen keyboard so it is above the track you want to record. This way, you can see the keyboard, the new track, and the Time Display without having to look away from what you're doing.

Understand the part you're about to record. Your goal is to record a new wind chime sound that starts around the beginning of the 37th measure and stops before the last measure of the song. Watch the Time Display for your cue, and when you get to the 37th measure, click the C5 note. Release the note when you get to the beginning of the 39th measure.

The Record button is the red button at the left end of the transport controls.

12 Click the Record button to start recording.

13 Select and hold the C5 note at the beginning of the 37th measure.

14 Release the mouse to stop the note when you reach the beginning of the 39th measure.

15 Press the spacebar to stop recording and playback.

Your finished recording should look something like the following picture.

Using Undo to Delete a Recording

Fortunately, GarageBand—like most software—has an Undo feature. Undo allows you to move back one step in your project to the way it was before the last thing you did.

In this case, we recorded a part. Undo will reset the project to the way it was before that recording. Not that there is anything wrong with your recording. This is just a good time to show you the Undo feature.

If you undo a recording immediately, before you save the song file, you delete the recording from memory. If you keep a recorded region in the Timeline, it is saved with your project file data and remains part of the project.

There are two ways to undo the last step:

- Press Cmd-Z.

- Choose Edit > Undo Recording.

Edit	Track	Control	W
Undo Recording		⌘Z	
Redo		⇧⌘Z	
Cut		⌘X	
Copy		⌘C	
Paste		⌘V	
Delete			
Select All		⌘A	
Split		⌘T	
Join Selected		⌘J	
Special Characters...			

Since you will be using the Undo feature frequently throughout your recording career, it's a good keyboard shortcut to memorize.

1   Press Cmd-Z to undo the last recording.

2   Move your playhead back to the beginning of the 34th measure.

3   Repeat steps 12 through 15 from the previous exercise to re-record the wind chime part. Make sure the Jazz Kit track is selected before you click the Record button.

4   Listen to the song with your new recording. If you're satisfied with your recording, move on to the next task. If you want to try again, press Cmd-Z to undo and repeat the process to record again.

Saving Your Song

Now that you have successfully recorded a Software Instrument track, it's a good idea to save the changes you've made to the song.

There are two ways to save your song:

•   Press Cmd-S.

•   Choose File > Save.

You can also Save As to save a new version of the song with a different name. Let's try that for this exercise.

To Save As, you can either press Shift-Cmd-S, or go to the File menu and choose Save As.

1   Choose File > Save As.

A Save As window appears so you can change the song name and location.

2 Delete the word *Starting* to leave the name as *2-1 Eyewitness* in the Name field.

If you have been working with **1-1 Eyewitness** from Lesson 1, change the name to *2-1 Eyewitness* also.

3 Click the blue downward-pointing arrow to the right of the Save As name field for an extended view of the Save As window.

Save As: 2-1 Eyewitness

Where: GarageBand

Cancel   Save

The window expands to show the extended view.

NOTE ▶ If you were already looking at the expanded view, clicking the downward-pointing arrow takes you back to the minimized view. Click the downward-pointing arrow again to see the full window.

It's a good idea to have a set destination for all the songs you create as you work through this book. To keep it simple, let's create a new folder on your Desktop for saving song files. By default, GarageBand songs are saved to the GarageBand folder in the Music folder on your computer.

4 Select the Desktop as the destination for your files.

5 Click the New Folder button in the lower-left corner of the Save As window.

☑ Hide Extension (New Folder) (Cancel) (Save)

A New Folder window appears so you can name the new folder.

6 Type your first name and *GarageBand Songs* in the Name field.

New Folder

Name of new folder:

Mary's GarageBand Songs|

(Cancel) (Create)

7 Click Create to create the folder on your Desktop.

8 Locate the Hide Extension box in the lower-left corner and make sure it is checked. If it's unchecked, click the box now.

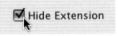
☑ Hide Extension

Now the .band extension will be hidden from your saved project.

NOTE ▶ The .band extension is useful if you are copying your projects and moving them to other computers, or posting them on a server. The .band extension makes it easier for the new computer to recognize the GarageBand file format. However, since you will be using one computer for the lessons in this book, let's leave the Hide Extension box checked to hide the extension on all the files that you save as GarageBand songs. (Note that the default setting for GarageBand is to hide the .band extension.)

9   Click Save to save the song into the new folder.

Now that you have saved the file to a new folder, let's go to the Desktop to see if it worked. First you will need to hide GarageBand. The easiest way to do that is to press Cmd-H.

10   Press Cmd-H to hide GarageBand and reveal your Desktop.

11   Locate your new GarageBand Songs folder on the Desktop.

12   Double-click the folder to see the contents.

Your newly saved song **2-1 Eyewitness** is inside the folder.

13   Click the Close button in the upper-left corner to close your folder.

14 Locate the GarageBand icon in your Dock.

15 Click the icon once to unhide the program.

Deleting a Region from the Timeline

Now that you have recorded a new Wind Chime region at the end of the song, you no longer need the originally recorded region on the Wind Chime track.

There are two ways to delete a selected region from the Timeline:

*   Press the Delete key.
*   Choose Edit > Delete.

Before you delete the original Wind Chime region, you should put away your onscreen keyboard, since you're finished with it.

1 Click the Close button in the upper-left corner of the onscreen keyboard to close the keyboard.

2 Locate the Wind Chime track.

3 Click the Mute button on the Wind Chime track to unmute the track.

4 Locate the third Wind Chime region in the track. It starts at the beginning of the 31st measure.

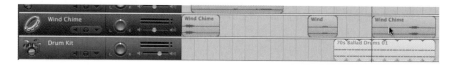

If you selected the Wind Chime track, all regions within that track become selected as well.

5 Click the empty track area to the left of the Wind Chime region to deselect all regions in the track.

6   Click once on the third Wind Chime region to select only that region.

7   Press Delete on your keyboard to delete that region.

NOTE ▶ When you press Delete, all selected regions will be deleted. Make sure you have selected only the regions you want to delete.

8   Press the Home key to move the playhead to the beginning of the song.

9   Press the spacebar to play your new and improved version of the finished song.

10   Press the spacebar to stop playback when the song is finished.

Nice job on the wind chime recording! It sounds a lot better than the original wind chime I recorded from my synthesizer.

Changing a Track Name and Icon

There's one last thing to do to this song before we move on to another project. Let's change the icon for the Jazz Kit track to reflect the instrument you actually recorded in that track. The track icon is the picture of an instrument on the left side of the track header.

To change a track's icon, you first need to double-click the current track icon to open the Track Info window.

1   Double-click the track icon for the Jazz Kit track.

The Track Info window for the Jazz Kit track opens.

2 Click the track icon in the Track Info window to reveal the Icons menu.

3 Click-drag the scroller on the right of the Icons menu to locate the Wind Chime icon.

The Wind Chime icon is located in the upper-right corner of the Icons menu.

4 Click the Wind Chime icon to select that icon for the track and close the Track Info window.

Now let's change the name of the track itself from Jazz Kit to Wind Chime.

5 Click the Jazz Kit track header to select the entire track (if it is not already selected).

6 Click the empty track area in the Jazz Kit track to deselect any regions within the track.

NOTE ▶ If any regions are selected when you change the name in the Track Editor, you will be changing the names of the regions instead of the track itself. Remember, anytime you select a track header, you also select all of the regions within that track.

7 Click the Track Editor button to open the Track Editor for the selected track.

The Track Editor opens at the bottom of the window. The word "Track" at the top left of the Track Editor shows that you're making changes to the track itself, not a specific region.

8 Type *Wind Chime* in the Name field to change the name of the track.

The Track Name changes to Wind Chime in the Timeline.

9 Press Cmd-E to close the Track Editor.

Project Tasks

Now it's your turn to change a track icon and name. Find the other Wind Chime track and change the icon from a tambourine to a wind chime. Then open the track in the Track Editor and change the track name to *Synth Wind Chime*.

1 Double-click the track icon to open the Track Info window.

2 Change the icon to a wind chime.

3 Click the Track Editor button.

4 Click the empty track space to deselect the regions in the track.

5 Type *Synth Wind Chime* in the Name field of the Track Editor.

6 Close the Track Editor.

Saving Your Project and Opening a New Project

You're now finished with the song **2-1 Eyewitness**. Let's save the project one last time, then open a different project. You can only have one GarageBand project open at a time, so by opening a new project, you will automatically close the other one.

1   Press Cmd-S to save the current project.

2   Choose File > Open, or press Cmd-O to open another project.

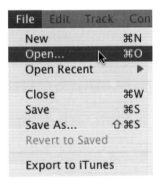

3   Locate your Lessons folder and select Lesson_02 > **2-3 Homecoming Starting**.

Open		
Lesson_02		
Lessons	Lesson_01	2–1 Eyewitness Starting
	Lesson_02	2–2 Eyewitness Finished
	Lesson_03	2-3 Homecoming Starting
	Lesson_04	2–4 Homecoming Finished

4   Click Open to open the song.

The song **2-3 Homecoming Starting** opens in the GarageBand window.

5 Choose File > Save As to save the project to your songs folder on the Desktop.

6 Click the Desktop icon in the Save As window.

7 Select your GarageBand Songs folder

8 Click Save.

Now all of the changes you make to this song will be saved to your version in your folder on the Desktop. The original song will remain "as is" in the Lessons folder.

Changing a Software Track Instrument

Not only can you edit Software Instrument regions, but you can also change the instrument itself. Imagine recording a music part using a piano sample, then deciding that you would rather have a guitar play that part—or vice versa. No problem. All you have to do is open the Track Info window and change the instrument for the track.

Before you go changing instruments, let's listen to the song to hear what it sounds like. You may notice that three of the tracks have been muted. We'll get to those in a few minutes. For now, leave them muted.

1   Press the Home key to move the playhead to the beginning of the Timeline, if it is not there already.

2   Press the spacebar and listen to the entire song.

I wrote this piece on my baby grand piano, then recorded the piano part using a MIDI keyboard and the Grand Piano Software Instrument.

3   Double-click the Grand Piano track to open the Track Info window for that track.

The Track Info window opens.

4   Select Guitars as the Software Instrument, and Steel String Acoustic for the specific guitar.

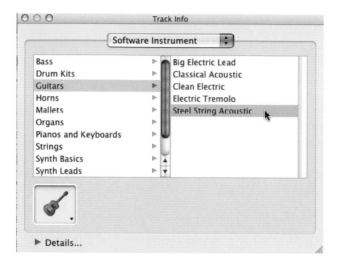

The Track Info window will automatically close after you have selected the instrument.

The first track in the Timeline is now called Steel String Acoustic, and the track icon is a guitar.

5   Press the Home key to move the playhead to the beginning of the song.

6   Listen to the first half of the song again with the new Guitar track as the lead instrument.

Now you see how easy it is to change one Software Instrument to another. This is incredibly useful if you only play keyboards but not guitar, for example, or the other way around.

I like the guitar as the lead for part of this song, but I miss the piano for other parts. Later on, when we work on song arrangement in Lesson 6, you'll learn how to break a song up into different parts on different tracks. For now, let's stick with one instrument for the lead.

Project Tasks

Change the lead instrument track (Steel String Acoustic track) back to a Grand Piano.

1   Double-click the top track header to open the Track Info window.

2   Choose Pianos and Keyboards > Grand Piano.

3   Close the Track Info window.

Using Solo and Mute to Evaluate Tracks

You've already worked with muting tracks, so let's take a look at soloing a track. When you mute a track, it silences that track. If you solo a track, it silences (mutes) all of the other tracks.

Our goal in this exercise is to use mute and solo to decide which percussion tracks to keep, and which to delete. When you build a song, it is common to have multiple versions of the same part. Then you can mix and match them, or pick the best one and delete the unwanted tracks.

Right now, the active percussion tracks consist of the 70s Ballad Drums 01 regions and several Shaker regions.

To solo a track, click the Solo button in the track header. The Solo button looks like a pair of headphones.

1   Click the Solo buttons for the active Drum Kit track and Shaker track (the second and third tracks from the top).

All of the other tracks will turn gray to show they have been muted.

2   Move your playhead to the beginning of the 16th measure.

3   Press the spacebar to play the song up to the beginning of the 32nd measure.

4   While the song is playing, click the Solo button for the Grand Piano track to hear it with the percussion tracks.

5   Click the Solo buttons on all three tracks again to unsolo the top three tracks.

One thing to remember when you're muting or soloing is that mute overrides solo on all other tracks. What does that mean? If you solo a track, it will mute all other tracks. If you unsolo a track, it will unmute all the other tracks, except tracks that have the Mute buttons turned on.

The three lower percussion tracks were muted separately. When you clicked the Solo button, they remained mute, and when you turned off solo, they remained mute. In other words, if you turn on a Mute button, you can't turn it off using the Solo buttons from another track.

Let's create a cycle region to make it easier to experiment with solo and mute and try out the different percussion tracks with the rest of the song.

6   Click the Cycle button in the transport controls.

7 Create a cycle region that starts around the beginning of the 15th measure and goes until the end of the 39th measure. (The cycle region should include all of the percussion regions in the lower three percussion tracks.)

8 Press the spacebar to begin playback of the cycle region.

9 Click the Mute buttons on the lower percussion tracks to turn mute off.

10 Mute the upper Drum Kit track with the 70s Ballad Drums regions.

11 Mute the Shaker track to hear the song with and without the shaker.

12 Solo the Grand Piano track and the lower percussion tracks to hear them by themselves.

13 Try different combinations of the lead instrument and the percussion tracks.

When you finish experimenting with solo and mute, press the spacebar to stop playback.

Well, what did you come up with? After much deliberation, I think the lower percussion tracks have much more personality, and they enhance the song, while the 70s Ballad Drums track seems a little too passive—this track keeps time but doesn't add anything to the song. I think it's time to delete the 70s Ballad Drums track. The Shaker track still works, so that track can stay with the others.

14 Click the Drum Kit header on the second track from the top.

15 Press Cmd-Delete to delete the track.

16 Click the Cycle button to close the cycle region.

17 Play the full song one more time to hear all the changes in the song.

Save and Close the Project

Now that you have finished the track changes to the **2-3 Homecoming Starting** song, you're ready to save and close the project.

1   Press Cmd-S to save the project.

2   Choose File > Close Window.

The GarageBand window closes along with the program.

What You've Learned

- You can add a new track for a prerecorded Apple Loop by clicking the loop in the Loop Browser and dragging it to the Timeline below the bottom track.

- To delete a track, select the track header and choose Track > Delete Track or press Cmd-Delete.

- To delete a region within a track, select the region and press Delete.

- The Time Display shows either musical time or actual time. It also shows the current playhead position.

- Mute silences an individual track.

- Solo silences all other tracks.

- To record a Software Instrument, you first need to create a Software Instrument track.

- The onscreen keyboard that comes with GarageBand is a MIDI interface that can be used to record Software Instruments.

- The onscreen keyboard works with the selected Software Instrument track.

- You can change a track icon in the Track Info window.

- You can change the location of saved songs. The default location is the GarageBand folder inside the Music folder on your computer.

- You can change the instrument of any Software Instrument track in the Track Info window.

- There can be only one GarageBand project open at a time.

3

Lesson Files Lessons > Lesson 3 > 3-1 SciFiShowBeats; 3-2 SciFiShowT1; 3-3 SciFiShowFinal

Time This lesson takes approximately 90 minutes to complete.

Goals Start a new song

Set the song's properties

Work with project tempo

Use the metronome to record a basic drum part

Build a rhythm track with Software Instruments

Connect a MIDI or USB keyboard to the computer

Record a Software Instrument keyboard part

Record a multipass drum region using a cycle region

Edit the length of a region

Edit a note or notes in a Software Instrument region

Transpose regions

Save a song in stages

Copy, paste, and duplicate regions

Lesson 3

Working with Software Instruments

You already have a basic understanding of the GarageBand window, and you have some experience working with tracks. Now it's time to dive in and start filling those tracks with custom music that you create with Software Instruments.

In this lesson, you are going to learn how to build a drum track out of Software Instrument regions. You'll also learn how to change the tempo, record your own beats, and copy, cut, and edit Software Instrument regions in the Timeline. After that, you'll record additional Software Instrument tracks, and edit and transpose them in the Track Editor. Along the way, you'll also learn some new keyboard shortcuts, recording tricks, and techniques for adding effects to your tracks.

NOTE ▶ Software Instruments require a Macintosh G4 or faster and at least 256 of physical RAM. If you are working on a G3, you will not be able to play or record Software Instruments in GarageBand. You will be able to open songs; you just won't be able to play them without overloading your processor.

If you are working with a slower computer, follow along with the exercises in the book using the actual lessons to learn how to work with Software Instruments. Then open the alternative version of the projects in the G3 folder included on the companion CD. The G3 versions of the songs are recreations of the songs using Real Instrument regions instead of Software Instrument regions. You will be able to play the songs in the G3 versions to hear the different tracks and the finished songs.

Starting a New Song

Launch GarageBand from your Dock, if it is not already open. GarageBand will automatically open the last project.

To start a new project, don't close the current project—doing so will also close GarageBand. Instead, let's create a new project, which will replace the current project in the window.

There are two ways to open a new song:

- Press Cmd-N.
- Choose File > New.

1 Choose File > New to open a new project.

The New Project window opens.

2 Type *Soft Inst Test* in the Save As field.

3 Click the Where pop-up menu to browse for a location on your computer to save your song.

The Recent Places pane at the bottom of the Where pop-up menu is a fast and easy way to navigate to recently visited folders on your computer.

4   In the Recent Places pane, choose your GarageBand Songs folder from the Desktop.

Setting Project Properties

Your next step is to set the properties for the project. The lower part of the New Project window shows the project properties.

The project properties are Tempo, Time, and Key.

- Tempo is the pacing of the song, measured by BPM (beats per minute).
- Time is the musical time signature used to count beats within a measure of the song. A song using 4/4 time means there are four beats per measure. A song using 3/4 time has only three beats per measure.
- Key is the musical key for the entire project. Once you set the key, all of the prerecorded loops will automatically match the project key. There are 12 different notes or keys you can set for your project.

The current settings are the default settings for each new GarageBand project.

1 Locate the Tempo slider in the middle of the New Project window.

The current tempo is 120 bpm, as you can see in the bpm field.

2 Click-drag the Tempo slider all the way to the left.

Tempo:
Time: 4 / 4   60 bpm
Key: C

The bpm field now shows 60 bpm, which is the lowest tempo.

3 Click the Time pop-up to see the various time signature choices.

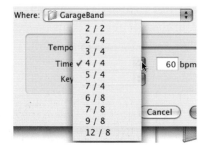

Time signature is a way of counting beats, and it is displayed as a fraction. The upper number indicates the number of beats per measure; the lower number is the basic beat value. The default time signature is 4/4, or four beats per measure.

Different types of music use different time signatures. A pop or rock song uses 4/4 time, or four beats per measure. If you count the beats out loud, they would be one-two-three-four, one-two-three-four. A waltz, on the other hand, uses a slower 3/4 time. The count sounds like one-two-three, one-two-three.

Let's leave the time signature at 4/4 for the new song.

4   Click the Key pop-up menu.

There are 12 different keys from which to choose. The default is a good key to work with, so let's leave it set to C.

5   Click Create in the lower-right corner of the New Project window to create your new project.

Your new project, titled Soft Inst Test, opens.

By default, every new song opens with the Grand Piano Software Instrument track in the Timeline.

Changing Project Tempo

Your new song has all of the properties that you set in the New Project window. Let's focus for a few minutes on the tempo, which you set to 60 bpm.

Tempo is pacing—the pulse or speed of the song. The slower the tempo, the slower the song sounds and feels. The faster the tempo, the faster the song sounds and feels.

1   Locate the Time Display at the bottom of the window.

The Time Display shows the tempo as 60 bpm.

To hear what 60 bpm sounds like, let's listen to some prerecorded Apple Loops.

2   Click the Loop Browser button to open the Loop Browser.

3   Click the Drum Kit button in the Loop Browser.

Each loop was originally recorded at a specific tempo and key. This information is part of the data that can be used to sort loops, and can be seen in different columns in the results list of the Loop Browser.

A loop will always conform to the project key and tempo.

4   Click any of the drum loops to hear it at 60 bpm.

How does it sound? Slow? Relaxed? Comatose? 60 bpm is slow even for a really slow song.

5   Click 80s Pop Beat 07 to listen to it at 60 bpm. Press the spacebar to stop.

Locate the Tempo column to the right of the Name column in the Loop Browser results list to see the native tempo of the selected loop.

Notice that the native tempo for the 80s Pop Beat 07 loop is 110.

Name	Tempo
70s Ballad Drums 01	80
80s Pop Beat 07	110
80s Pop Beat 08	110
80s Pop Beat 09	110
80s Pop Beat 10	110
Classic Rock Beat 01	140
Classic Rock Beat 02	140

Now let's add the loop to the Timeline.

6 Click-drag the 80s Pop Beat 07 loop from the results list in the Loop
Browser to the beginning of the Timeline below the first track. Release
the mouse.

A Drum Kit track appears in the Timeline with the 80s Pop Beat 07 region
at the beginning of the track.

7 Press the Home key to move your playhead to the beginning of the
Timeline.

8 Press the spacebar to listen to the 80s Pop Beat 07 region in the Drum Kit
track at 60 bpm. Press the spacebar again to stop playback.

Let's speed things up a bit by changing the
tempo. To change the tempo, you will need to
access the Tempo slider in the Time Display.

9 Click and hold the Tempo slider. Don't release
the mouse.

The Tempo slider appears with the slider arrow
in the lowest position (60).

10 Drag the Tempo slider to the highest position (240).

11 Play the region in the Timeline again at the new tempo.

Unlike the 60 bpm tempo, which sounded very slow and sleepy, this tempo is wide awake and in a serious musical hurry.

When you change the project tempo, all the loops in the Loop Browser play at that tempo to match the project.

Preparing the Project

Now that you know how to change the tempo, let's change it back to the GarageBand default of 120 bpm. This is also a good time to do a little Timeline housekeeping to prepare for the next exercise.

1 Change the project tempo to 120 bpm using the Tempo slider in the Time Display.

2 Press Cmd-L to close the Loop Browser.

3 Click the Drum Kit track header to select the Drum Kit track.

4 Press Cmd-Delete to delete the entire track from the Timeline.

5 Double-click the Grand Piano track header to open the Track Info window.

6 Change the instrument for the Grand Piano track from Grand Piano to Drum Kit > Hip Hop Kit.

7 Close the Track Info window.

Recording a Simple Drum Part

You have listened to the drum and percussion loops in the Loop Browser, and the regions used in the songs for the previous lessons. Now it's your turn to create a drum region of your own. This exercise will be challenging, especially if rhythm isn't one of your specialties. Fortunately, GarageBand comes with a built-in metronome to help you.

Turning on the Metronome

A metronome is a device used by musicians to keep time. The metronome clicks at a steady beat based on the tempo of the project. You can use the clicks as a guide for "practicing" instrument parts during playback and for recording them.

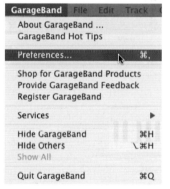

To hear the metronome during playback, you need to turn it on in the General Preferences.

1 Choose GarageBand > Preferences.

The General Preferences window opens.

2 Locate the Metronome settings near the top of the window.

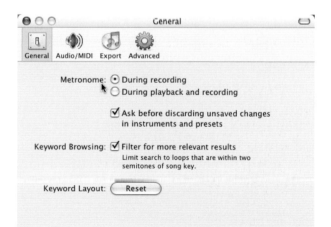

There are two settings for the metronome: "During recording" or "During playback and recording."

3   Select the "During playback and recording" setting.

The metronome will now play during playback (as you practice) and while you record.

4   Click the Close button (red X) on the General Preferences window to close the window.

5   Press the Home key to move the playhead to the beginning of the Timeline.

6   Locate the Time Display at the bottom of the GarageBand window.

The Time Display shows you are at the first beat of the first measure. Remember, this project is in 4/4 time, so there will be four steady beats in each measure. The metronome will count off the beats (4) to the project tempo (120).

7   Press the spacebar to hear the metronome. Watch the beats count 1 through 4 in the Time Display for each measure.

Notice that the measure counter advances one for every four beats.

The beat changes with each click of the metronome. The first beat of every measure is louder and of a slightly lower pitch.

8   Press the spacebar again to stop playback.

Practicing with the Metronome

Before you record the actual drum part, it's a good idea to practice a few times first. For this exercise, you will use the onscreen keyboard to play a drum part and practice using the metronome.

1   Press Cmd-K to open the onscreen keyboard.

2 Click the Lower Octave arrow on the left edge of the onscreen keyboard until the first note on the keyboard is C1.

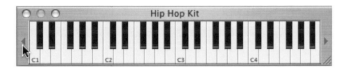

NOTE ▶ If your keyboard starts lower than C1, press the Higher Octave arrow on the right edge of the keyboard until the first note is C1.

To keep this exercise simple, you will only be working with the first five notes (white and black keys), which are C1, C1#, D1, D1#, and E1. Each note triggers a different sampled drum sound from a Hip Hop Drum Kit.

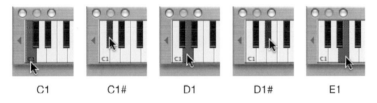

| C1 | C1# | D1 | D1# | E1 |

3 Click each of the five notes with your pointer to hear what each one sounds like.

4 Select one of the five sounds to practice your timing.

5 Press the spacebar to start the metronome.

6 Click the drum sound—the note you've selected on the keyboard—on each beat of the metronome.

Okay, so that's kind of boring. Let's make it a little more interesting.

7 Play every other beat with the metronome.

8 Play between metronome beats.

9 Press the spacebar to stop playback.

Now that you are warmed up, you can try recording a simple drum beat. Notice that the emphasis is on *simple* at the moment. You'll get to try a more complex beat in a few minutes.

Recording a Single Take

Here is the plan: you are going to record a simple drum part that is four measures long. You will press the same instrument key as before, only this time you'll record it to the Timeline. Watch the Time Display so you'll know to stop when you have finished recording four measures.

1   Press the Home key to move the playhead to the beginning of the Timeline.

Let the first measure pass (four metronome clicks) before you start playing. That will give you a chance to get in the groove.

Try whatever pattern you want. If you are not sure what to record, try hitting the first, third, and fourth beats. Then skip a beat and repeat the pattern.

When you are ready to try, click the Record button. Remember, skip the first measure to get your timing. Then begin recording.

2   Click the Record button and record your part.

3   When you finish, press the spacebar to stop recording.

Your finished recording will look something like the following picture.

4   If you are unhappy with your recording, press Cmd-Z to undo the recording and try again.

Don't worry if it isn't perfect. The idea of this exercise is to learn how to record a single take in the Timeline, not how to record perfect drums.

Did you notice that although you started your recording at the beginning of the first measure, the recorded region actually begins wherever you played the first note event?

This is a great feature because it means you can click the Record button *before* you need to start recording to get into the groove of the song. The recorded region will begin wherever you record the first event.

Extending Your Recorded Region

One of the best things about recording Software Instruments is that you don't have to play the same part over and over. You only have to get it right once. Let's assume the drum part you recorded is perfect. Now you can loop the region by extending it.

1   Click-drag the upper-right corner of your recorded region and extend it to the right to repeat four more measures.

The extended region will have a notch in the middle to show where the original region ends and the extension begins.

2   Move your playhead to the beginning of the recorded region and press the spacebar to listen to the track. Press the spacebar again to stop playback.

3   Click the Mute button on the Hip Hop Kit button to silence the track before we move on to the next recording.

Congratulations! You just recorded your first drum track in GarageBand. Now let's move on to creating some more complicated beats.

Multipass Recording

You just recorded a simple drum part in one take. To create a mixed drum part, you may wish to try multipass recording. With multipass recording, you can record into the same region over and over, adding different sounds with each pass.

Your goal in this exercise is to record a drum region that has different drum sounds. You'll then use that region as a drum loop.

Creating a Recording Cycle Region

The first step in multipass recording is to create a cycle region for the number of measures you wish to record. For this exercise, you will set a cycle region that is two measures in length.

1   Click the Cycle button in the transport controls to show the cycle region.

The cycle region appears beneath the Beat Ruler at the top of the Timeline.

2   Click-drag the Cycle Region Ruler between the 2nd and 4th measure to create a cycle region two measures long.

Creating a New Software Instrument Track

Before you record, you'll need to create a new Software Instrument track.

1   Choose Track > New Track to open the New Track window.

2   Select Drum Kits > Hip Hop Kit from the Software Instrument choices.

3   Click OK to create the new track.

4   Click the first five keys (C1–E1) to hear the sounds again.

Recording a Rough Draft

Brace yourself—the first time you try multipass recording will likely be rough. Don't worry—with the Undo command, you can always do it again.

Select one drum sound, perhaps the kick drum (C1) or the snare (E1), and play only that drum part for the first pass. Choose a second drum part for the next pass. Each time you finish recording a drum part, switch to a different sampled drum sound (a different key on the keyboard) to add a new part.

Experiment with the different drum parts to come up with one that you like. If you are having trouble coming up with a pattern, start with the pattern I describe below for the kick drum and snare. Keep in mind that your drum pattern will be two measures in length, making it a total of eight beats, four per measure.

Try recording the kick drum once on the second beat and twice on the fourth beat. Then again in the next measure, record once on the second beat and twice on the fourth beat.

Now try the snare twice on the first beat, once on the second beat, twice on the third beat, and once on the fourth beat for both measures.

Keep the recording going until you have recorded a pass with all five of the different sounds.

The key (pun intended) to making this work is that you *can't* stop recording. If you stop recording, the multi-take option is over. If you try to record in that region again, you'll erase the previous recording.

One more thing: let's slow things down a bit for this first version. Remember, if you slow the tempo down for a Software Instrument, you can always speed it up again after you record.

1   Change the project tempo to 100.

    The metronome will change to match the new project tempo.

TIP ► Let the metronome count off a few measures first to get a feel for the tempo before you start recording.

2   Click the Record button to start the multipass recording.

3   Record each instrument one at a time through each pass.

4   When you finish, press the spacebar to stop recording.

NOTE ► If you hold a note at the end of the loop region, it may cause the finished loop to extend longer than two measures.

5   Change the project tempo back to 120 to hear your recorded loop at a faster tempo.

So, how did it go? Recording drum loops takes a lot of practice and patience. Fortunately, you can always press Cmd-Z to undo the recording and start over.

If you had a rough time creating your own drum tracks, there's good news. GarageBand includes hundreds of prerecorded drum loops from which to choose. For those of you who like creating your own beats, you now have the tools to do it.

Resizing a Recorded Region

What if your finished recorded region appears longer than the two measures you set in the cycle region? You can easily resize the region to trim the empty space at the beginning and end.

To resize a Software Instrument region in the Timeline, simply click-drag the lower-right or lower-left corner and resize.

1   Move your pointer over the lower-right corner of the recorded region.

The pointer becomes a resize pointer.

2   Click-drag the lower-right edge of the loop to resize it so that it fits the two measures of the cycle region.

3   Move your pointer over the upper-right corner of the recorded region to turn it into the loop pointer.

4   Click-drag the upper-right corner to extend your recorded region another two measures.

As you can see, your recorded software regions can be resized or extended into loops depending on which corner you click-drag.

Saving Your Project

Now that you've created three different drum loops, let's save your work so you can come back and listen to it another time for pleasure—or torture, depending on the quality of your recordings.

1   Click the Mute buttons on the first two tracks to turn them back on.

2   Click the Cycle button to turn off the cycle region in the Timeline.

3   Press Cmd-S to save the project into your GarageBand Songs folder on the Desktop.

Project Tasks

Now it's time to practice your skills by recording another multipass drum loop at full tempo. For those of you who feel like creating a really fat beat, feel free to try some of the other drum sounds (keys) within the Hip Hop Kit.

1   Create a new Software Instrument track and select the Drum Kit > Hip Hop Kit for the instrument.

2   Turn the cycle region on and record a new drum loop using multiple drum sounds.

3   Extend your finished region so that it loops three times in the Timeline.

Building a Song from Scratch

The next series of exercises will walk you through the steps of building a song using Software Instruments. Some of the instrument parts will be prerecorded Apple Loops; others you will record using the onscreen keyboard. Once the parts are in place, you will open the different regions in the Track Editor to edit and transpose them.

Previewing the Finished Song

Let's take a sneak preview of the finished song, so that you'll have an idea what you're going to build from scratch. I've called this song **SciFiShow,** because it's the sort of thing I would score for the opening title sequence of a hip science fiction show.

1   Choose File > Open to open an existing song file.

2   Select Lessons > Lesson_03 > **3-3 SciFiShowFinal**.

3   Double-click **3-3 SciFiShowFinal** to open the song.

    The song opens in the GarageBand window.

4 Press the Home key to move the playhead to the beginning of the song.

5 Press the spacebar to listen to the song once.

There you have it. Let's get started.

Starting a New Song

First, you need to start a new song and create a few instrument tracks for recording.

1 Choose File > New, or press Cmd-N to open the New Project window.

2 Type *SciFiShowStarting* in the Save As field.

3 Select your GarageBand Songs folder from the Where pop-up menu.

4 Click Create to create the new song.

Adding Software Instrument Tracks

You're going to be recording two Software Instrument tracks using synthesizer sounds. Let's go ahead and add another Software Instrument track before we start building the drum tracks.

1 Choose Track > New Track, or press Option-Cmd-N to add a new track.

The New Track window opens.

2 Scroll down through the Software Instruments and select Synth Pads from the left column.

3 Select Falling Star for the specific Synth instrument.

4 Click OK to create the Falling Star Synth track.

The new Falling Star track appears in the Timeline.

5   Double-click the Grand Piano track header to open the Track Info window.

6   Select Synth Pads for the Software Instrument and Angelic Organ for the specific instrument.

7   Close the Track Info window to change the track.

The top track in the Timeline is now titled Angelic Organ.

8   Press Cmd-S to save the project with the new tracks.

Building Rhythm Tracks

Sometimes you start a song by recording the melody. Other times you start with the rhythm tracks. With the SciFiShow song, it will be much easier to record the melody if we already have the rhythm tracks in place.

Rhythm tracks can consist of a bass line, a steady rhythm guitar, or drums—whatever the song uses to convey the rhythm. For this song, the drums will carry the rhythm.

Instead of recording the drum parts, you'll use some prerecorded drum loops.

Selecting Software Instrument Drum Loops

The first step in building a solid rhythm track is selecting (or recording) several different loops that will work well together. Let's select some loops.

1   Click the Loop Browser button to open the Loop Browser.

2   Click the Drums button to narrow the search results to drums only.

3   Click-drag the scroller to the right of the results to scroll through the various choices.

4   Locate the far-left column in the search results.

There are two symbols in this column: a green note, which indicates a Software Instrument loop, or a blue waveform, which indicates a Real Instrument loop.

You can sort the search results by clicking the top of any of the different columns. Usually you sort by name and look at the results in alphabetical order. For this exercise, you want to look at only Software Instrument loops, so let's click the top of the Loop Type (left) column.

5   Click the top of the Loop Type column to sort the loops by type.

The loops are now sorted by type.

NOTE ▶ If you want to reverse the order of a column, just click the column header again.

6   Scroll down to locate the Software Instrument loop called Hip Hop Beat 01.

7   Click-drag the Hip Hop Beat 01 loop from the browser to the beginning of the Timeline below the Falling Star track.

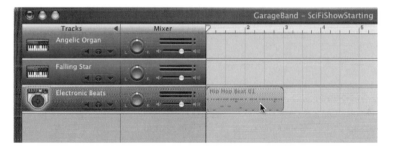

A new Electronic Beats track appears in the Timeline with the Hip Hop Beat 01 region inside.

8   Click-drag the upper-right corner of the Hip Hop Beat 01 region to extend it until it repeats a total of four times.

9   Listen to the entire Hip Hop Beat 01 region in the Timeline.

It starts out cool, and it is. However, if you listen to that same beat for almost a minute, it's going to lose its coolness real fast. The song needs additional drum parts. We'll find them next.

NOTE ▶ If you use only one drum loop for an entire song, no matter how good the loop is, eventually it becomes nothing more than a complex metronome. Try to mix it up and add some variety to your drum tracks to keep them from being so "loopy."

Selecting Additional Drum Parts

You're off to a good start, but it's time to dive into the Loop Browser and find a few more loops that will complement your **SciFiShow** song.

1   Move the playhead to the beginning of the 12th measure in the Timeline.

Check your Time Display to make sure you are at the beginning of the 12th measure.

2   Click-drag the Hip Hop Beat 02 from the Loop Browser to the playhead position below the bottom track in the Timeline.

A new Electronic Beats track appears in the Timeline with the Hip Hop Beat 02 region starting at the beginning of the 12th measure.

Now you need to add an interesting loop to overlap the first drum region and fill the gap between the first two Hip Hop Beat tracks.

3   Move the playhead to the beginning of the 8th measure.

4   Locate the Ambient Beat 01 loop in the search results.

5   Click-drag the Ambient Beat 01 loop from the Loop Browser to the playhead position below the lowest track in the Timeline.

A new Electronic Beats track appears in the Timeline with the Ambient Beat 01 region starting at the 8th measure.

Your three new tracks should look like the following picture.

6   Press the Home key to move your playhead to the beginning of the Timeline.

7 Press the spacebar to listen to the drum tracks.

8 Press the spacebar again to stop playback when you reach the end of the song.

9 Click the Loop Browser button to hide the Loop Browser.

Viewing Actual Time in the Time Display

Up to this point in the book, you have been using musical time as a reference for the playhead position. The Time Display also shows actual time.

The lower-left corner of the Time Display shows a musical note. This note is a button that selects the type of time to be displayed.

1 Locate the Musical Time button in the lower-left corner of the Time Display.

2 Click the empty space above the Musical Time button to change the display to actual time.

A small clock button appears, and the time in the display changes to actual time (hours, minutes, seconds, and fractions of seconds).

3 Move the playhead to the end of the last region in the Timeline to see the length of the song in actual time.

According to the Time Display, the song is currently 30 seconds long. This song is supposed to be 50 seconds in length, so you're going to have to extend it.

Copying and Pasting Regions in the Timeline

Copying and pasting regions in the Timeline is an easy way to duplicate regions without having to go back to the Loop Browser.

There are two ways to copy regions in the Timeline:

*   Choose Edit > Copy.
*   Press Cmd-C.

To paste a region, you first must select the track where you wish to paste the region, then, move the playhead to the desired position on the track.

There are two ways to paste regions in the Timeline:
*   Choose Edit > Paste.
*   Press Cmd-V.

Let's try copying and pasting a region now.

1   Select the Hip Hop Beat 01 region in the Timeline.

2   Press Cmd-C to copy the region, or Choose Edit > Copy.

The region has been copied into the computer memory.

3   Move the playhead to the end of the last region (30 seconds) in the Timeline. (It should be there already.)

4   Make sure the top Electronic Beats track is selected.

5   Press Cmd-V or Choose Edit > Paste to paste the region at the playhead position on the selected track.

The new pasted region appears in the Timeline.

NOTE ▶ If the pasted region appeared on a different track, or you accidentally copied and pasted the wrong region, press Cmd-Z to undo the edit, then repeat steps 1–5.

Backing Up a Song File in Stages

It's a good idea to save your song with different names as you build it. That way, you can go back to an earlier stage of the song to change the outcome or to create different versions. Up to this point, you have only created the rhythm tracks or *beats* for this song. Let's save the project and identify it as beats only, so later you can go back to the song at this level and record different tracks to the beats.

1   Choose File > Save As or press Shift-Cmd-S to open the Save As window.

2   Change the name to
SciFiShowBeats.

3   From the Where pop-up,
choose your GarageBand
Songs folder on the Desktop.

4   Click Save to save a copy of the project as **SciFiShowBeats**.

Finishing the Basic Beats Tracks

Now let's apply what you have learned so far in this lesson to finish the basic beats tracks for this song. In this review exercise, you will copy and paste the Hip Hop Beat 02 region in the Timeline.

1   Select the Hip Hop Beat 02 region and press Cmd-C to copy it.

2   Move the playhead to the beginning of the 19th measure.

3   Paste the Hip Hop Beat 02 region to the playhead position.

4   Locate the second Hip Hop Beat 01 region in the Timeline.

It is located in the third track from the top.

5   Extend the second Hip Hop Beat 01 region so it loops a total of five times and ends at the end of the 26th measure, which is 50 seconds in the Time Display.

6   Listen to the rhythm tracks in the Timeline.

7   Press Cmd-S to save the changes to your song.

Recording a New Software Instrument Part

Now that the rhythm tracks are in place, it's time to start recording the additional parts. Another terrific feature about Software Instruments in GarageBand is that you can edit them once they have been recorded.

In this next exercise, you'll record an organ part for the song. The part is very simple to play, so you can use the onscreen keyboard. If you have a different musical keyboard that you wish to use for this recording, you're welcome to use it.

Connecting a MIDI Keyboard to the Computer

If you prefer to use an external music keyboard instead of the onscreen keyboard, you can connect a MIDI-compatible keyboard through a USB connection or MIDI interface.

To connect a USB MIDI keyboard, all you need to do is connect the USB cable to the computer and to the keyboard.

To connect a standard MIDI keyboard, you will need a USB-to-MIDI interface. Connect the keyboard to the MIDI interface device using standard MIDI cables. Then connect the interface to your computer using the USB cable.

Carefully read the instructions that come with the keyboard and MIDI interface, and be sure to install all of the necessary drivers.

> **MORE INFO** ▶ *For more information about GarageBand accessories, including MIDI keyboards, USB keyboards, or MIDI interfaces, visit Apple's Web site: www.apple.com/ilife/garageband/accessories.*

Preparing to Record

As you prepare to record new tracks, your first step is to select the Software Instrument track where you wish to record—in this case, it's the Angelic Organ track.

1   Click the Angelic Organ track header to select the track.

2   Press Cmd-K to open the onscreen keyboard.

NOTE ▶ If you are using an external music keyboard, you don't need to open the onscreen keyboard. Whenever I refer to pressing specific keys on the onscreen keyboard, locate the correct keys on your external keyboard to play along.

3   Click any note to hear the Angelic Organ sound.

4   Click another note and watch the Time Display carefully.

A small blue dot flashes near the bpm number (120). That flashing dot is the MIDI status light that indicates a MIDI signal. This indicates any MIDI signal, whether it comes from an external MIDI device or the onscreen keyboard.

Practicing the Part Before You Record It

Now that the onscreen keyboard is active, you have selected the Software Instrument track, and you have a MIDI signal, it's time to practice the part you will be recording.

The part you are about to record uses only five notes played sequentially. I made this part simple for those of you who are beginners. Feel free to record a more elaborate part after you finish this lesson.

There are a total of 12 notes (black and white keys) in an octave. The keys are: A, A#, B, C, C#, D, D#, E, F, F#, G, and G#. The sharp (#) keys are the black keys. If I ask you to move two white keys to the right, I will say "move two steps to the right." Moving to a black key from the nearest white key would be considered a half a step.

To communicate the notes, I'll give the key plus the octave number. For example, C2 would be the C key in the second octave. All notes run consecutively from A through G, then they repeat. If you move toward the right on the keyboard, you are moving toward a higher octave, and the notes get higher in pitch. If you move toward the left on the keyboard, you are moving toward a lower octave and lower pitch.

If you work with a full-size external keyboard, C1 is the first key on the left side of the keyboard, and C2 is one octave higher (12 notes/keys) to the right.

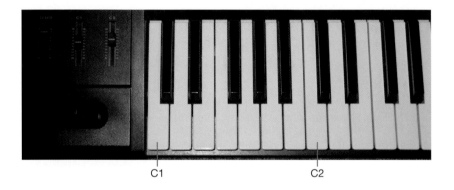

C1   C2

1   Locate the C2 note on your onscreen keyboard.

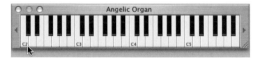

2   Click the arrows to the right or left of the keyboard to change the octave until C1 is the first note on the left of the onscreen keyboard.

3   Move two steps (two white keys) to the right to E2.

This is the first note of the organ part you will be recording.

4   Click the first note E2 to hear how it sounds.

5   Move three steps (three white keys) to the right to A2, and click A2 to hear how it sounds.

A2 is the second key you will play.

6   Move two steps to the right to C3 and click to hear the third note.

7   Move one step to the left to B2 and click to hear the fourth note.

8   Move back four steps to E2 and click to hear the fifth and final note.

You'll notice that the first and fifth notes are the same in this five-note organ part.

Let's save your progress, then reopen the piece to hear the finished organ part one more time.

9   Press Cmd-S to save the song up to this point.

10 Choose File > Open Recent > **3-3 SciFiShowFinal** to open the final song.

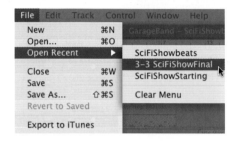

11 Click the Solo button on the Angelic Organ part to silence the other tracks.

12 Play the first Angelic Organ region in the Angelic Organ track.

13 Click the Solo button again to unsolo the track.

14 Play the first Angelic Organ region again to hear it with the rhythm track.

15 Choose File > Open Recent > **SciFiShowBeats** to open your work in progress.

NOTE ▶ Open Recent is a convenient way to open recent projects. If the Open Recent submenu gets too cluttered, you can choose Clear Menu from the bottom of the Open Recent submenu to clear all of the recent files and start fresh with the current file.

Project Tasks

That's it. You've played all five notes, and you've heard how they are supposed to sound in the final recording. Now all you need to do is practice a few times before you record. Practice playing all five notes one at a time until you get a feel for the part. Remember, you need to play only the first region in the Angelic Organ track. We will use that region to create the other regions in the track.

1   Practice clicking each note until you can play the part (E2-A2-C3-B2-E2).

2   If you want to practice with the finished part, Choose File > Open Recent > **3-3 SciFiShowFinal**, create a cycle region around the first Angelic Organ region, and play along with the finished part.

3   Open your **SciFiShowBeats** project.

When you feel comfortable playing the part, move on to the next exercise.

Recording a Single-Take Organ Part

Let's put your practice to the test and try recording this part into the Timeline. You will use the single-take method to record the Angelic Organ part. Make sure your Cycle button is turned off (the cycle region is not showing) before you begin.

The Angelic Organ part you will be recording starts at the beginning of the 3rd measure and ends at the beginning of the 7th measure. It's a good idea to change the Time Display back to musical time so you can use it as a reference as you record.

1   Click the lower-left corner of the Time Display to change it to musical time.

2   Press the Home key to move the playhead to the beginning of the Timeline.

3   Press Cmd-K to open the onscreen keyboard, if it is not already open.

4   Click the Record button and try recording a take.

Press the spacebar to stop recording when you finish.

5   Listen to your recording. If it sounds good, skip down to the next exercise.

6   If you want to try the recording again, press Cmd-Z to undo the recording. Repeat steps 2 through 5 a few more times.

NOTE ▶ If you are totally frustrated and want to move on, choose File > Open and select **3-2 SciFiShowT1** from the Lesson_03 folder to open a version of the song with the part already recorded for you.

7   Press Shift-Cmd-S to save the new version of your song.

8   Change the name to *SciFiShowT1* to show that it is your song with the beats and the first recorded instrument track. Save the song to your folder on the Desktop.

Editing a Software Instrument Region in the Track Editor

The next step in building this song is to copy the Angelic Organ region in the Timeline to duplicate the part. You will keep the original region as is, and edit the duplicate to vary the part.

Using Option-Drag to Duplicate a Region

You've already learned that you can copy and paste regions using the Edit menu. This exercise will show you another way to duplicate a region—using the Option key.

1   Select the Angelic Organ region in the top track of the Timeline.

2   Move the playhead to the beginning of the 8th measure in the Timeline.

3   Press and hold the Option key to create a copy when you click the region. Don't release the key.

4   Click and hold the Angelic Organ region to create a copy. Don't release the mouse.

5   Drag the copy to the playhead position in the Timeline. Release the Option key and the mouse.

The shorthand for this process would be Option-drag the Angelic Organ region to the playhead position in the Timeline.

6   Press Cmd-S to save your progress.

> **TIP**   You should save often when you are creating any project. It just takes a moment and can prevent a lot of frustration.

Opening the Copied Region in the Track Editor

It's time to venture back to the Track Editor and use it to change the copied Angelic Organ region. Why do we want to change the region? Because if you just repeat the same part over and over, it sounds like you just copied the same part over and over. But if you change the part slightly, it will sound different from the first, and nobody will know that the entire Angelic Organ track in your song came from only five recorded notes.

In this exercise, you will open the copied region in the Track Editor, then delete the last note and transpose the part to a different key so it won't sound like the same notes as the original.

1   Double-click the second Angelic Organ region in the top track of the Timeline to open that region in the Track Editor.

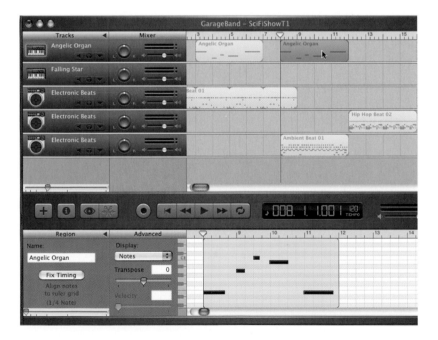

The five dark lines in the Track Editor region are the note events for that region.

2   Click each note to hear it in the Track Editor.

NOTE ▸ You may need to adjust the Zoom slider in the Track Editor to see the entire region.

On the left edge of the Track Editor is a vertical keyboard so you can see the key for each note in the region.

These keys are the exact keys you played when you originally recorded the part.

3   Notice that the lines are all very dark, and the velocity is 127—the highest velocity.

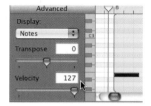

When you record notes with the onscreen keyboard, they will always be played at the highest velocity. Other MIDI keyboards are touch sensitive, so the harder or softer you play a note, the higher or lower the velocity of the note.

There is no need to change the velocity for this part.

Changing a Note in the Track Editor

Now let's change the last note in the region.

1 Locate the last note in the region.

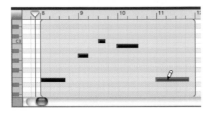

2 Locate C3 on the vertical keyboard to the left of the region.

3 Click-drag the note straight upward in the Track Editor. Stop when it is at the C3 line in the vertical keyboard.

You just changed the last note to C3.

Deleting a Note in the Track Editor

You can also delete a note in the Track Editor by selecting the note and pressing the Delete key.

1   Select the last note in the region (if it is not already selected).

You may have already noticed that it isn't the most ear-pleasing note of the keyboard part, and certainly doesn't work in its current location. That's as good a reason as any to delete it.

2   Press the Delete key to delete that note from the region.

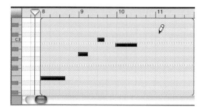

Easy, right? Deleting is deleting, whether you do it in the Timeline or the Track Editor.

NOTE ▶ Delete will delete all of the selected items in either the Track Editor or Timeline. It's a good idea to double-check what you have selected before you press the Delete key.

Transposing a Region in the Track Editor

You know how to change a single note by clicking it and dragging it up or down in the Track Editor. You can change all of the notes in the region at once by transposing the region. *Transposing* means to change the key. Remember, there are only 12 different keys (black and white) before a note repeats an octave higher or lower. To transpose a region by −12 would be to lower the entire thing one full octave. To transpose a region by 12 would be to raise the entire region to a higher octave. Anything other than a full octave will change each note in the region to a different key.

Let's transpose this region to make it sound like different notes than the original recorded region.

1   Locate the Transpose slider and field in the Advanced portion of the Track Editor.

The current Transpose setting is 0, which indicates the region is in the original recorded key.

2   Type *12* in the Transpose field and press Return to raise the entire part by one octave.

3   Play the region in the Track Editor to hear it at the higher octave.

4   Type *–5* in the Transpose field and press Return to transpose the region by five notes lower than the original recording.

5   Click the Track Editor button to close the Track Editor.

Resizing a Region in the Timeline

Now that you have deleted a note and transposed the region, there's some empty space in the region that can be trimmed.

1   Locate the beginning of the 11th measure in the Beat Ruler.

2   Click-drag the lower-right corner of the selected region in the Timeline and drag it left to the beginning of the 11th measure.

3   Play the first half of the song to hear your progress with the Angelic Organ regions.

Copying and Pasting Multiple Regions in the Timeline

The first two Angelic Organ regions sound great. Instead of repeating all of that work from scratch, you can simply copy and paste both regions at the same time to repeat them later in the song.

To copy multiple regions, you can click-drag the empty space to the left of the first region and drag your pointer toward the right across both of the regions you wish to select. You can also press the Shift key and click each of those regions.

1   Click-drag the empty space to the left of the first Angelic region and drag your pointer to the right across both regions to select them.

2   Press Cmd-C to copy the selected regions.

3   Move the playhead to the beginning of the 16th measure.

4 Press Cmd-V to paste the copied regions at the playhead position.

The pasted regions start at the beginning of the 16th measure.

Let's move the second pasted region to the right by one measure to create a larger gap between the last two Angelic Organ parts.

5 Move your playhead to the beginning of the 22nd measure.

6 Click the gray, empty track space between last two Angelic Organ parts to deselect them in the Timeline.

7 Click-drag the last Angelic Organ region (fourth region) to the playhead position so that it starts at the beginning of the 22nd measure.

Recording and Editing a New Region

Now it's time to put everything you have learned so far together and record and edit a new region. This region will be very easy because it is only one long note that will last from the beginning of the 10th measure to the end of the 13th measure.

1 Select the Falling Star track header to select the track.

2   Press Cmd-K to open the onscreen keyboard.

3   Move the playhead to the beginning of the 9th measure in the Timeline.

4   Click the Lower Octave arrow located at the left edge of the onscreen keyboard to lower it an octave.

C1 should now be the first key on your keyboard.

5   Click-hold C1 to hear how it sounds. Release the mouse to release the note.

You will be holding this note during the recording for a total of four measures.

6   Click the Record button and wait for the playhead to reach the beginning of the 10th measure. Then press the C1 key.

7   Press the spacebar to stop recording when you reach the beginning of the 15th measure.

NOTE ▶ If your recording is slightly longer or shorter, you can always fix it in the Track Editor.

8   Double-click the Falling Star region you just recorded to open it in the Track Editor.

9 Click-drag the single note event down one step to change the note to B0.

10 Click the Track Editor button to close the Track Editor.

11 Close the onscreen keyboard window.

Duplicating the Region in the Timeline

This is a good opportunity for you to practice some of your new skills by duplicating the region and editing it in the Track Editor.

1 Move the playhead to the beginning of the 19th measure.

2 Option-drag the Falling Star region so that it begins at the playhead position.

3 Double-click the copied region to open it in the Track Editor.

Duplicating and Editing Notes in the Track Editor

The region you just opened in the Track Editor consists of one long note. In this exercise, you will change the length of the note, duplicate it, and then change both notes to a different key.

You can click-drag the edge of a note in the Track Editor to resize a note the same way you resize a region in the Timeline.

> **NOTE ▶** If the note starts and ends at the edge of the region, you will need to extend the region in the Timeline so you can grab the edge of the note in the Track Editor.

1 Click the right edge of the note event and drag it left to shorten the length of the note so that it is about half the length of the original recorded note.

The original note was about four to five measures long, so the new one will be two to two-and-a-half measures long.

The note will appear shorter in the region.

2 Click-drag the note upward in the Track Editor and release it on the E2 line.

E2 is four lines (black and white keys) above C2 on the vertical keyboard.

3   Option-drag the note down and to the right to duplicate the note and move the duplicate to B1 (one line below C2), so that it starts right after the end of the first note.

The first note ends part way into the 21st measure, and the second note starts immediately afterward.

Finishing the Part

Now let's edit these two notes to get them just the right length for the part. For this exercise, you'll use the Beat Ruler in the Track Editor and the screen shot as a guide to move and resize the notes. When you finish, save your work and close the Track Editor.

1   Use the Track Editor Zoom slider for a clear view of the two notes in the Track Editor.

2   Click the 4th beat (beat mark) of the 19th measure in the Beat Ruler to move the playhead to that position.

3   Click-drag the first note to move the note to the playhead position.

4   Move the playhead to the 4th beat of the 20th measure.

5   Click-drag the right edge of the first note and resize it to the playhead position.

The first note should start on the fourth beat of the 19th measure and end on the 4th beat of the 20th measure.

6 Edit the second note so that it starts at the beginning of the 21st measure and ends on the 2nd beat of the 22nd measure.

Finishing the Song

The last step to finishing this song is to add a Software Instrument part from the Loop Browser.

1 Click the Loop Browser button to open the Loop Browser.

> **NOTE ▶** If your Loop Browser still shows your last search, click the Reset button to clear any previous selections.

2 Click the Elec Piano button.

3 Select Deep Electric Piano 05 from the search results.

4 Move the playhead to the beginning of the 11th measure in the Timeline.

5   Click-drag the Electric Piano 05 loop from the browser to the playhead
    position below the lowest track.

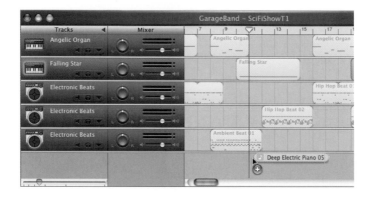

A new track appears with the Deep Electric Piano 05 region starting at
the beginning of the 11th measure in the track.

6   Click-drag the upper-right corner of
    the Deep Electric Piano 05 region to
    extend the loop so it repeats a total of
    three times.

7   Double-click the region to open it in the Track Editor.

8   Transpose the entire region down by –3.

9   Close the Track Editor.

10   Click-drag the first Falling Star region in the Timeline so the note begins at the same time the Deep Electric Piano 05 region begins.

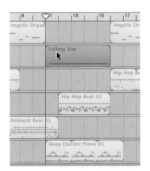

Project Tasks

The last step is to add and edit two more Deep Electric Piano 05 regions in the Timeline.

1   Locate the Deep Electric Piano 05 loop in the Loop Browser.

2   Drag the Deep Electric Piano 05 loop to the Electric Piano track and release it at the beginning of the 20th measure.

3   Option-drag the same region to the beginning of the 25th measure to duplicate it.

4   Open the duplicated region in the Track Editor.

5   Delete the long sustained notes at the bottom of the region and the first five short notes.

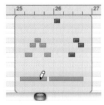

6   Move the edited region in the Timeline so the first note starts at the beginning of the 25th measure.

7 Save the finished project.

8 Play the project to see how it sounds.

Congratulations! You just created a song from scratch using all Software Instruments in GarageBand.

What You've Learned

- When you open a new song, you can set the project properties.
- Project properties include Tempo, Time (time signature), and Key.
- The default time signature is 4/4, and the default tempo is 120.
- There are 12 different keys to choose from for a project. The default is C.
- You can change a project tempo by clicking the Tempo portion of the Time Display and adjusting the Tempo slider.
- You can record a single-take Software Instrument region or a multipass Software Instrument region.
- Multipass recording requires using a cycle region to repeat the region you are recording over and over.
- The metronome clicks once for each beat in a measure and can be used during playback or recording.
- You can loop a recorded region by clicking and dragging the upper-right corner of the region.
- You can resize a recorded region by clicking and dragging the lower-right corner of the region.
- The Track Editor can be used to move, delete, duplicate, or resize notes within a region.
- The Track Editor can also be used to transpose an entire region, which changes the key of the region.

4

Working with Real Instruments

GarageBand gives you many choices of instruments, tracks, regions, and methods of recording. In the previous lesson, you worked with flexible, editable Software Instruments. This lesson is dedicated to what GarageBand calls Real Instruments.

Real Instruments are exactly what they sound like: regions recorded from real instruments. With GarageBand, you can record a real instrument such as a guitar, bass, or keyboard directly into the Timeline. You can also use a microphone to record instruments that don't have an output jack, such as a trumpet, violin, grand piano, drum kit, acoustic guitar, or even vocals.

To record a Real Instrument into the Timeline, you have to physically perform/play the part using a real instrument in real time. In contrast to Software Instruments, Real Instrument recordings are "as is." Once they're recorded, you can't change tempo, edit individual notes, or transpose a Real Instrument region.

With all of these limitations, why would you record real instruments when you can use Software Instruments? Because they're *real* instruments! Certain instruments can't be simulated very well, so you want to record the real deal.

Suppose you're in a band and you want to record one of your new songs. How do you explain to your drummer that he has to play drums on a MIDI keyboard to get them into the computer? What about the lead vocal, guitar, and bass? Most musicians play best on their chosen instruments, not on a keyboard simulation. (Nothing against keyboards, which happen to be my instrument of choice.)

In this lesson, you'll learn how to work with Real Instruments once they are recorded into the Timeline. You'll learn how to record Real Instruments, edit and loop the recorded regions, and add effects to enhance the tracks.

Connecting Musical Instruments to Your Computer

There are basically two types of musical instruments: electric and acoustic. An electric instrument has a built-in interface to output its sound, but an acoustic instrument needs a microphone to record its sound.

Electric instruments include electric guitars, keyboards, and electric bass. You can connect an electric instrument directly to the computer's audio-in port, if your computer has one. The computer audio-in port is a ⅛-inch mini input, so you will need an adapter or cable to convert the ¼-inch phono output from your instrument to the ⅛-inch audio line-in port (mini input) on the computer.

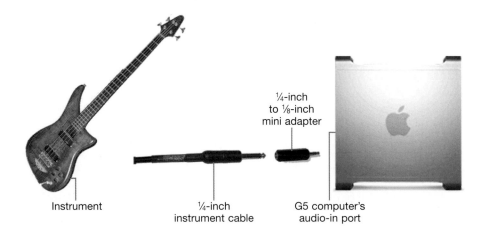

Instrument   ¼-inch   G5 computer's
                 instrument cable   audio-in port

To record an acoustic instrument or vocals, you can connect a microphone to your computer through the audio-in port, which is located on the back of the computer.

Mini cable into audio-in port

You can also connect an audio interface to your computer, and then connect your microphone or instruments to the audio interface. There is a wide range of audio interfaces and compatible formats, including USB, FireWire, PCI, and PC cards.

If you want to record more than one instrument or microphone at a time, you can also connect an audio mixer or console to your computer.

For this lesson, I'm using the EDIROL PCR-A Audio Interface/MIDI Keyboard Controller. This interface is both a MIDI controller and an audio interface.

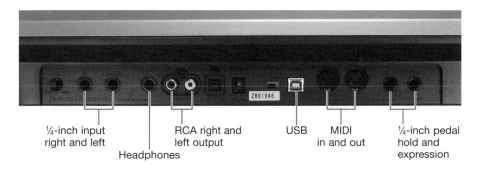

¼-inch input right and left

Headphones

RCA right and left output

USB

MIDI in and out

¼-inch pedal hold and expression

Make sure any audio interface is compatible with Mac OS X 10.2.6 or later, and that the format used by the interface is supported by your computer.

Also, always follow the manufacturer's instructions, and be sure you install the correct driver on your computer.

> **MORE INFO** ▶ *You can find more information about GarageBand accessories at www.apple.com/ilife/garageband/accessories.*

Setting Preferences for the Audio-In Port

If you plan to record through the audio-in port on your computer, you will need to set the System Preferences accordingly. The System Preferences are located under the Apple menu (blue apple) in the upper-left corner of the computer screen.

Let's change the preferences to record through your audio-in port. If your computer doesn't have an audio-in port, you won't be able to make the changes, but you'll know how to do it if you ever use GarageBand on a Mac with audio-in.

1 Click the blue apple to open the Apple menu.

This menu is always available, even when you're running an application.

2 Choose System Preferences from the Apple menu.

The System Preferences window opens.

3 Click the Sound button to open the Sound Preferences window.

The Sound Preferences window opens.

4 Click the Input button to see the sound input pane in the window.

The input options on your computer will reflect the current audio devices and hardware that you are using. It is very likely that your input options will be different from the ones shown in the screenshots.

5   Select the audio interface that you will be using for the recording.

If you are using the audio line-in port on your computer, select Line In from the sound input list.

6   Play a riff on your instrument and notice the input level on the Input level meter.

7   Click-drag the Input volume slider to raise or lower your input volume levels as needed.

The Input level meter shows the level of your input from left to right. Left is the lowest input level (quietest), and right is the highest (loudest). If your input levels are too high, you will "overdrive" the input, which means the recording is louder than the device can handle and your music will be distorted.

If the device you select does not have input controls in the Sound Preferences window, you can raise the output volume on your instrument or device.

For this exercise I'm using the EDIROL PCR-A Audio Interface/MIDI Keyboard Controller as an input device. As you can see in the illustration, this device does not have an Input volume slider in the Sound Preferences window.

Preparing the Project

Before you start working with Real Instruments, you need to create a new GarageBand project.

1   Launch GarageBand if it is not already open.

2   Chose File > New to open the New Project window.

3   Name the new project *Guitar Test*.

4   Save the new project to your GarageBand Songs folder on your Desktop.

5   Click Create to open the new project.

Your new project titled Guitar Test opens.

Creating a Real Instrument Track

By default, your new Recording Test project opens with an empty Grand Piano Software Instrument track.

When you set up a Real Instrument track, you also need to set which channel or channels you wish to record to, whether you're recording mono or stereo, and whether you want to monitor (hear) the sound through your speakers or headphones.

For this exercise, you will create a guitar track with no effects recorded on Channel 1, in mono, and with the monitor on. First, you need to delete the unnecessary Grand Piano track.

1   Choose Track > Delete Track, or press Cmd-Delete to delete the Grand Piano track.

You now have a project with no tracks at all.

2   Click the Add Track button (+) located in the bottom-left corner of the GarageBand window to add a new basic track.

A new empty track appears, along with the New Track window.

Real Instrument should be selected by default as the track type. If it isn't, click it.

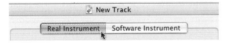

3 Click Guitars as the instrument and No Effects as the type of guitar.

4   Click the Icon button to open the icon menu.

5   Select an electric guitar as the track icon.

Stereo vs. Mono Recording

How do you know when to record mono and when to record stereo? Well, it depends on the instrument and the recording. A single instrument with only one output jack is a mono output. An instrument like a keyboard with multiple outputs (left and right) gives you a choice of stereo (both left and right outputs) or mono (only the left output).

If you're recording a number of musicians at the same time through a mixing board or console, their sound may go into a board as mono input. Then the signals are mixed in the board and sent out of the mixer into the computer as a stereo signal.

You can also record a single guitar as a stereo input by changing the track settings to stereo. It just depends on what type of signal you're working with and what you're trying to accomplish. You will explore the different options throughout this lesson.

Each track in GarageBand has two channels for audio recording and playback, Channel 1 and Channel 2. If you record a track in stereo, you use both channels. If you record mono, you record only Channel 1 or Channel 2. You can set which channel you record to in the New Track window's Input pop-up menu.

In this exercise, you're working with a single electric guitar with a mono output, so the input into the computer will be mono as well.

1   Select Mono as the Format to record only one channel of audio.

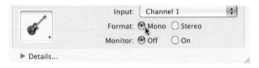

2   Locate the Input pop-up menu. It should be set to Channel 1.

Monitoring Your Input

Monitoring is a musical term for being able to hear yourself play. Musicians monitor their performance in the recording studio and on stage. If you've ever performed live, you know it's nearly impossible to play if you can't hear the sound coming from your own instrument. That would be like painting a picture blindfolded.

Just as you would in a recording studio, you will probably want to monitor your performance when you record a Real Instrument track in GarageBand. If the Monitor setting is off, you won't hear the sound of your instrument or any sound going through the microphone to the computer.

You should always turn Monitor off when you're not recording. Leaving a microphone input on can cause feedback, which is painful to the ears. Avoiding feedback is the reason that Monitor is set to off by default.

TIP ▶ Don't wear headphones when connecting, disconnecting, or moving an instrument or microphone. There is always the possibility of hearing loud pops when you plug and unplug, as well as feedback that can be a real pain in the ear! Also, if you're using more than one microphone, don't put them too close together or they are likely to cause feedback.

When do you turn Monitor on? When you're practicing or recording a specific track. Once the instrument part is recorded into the Timeline, you will hear it on playback, just as you would any other region in the Timeline.

1 Click the On button for the Monitor.

NOTE ▶ If you are using a microphone to record and speakers to monitor your sound, you are likely to get feedback when you turn monitoring on. To avoid this feedback, listen to your sound through headphones, or turn Monitor off.

2 Click OK to finish creating the new track.

Your new track, currently called No Effects, appears in the Timeline. Notice the guitar icon in the track header.

Plan Before Recording

There are a few obvious yet essential things to consider before you start recording. First, make sure that the instruments or microphones you plan to use are connected properly and working. Second, be sure you have enough hard-drive space for your recordings. Audio recordings use a fraction of the space of video, but they can accumulate over time, especially if you record many takes. The last thing you want to do is stop your recording session because you're out of drive space.

Stereo audio recorded at CD quality uses around 10 MB of disk space per minute. So 10 recorded stereo tracks, for a song that is 3 minutes long, would fill up around 300 MB.

Recording and Saving a Real Instrument Part

The next series of exercises will walk you through some different techniques for recording a Real Instrument part.

Recording Long vs. Short Regions

Before you start recording, there are some recording techniques to consider. Should you record the entire song in one take, or break the instrument part into smaller pieces? I think the answer depends on the musician. If there is a song that you have played so many times you don't even have to think to play it, feel free to record it in one long and perfect take. Some musicians record multiple takes of a whole song, then edit together the best parts from each take into a master track that becomes the final song. If playing the entire song flawlessly is unlikely, it is very easy to record smaller sections, then put them all together in the Timeline. Most songs in the world of music recording are recorded in smaller pieces, then arranged together to form the final master track. You can also record punch-ins to record over a specific part of a song if necessary.

Let's start with the basics—recording a short musical part, also known as a *riff*.

> **NOTE** ▶ The following recording exercise uses a guitar as an example. However, you are welcome to record whatever instrument you have available.

Setting Up Your Instrument

Take a moment to set-up your guitar, keyboard, bass, microphone, or whatever instrument you want to use for the recording exercise. If you don't have an instrument and your computer has a built-in microphone, you can record finger snaps, or you can whistle. If you don't have an instrument or a microphone, read through the following steps anyway to get a sense of how recording a Real Instrument works.

If you do have an instrument, play a riff on it now. Do you hear a delay between when you play and when you hear the sound? Depending on the audio hardware and computer you are using, there may be a slight delay when playing and recording Real Instruments. It takes a short amount of time for the Real Instrument input to reach the computer's input port and be processed. This delay is referred to as *latency*. You may not be able to eliminate latency completely, but you can reduce the amount of latency in the GarageBand Preferences. Let's take a look at the Preferences setting to reduce latency.

1   Choose GarageBand > Preferences to open the General Preferences window.

2   Click the Audio/MIDI Interfaces tab at the top of the window to open the Audio/MIDI interfaces pane.

3   Locate the "Optimize for" section and click the "Minimum delay when playing instruments live" button if you are experiencing latency delays when you play your instrument.

Selecting "Minimum delay when playing instruments live" will reduce latency by using more of the computer's processing power to process the audio input signal faster. However, this can affect performance on slower computers. If you don't have a latency issues or if you're running a slower computer, you may wish to change the setting to "Maximum number of simultaneous tracks." For more information, see Lesson 9.

4   Close the General Preferences window.

Recording a Short Take

Since the track you are about to record has no effects applied to it, the sound of whatever instrument you record will not be altered. You will learn to add effects to the tracks in the next exercise.

1   Select the No Effects track header to make the track active.

2   Choose Control > Metronome, or press Cmd-U to turn on the metronome during practice.

3   Press the spacebar to start the metronome and playback of the empty track in the Timeline.

   NOTE ▸ You can only hear the metronome if the playhead is moving—that is, only while you are playing a song in the Timeline or while you are recording.

4   Play a simple musical riff.

5   Practice a few times until you're ready to record.

6   Click the red Record button and record your musical riff.

7   Press the spacebar to stop recording when you're finished.

8   Press Cmd-S to save your project.

That's it! You've recorded an instrument part into GarageBand.

Project Tasks

Now that you've successfully recorded one part, why not try another? Create a new track in the same project and record another part to go along with the first piece you recorded.

1   Click the New Track button to create a new Real Instrument track.

2   Select the instrument you wish to record, and choose No Effects for the track.

3   Mute the top track in the Timeline if you don't want to play along with it.

4   Select the new track and record the second musical part.

5   Listen to your new recording.

6   Press Cmd-S to save your work when you are finished.

Recording a Long Take

There is nothing wrong with recording the entire song—or even a long part of the song, such as the first half—in one take. If you can play it, by all means record it.

This method is also fantastic for recording song ideas. If you have a melody, lyrics, or instrumental parts floating around in your head, I strongly encourage you to sit down right away and record it. Who cares if it's a rough draft and full of mistakes? The important thing is to document it so you won't forget the subtle creative nuances of the idea while it's fresh. The human brain isn't the most reliable storage medium. Instead of carrying 50 songs around in your head, trying to remember all of them, commit them to your computer instead. You can always delete them later.

Another thing to remember about recording one long take is that you can always punch in and record over, or re-record any mistakes you make along the way.

Recording one long take is simple. You do everything the same way as you would when recording a short take, only you play longer.

Adding Preset and Custom Effects

In the old days of recording electric guitars—less than a decade ago—the particular sound the guitar made was determined by the amplifier, stage, and additional recording equipment used by engineers to alter the sound. Amplifiers were just big black speakers used to project the sound of an electric instrument. Now that digital recording has emerged, the new amplifiers have settings to alter the sound of the guitar itself.

GarageBand builds this extraordinary technology into the software with an effect called amp simulator. Amp simulation lets you change the sound of the guitar as you play and record. All you have to do is play your guitar, and then select the type of amplifier simulation sound and feel for your guitar. For those of you raised on a computer, this may not seem like a big deal, but for those of us who used to perform on stage with amplifiers and racks of equipment, it's huge.

Preparing the Project

If you recorded a guitar riff, keep your project open as is. If you didn't record with a guitar or you prefer to use the prebuilt project, follow these steps:

1   Choose File > Open and select **4-1 GuitarTest Starting** from the Lesson_04 folder.

2   Choose File > Save As and save the **4-1 GuitarTest Starting** project to your GarageBand Songs folder on the Desktop.

Using Amp Simulation

At this time, there is only one track, titled No Effects, in the Timeline, with a recorded Real Instrument region that is also titled No Effects.

1. Press the spacebar to play the guitar region in the Timeline so that you can hear the part with no effects.

   Now let's listen to it with one of the different guitar amp simulators. To change the sound, all you have to do is change the track info.

2. Double-click the track header to open the Track Info window.

   The Track Info window opens.

3. Click-drag the top of the Track Info window to move it below the track in the Timeline.

   You want to be able to see both the track and the Track Info window at the same time.

4. Click Arena Rock to change the sound of the guitar amplifier to Arena Rock.

   The name of the track changes as well as the sound.

5. Press the Home key to move the playhead to the beginning of the Timeline.

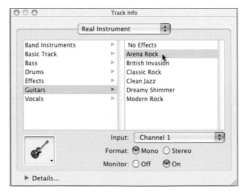

6   Play the track and listen to the guitar part using the Arena Rock amplifier sound.

7   Click the Cycle button and create a cycle region above the recorded guitar region in the Timeline.

8   Play the track again. This time, click through all the different guitar amplifier sounds as the track plays to hear them one at a time.

Notice that each guitar amp simulator sounds different.

9   Select No Effects in the Track Info window.

Our next step will be to add some effects to our No Effects track.

Adding Custom Effects to a Track

The fact that your current track is called No Effects and has no effects doesn't mean that you can't add effects to it. This exercise will acquaint you with the effects included in GarageBand and how to add one to a track. You will work more with effects later in this book. For now, you will just add a simple effect like Reverb.

1   Double-click the No Effects track again to reopen the Track Info window, if it isn't already open.

NOTE ▶ When you select No Effects, the track icon changes back to a speaker.

2   Locate the Details triangle at the bottom-left corner of the Track Info window.

3 Click the Details triangle to get more details about the effects used in the track.

The Track Info window expands to reveal additional information about the track.

4 Locate Reverb in the list of effects.

Notice that all of the sliders to the right of the effects are disabled (gray).

5 Click the box to the left of Reverb to add reverb to the track.

You can now adjust the slider to the right of the Reverb effect. By default the slider is set to 0 (no reverb). The highest setting is 100.

6 Click-drag the Reverb slider around halfway (to approximately 50).

Let's test the new reverb before closing the Track Info window.

7 Press the Home key and then the spacebar to listen to the track with the reverb.

You can also adjust the effect while you listen to playback by moving the slider.

8 Press the Home key and spacebar again and adjust the slider as you listen.

Repeat this process until you get the reverb just the way you like it. I'm going to stick with around 50 on mine. Don't close the Track Info window yet.

You have successfully added the Reverb effect to your track.

Saving an Instrument

Now that you've added an effect to your track, you can save the instrument with your custom effect to your list of instruments. Once you have saved an instrument sound, you can use it again on different tracks or projects.

1 Click the Save Instrument button in the lower-right corner of the Track Info window.

The Save Instrument window opens.

2 Type *Guitar with Reverb* in the Save as field.

3 Click Save to save the instrument.

Guitar with Reverb appears in the Guitars instrument list.

4 Click the Details triangle to hide the details portion of the window.

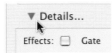

5 Close the Track Info window.

The track in your Timeline is now called Guitar with Reverb.

You can use this method to create and save different instruments that you want to use later.

Deleting a Saved Instrument

Sometimes you may wish to delete a saved instrument. Maybe you have too many saved instruments, and you want to clean up the cluttered instrument list. Or maybe you don't need a saved instrument anymore because you created a new instrument you like better.

Whatever the circumstances, deleting a saved instrument is quite easy. All you have to do is open the Track Info window, select the saved instrument you wish to delete, and click the Delete Instrument button.

Let's delete the Guitar with Reverb saved instrument from the list in the Track Info window.

1 Double-click the track header to open the Track Info window.

2 Select Guitar with Reverb from the list. (It should already be selected.)

3 Click the Details triangle to show the track details.

4   Click the Delete Instrument button in the lower-left corner of the Track
Info window.

A dialog box opens to ask if you really want to delete the instrument.

5   Click Remove to remove
the instrument.

6   Close the Track Info
window.

The track retains the name and effects you originally added, but it is no
longer a saved instrument in the Track Info window.

There you have it. Now you can add effects, save the instrument with effects,
and delete saved instruments.

Creating Guitar Test Tracks

In this exercise, you'll build a test project so you can hear a guitar part with all the different amplifier sounds at the same time.

First, you need to make some new basic tracks.

1 Click the Add Track button (+) to add a new Real Instrument track.

2 Choose Guitars and Arena Rock for the new track.

3 Set the input to Mono, Channel 1.

4 Click the Off button for the Monitor (if it is not already selected) so you don't have to listen to amplifier noise.

   To sound realistic, the amp simulators include the static noise that is inherent with each amplifier sound. If you want to hear the static amplifier noise for the different amp simulators, you can turn the Monitor on.

5 Click OK.

6 Repeat steps 1 through 5, but this time, choose a different amp setting in step 2. Go down the list of guitar instruments until you have selected all six of the different guitar sounds.

NOTE ▶ If you have installed the Jam Pack expansion, you will have more guitar instruments. Select any six for this test.

Once the test tracks have been created, you can click any of the track headers and play your guitar to hear it using the new sound.

Moving a Region to Different Tracks

Now that your test tracks are complete, you can also click-drag the original recorded region to a different track to hear the changes in sound.

1   Click-drag the recorded Real Instrument region from the Guitar with Reverb track to the Arena Rock track.

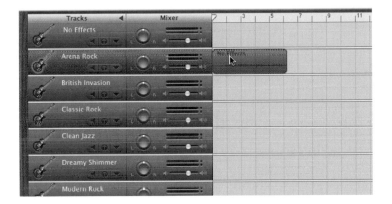

2   Click-drag the region down to the next track and listen to the British Invasion sound.

As you can see, it's easy to test-drive the different amp simulators in the Timeline. You can also use this method when practicing or recording your guitar. Simply click the track header of the amp simulator that you want to hear to select that track. Then play your guitar and practice with the amp simulator sound, or record the part.

Trimming and Looping a Real Instrument Recording

Now that the guitar riff has been recorded to the Timeline, let's do a little cleanup on the region so it will make a better loop.

Before you can start trimming, you need to understand grid lines.

Understanding Grid Lines

You're probably wondering what the heck a grid line is, and why we are learning about them now. Great question. Grid lines are the vertical gray lines in the Timeline.

Grid lines act as a guide for aligning the playhead and your regions in the Timeline. They are also used for trimming, which is why they are pertinent at this point in the book.

Grid lines are like the lines on a highway. They maintain order and safety by keeping all traffic separate and moving at the right speed and direction.

In the same way, GarageBand uses grid lines to govern the musical traffic within the Timeline. The grid lines keep order by adhering to the laws of musical time. Remember, musical time consists of separate measures, beats, and clicks within a beat. Grid lines keep all of the regions in the different tracks orderly and in time with one another.

When it comes to trimming a region, grid lines are important because they restrict your ability to trim.

Your goal for this exercise is to trim the silent portion of the recorded region. The sample region has silence at the beginning and end of the region. Silence is no big deal if you're only playing this region once, but what if you want to loop the region? Silence doesn't work well with a loop. Let's demonstrate.

1 Click-drag the upper-right corner of the No Effects region in the Timeline and extend it to repeat by one full segment.

2 Play the entire track to hear the looped region.

Notice the loooonnng pause in the middle before the riff repeats.

That pause would be a song killer if it happened onstage. But if you first trim the pause off the clip, then loop it, the riff will repeat seamlessly.

3 Locate the pause in the region's waveform.

The pause is the flat horizontal line, which indicates no sound.

4 Press Cmd-Z to undo the looping of the region.

Now that you're aware of the problem with the silence, you have an incentive to get rid of it.

5 Locate the Zoom slider for the Timeline.

It's located in the lower-left corner of the Timeline.

6 Click-drag the slider all the way to the left to zoom out of the Timeline as far as possible.

Your recorded region becomes very small in the track, and there are very few grid lines in the Timeline.

7 Move the playhead to the first grid line to the right of the 1st measure and read the Time Display.

The first grid line is at the beginning of the 5th measure.

8 Press the Home key to move the playhead back to the beginning of the Timeline.

9 Click-drag the region slowly to the nearest grid line on the right.

The clip pauses three times as you move it to show you the different options for placement. You have four automatic options for placing the clip between the grid lines.

Those four stops are the only four placement options you have at this moment if you want to move the clip between the 1st and 5th measure. That's definitely restricting your movement in the Timeline.

10 Click-drag the region back to the beginning of the Timeline and count the four stops along the way.

11 Go back and move the Zoom slider toward the right about one-half of the distance from the left edge.

As you zoom in, you get more grid lines in relation to the region.

Notice there is now one grid line for each beat in the Beat Ruler. Since there are four beats per measure, there are also four grid lines per measure when you are zoomed in at this level.

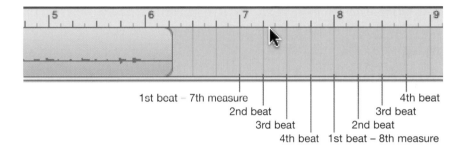

1st beat – 7th measure
2nd beat
3rd beat
4th beat   1st beat – 8th measure
2nd beat
3rd beat
4th beat

12 Move the region to the beginning of the 5th measure again.

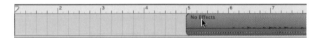

Notice that you have more choices for moving your clip. The more you zoom in to a track, the more grid lines per region, and the more choices you have for moving and editing.

Snapping to the Grid

You can override the grid lines for more freedom of movement by turning off the Snap to Grid feature.

1 Choose Control > Snap to Grid, or press Cmd-G to turn off the snapping feature.

> **NOTE ▶** The Snap to Grid selection in the Control menu becomes unchecked when snapping is turned off.

Control	Window	Help
✓ Metronome		⌘U
Count In		
✓ Snap to Grid		⌘G
Show Loop Browser		⌘L
Show Editor		⌘E

2 Click-drag the region back to the beginning of the Timeline.

Could you feel the difference in movement?

3 Press Cmd-G to turn snapping back on.

With snapping off, you can move the region anywhere. The downside is that you can move the region anywhere. This isn't a problem when you have only one region, but if you have different regions haphazardly placed on different tracks, the parts will be completely out of time with one another. Instrument parts played out of time sound like an orchestra tuning up. It may be interesting, but it sure isn't music.

TIP ▶ Always work with snapping on unless you absolutely have to turn it off. Remember to turn it back on as soon as possible.

Changing Snapping Parameters

Occasionally, you may want to change the snapping parameters within the grid without turning snapping off. The Timeline Grid button looks like a small ruler and is located in the upper-right corner of the Timeline.

1   Locate the Timeline Grid button in the upper-right corner.

2   Click the Timeline Grid button to open the Timeline Grid menu.

These settings change the note value of the snapping feature. If you leave it set to Automatic, the note value will automatically scale with the grid as you zoom in and zoom out of the track.

3   Click outside of the menu to leave it set to Automatic and close the menu.

Working with Grid Lines in the Track Editor

Now that you have a better understanding of grid lines and how they keep order in the Timeline, let's look at the grid lines in the Track Editor.

1 Double-click the recorded region in the Timeline to open it in the Track Editor.

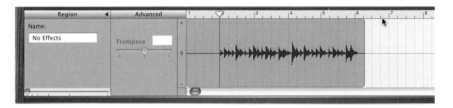

Notice the grid lines within the Track Editor.

Since the Track Editor has a Zoom slider that is independent of the Timeline, you can also adjust your grid lines in the Track Editor by zooming in and out of it.

2 Click-drag the Track Editor's Zoom slider to zoom in to the region.

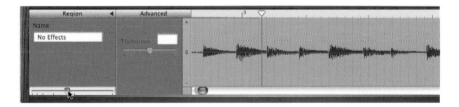

The Track Editor also has a Grid button, independent of the button in the Timeline.

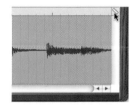

Trimming a Region in the Track Editor

To trim a recorded Real Instrument region in the Track Editor, all you need to do is click and drag the right or left edge of the region. Your trimming will be restricted to the grid, so you should always zoom in as much as needed for the desired result.

1   Zoom in or out of the Track Editor until you can clearly see the beginning of the region, as well as the beginning of the music's waveform.

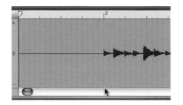

2   Move your pointer over the region to see the pointer change to a crosshair.

The crosshair can be used for editing inside of a region.

In Lesson 9, you learn more about how to edit inside a region using the Track Editor.

3   Move your pointer over the lower-left corner and click the mouse to change to a resize pointer.

When you are in the lower-left corner, the resize pointer looks like a line with a small arrow pointing to the left. The resize pointer for the lower-right corner looks like a line with a small arrow pointing to the right.

If your pointer turned to a crosshair when you clicked, click again to change to the resize pointer.

4   Click-drag the lower-left corner of the region with the resize pointer and trim to the beginning of the 2nd measure.

The trimmed region will start right on the 1st beat of the 2nd measure. When you trim regions that will be used as loops, it's extremely important to make sure that the region starts and ends on a beat.

NOTE ▶ Trimming a region so it begins and ends on a beat is the basis for loop-based production. If your region does not end on a beat, it will gradually drift from the counter and the grid lines as you loop the region over and over in the Timeline.

5   Click-drag the scroller in the Track Editor to view the end of the recorded region.

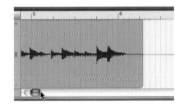

6   Locate the end of the recorded sound at the end of the waveform, and find the 1st beat mark in the Beat Ruler after the waveform ends (2nd beat of the 6th measure).

You will be able to trim to the grid line and get as close as possible to the waveform without cutting off any of the sound.

7   Click-drag the lower-right corner toward the left and stop at the 2nd beat in the 6th measure.

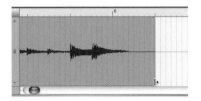

Remember, when you trim your region, you need to make sure that it starts and ends on a beat. The new trimmed region starts on the 1st beat of the 2nd measure and ends on the 2nd beat of the 6th measure.

8   Press Cmd-E to close the Track Editor.

9   Click-drag the region and move it to the beginning of the track in the Timeline.

10 Click-drag the upper-right corner of the region in the Timeline to extend it by one full loop segment.

11 Play the two loops to hear the new looped region.

> **NOTE ▶** If you have trouble extending exactly one loop segment, it may be because of the odd size of your trimmed loop. Reopen your loop in the Track Editor and resize the left and right edges of the loop until it starts and ends exactly on a beat.

Project Task

It's your turn to create another instrument test. This time you will work with a bass riff performed by my friend Stephen Kanter. Open the project titled **4-3 BassTest Starting** from the Lesson_04 folder. Your goal is to trim the silent parts from this recorded region to make a good loop, and then to extend the trimmed region until it repeats one full loop segment. Finally, you'll create a cycle region over the looped bass region and listen to it with different bass sounds while it is playing.

1 Choose File > Save As and save the project to your Songs folder on the Desktop.

2 Double-click the region to open it in the Track Editor.

3 Trim the silence off the beginning and end of the region so that it starts on the 2nd beat of the 1st measure and ends on the 2nd beat of the 3rd measure.

4 Loop the region in the Timeline so it plays twice.

5 Open the Track Info window and add Reverb to the No Effects track, and save the instrument as *Bass with Reverb*.

6   Turn on the cycle region and set it to cover the entire extended region in the Timeline.

7   Listen to the different bass sounds to pick a favorite for this part.

8   Save your finished project.

Arranging and Editing Regions into Songs

The next series of exercises will focus on the same piano part recorded multiple times using different methods. When you're on your own, you can decide on the method that works best for a given recording. For now, it's a good idea to get your feet wet by trying to edit and arrange regions that were recorded using both long and short takes.

As discussed earlier, many musicians record an entire song in one take, then go back and record punch-ins to fix mistakes in the live performance, or record multiple long takes and edit the best parts of each take together. Others record songs using multiple short takes, which are then arranged in the Timeline to form the complete song. Keep in mind that no matter what recording method you use, your audience will probably never know. When people listen to your finished song, they'll have no idea if you recorded it all in one take or in small sections. So your job is to do whatever is necessary to get the song recorded—period.

Re-Recording Part of a Song

Now that the long region has been recorded in the Timeline, what if you want to re-record just part of the region? Re-recording is easy. You can use a cycle region to narrow down the section you wish to re-record. This is known in recording circles as *punching in*.

Recall that when you recorded with a cycle region using a Software Instrument, you were able to record multiple passes and keep adding to the part within the cycle region.

Recording Real Instruments with cycle regions is different because it records only the first pass. After the first pass, you can only monitor the newly recorded section. This is a good thing. If you don't like the recording, you can undo and try again. But if you got lucky and recorded the perfect take, you won't accidentally record over it because it took you too long to hit the spacebar to stop the recording.

Let's take a look at a long recorded region with a major mistake that I had to punch in and record again.

1   Choose File > Open to open a song file.

2   Select **4-7 Piano punch ins** from the Lesson_04 folder.

The project opens in GarageBand.

I created this project to illustrate the punch-in process.

3   Locate Track 1 and make sure the Solo button is selected. (It should be already.)

4   Press the spacebar to stop playback when you reach the end of Track 1.

Notice the huge mistake near the middle of the recorded region. Once you have located a mistake you want to re-record, you can set up a cycle region over the mistake to designate which part of the region you want to re-record.

5   Click the Cycle button to see the cycle region that I used to punch in and re-record over the original mistake.

6   Click Play to hear the mistake that has been isolated by the cycle region.

Normally, you can re-record directly in your original recorded region. Since I was creating this project as a demonstration of punch ins, I copied my original recording to two other tracks so you could see the different takes and compare the recordings.

The next step is to select the track you want to record.

7   Click the Solo button on Track 1 to unsolo that track.

8   Click the second track (Punch in Take 1) to select that track.

Before you record a part of a region, you also want to be sure the metronome is turned on, and that Count In is also selected so you can hear the meas-ure prior to the region you are about to record. Both selections will be checked in the Control menu if they are on.

9   Click the Solo button to hear the first punch-in recording.

10 Click the Cycle button to close the cycle region.

11 Play the entire track to hear the original recording with the first take of re-recorded section.

When you re-record part of a region, the new recording will be named after the track instead of the original region.

12 Click the Solo button again to unsolo the track.

13 Repeat the previous steps to hear the Punch in Take 2 track.

Re-recording part of a region is a great method for masking mistakes in an otherwise terrific performance.

Project Tasks

Now that you've seen how I recorded a punch in to fix the song, it's your turn to try recording and punching in. Use the same instrument that you recorded with earlier in this lesson. Record a region with a mistake, then create a cycle region to punch in and fix the mistake. This exercise will truly be an example of learning from your mistakes.

1 Select one of the empty tracks in this project.

2 Record a simple scale (series of consecutive notes) with one or two wrong notes in the middle.

3 Set a cycle region over your mistake.

4 Click the Record button and try punching in to repair the recording with the correct notes.

5 For more practice, record the same riff that you recorded earlier. Intentionally make a mistake somewhere in your recording.

6 Set a cycle region over your mistake and try punching in to repair it.

Punch-ins get easier the more you practice with them.

Preparing the Project

Now that you understand punch-ins, let's work with a project that I created to illustrate the different recording techniques.

Open **4-5 Piano Starting** from the Lesson_04 folder.

Editing and Arranging Long Takes to Build a Song

Earlier in this lesson, you learned how to trim the edges of a region in the Track Editor. But what if you want to edit the *middle* of a region? Maybe it's a long region, and you want to split it into smaller pieces so you can loop certain sections or duplicate them for reuse later in the song.

When would you do this? Most songs consist of two or three parts (verses and chorus parts) that repeat several times before the end of the song. If the music in the second and third verse of your song is the same as the first verse, you don't need to record it three different times. All you need is one good take that you can copy and paste when needed. If you record the first verse and then the first chorus together in one long take, you can use the techniques you'll learn next to split the track so that you can separate the different parts, then duplicate or loop them when needed.

Splitting a Track

Splitting the track means that you physically slice the track at the playhead position, creating two regions on either side of the split. To split a region with a track, you need to first select the region, then press Cmd-T or choose Edit > Split.

The trick in splitting a track is finding the right spot to create the split.

This project illustrates two examples of the same long take. The first example on Track 1 was played straight through using the sustain pedal throughout and never pausing for any reason—as if it was a live performance.

I recorded the second example, on Track 2, slightly differently, with the idea of track splitting in mind. I paused a beat and released the sustain pedal between the different sections of the music to create spots within the recording where we will be able to easily do some editing. Think of them as "edit-friendly" spots.

Let's compare the two recordings and split both tracks.

1   Choose File > Open and select **4-5 Piano Starting** from the Lesson_04 folder.

2   Click the Solo button on Track 1 to solo the track (if it's not already selected).

3   Play Track 1 and listen for the change in the song around the beginning of the 10th measure.

This is part of a song called *Coming of Age* about teen angst and moving to a new city. I wrote this piece back in high school before digital recording, before the Internet, before Apple changed the world of computing, back when computers used the Basic language and were pretty much useless as far as I was concerned. What did I know? I was 15, and parachute pants were in style.

This long region is the first of four parts to this song.

4   Move the playhead to the beginning of the 10th measure.

5   Click the recorded region in Track 1 to make sure it is selected.

You can tell a region is selected because the color is darker in the Timeline. In this case, it is the only colored region because the others have been muted.

6   Press Cmd-T or choose Edit > Split to split the track at the playhead position.

A new region begins at the beginning of the 10th measure.

Ganging the Playhead

This is a good time to mention the two different ways you can watch the play-head in action. When you play a long take or a full song, your playhead may actually leave the screen. If you like to watch your playhead scrub across the tracks, you should click the Playhead Lock button. It's called that because it also lets you lock, or *gang*, the playhead in the Timeline with the playhead in the Track Editor. When you click the button, the playhead remains in the center of the screen, and the tracks move behind the playhead.

The Playhead Lock button is located on the far-right side of the window, and it looks like two playheads, one on top of the other.

If the two playheads are lined up in the middle of the button, it means that the playheads in the Timeline and the Track Editor are moving in sync with one another (ganged). It also means that the playheads will stay locked in the center of the Timeline, and the tracks will move behind the playhead.

If the button shows two playheads that are not aligned, the playheads in the Timeline and Track Editor are not locked to the center of the screen. The play-head will continue moving left to right and can continue to move offscreen as it plays the tracks in the Timeline.

By default, the playheads in the Timeline and the Track Editor stay centered in the middle of the GarageBand window once they reach the center. Sometimes you may want to see a different part of the song in the Track Editor than the one shown in the Timeline. To do this you can "unlock" the two playheads, so that the Timeline and Track Editor can show different parts of the song. Let's try it.

1   Press Ctrl–right arrow several times to zoom into the Timeline.

2   Press the spacebar to continue playback in the Timeline.

3   While the track is playing, click the Playhead Lock button once.

    Notice the change in the playhead.

4   Click the button again to see the playhead in the other mode.

5   Click the button until it is in the locked position (two playheads aligned in the center of the button).

6   Press the spacebar to stop playback.

7   Press Cmd-G to turn off snapping.

8   Move the playhead to 17.4.4.049 in the Time Display.

    You will need to zoom in to move the playhead to that specific location in the Timeline.

9   Press Cmd-G to turn snapping back on.

As you can see, manually moving the playhead to a specific location can be a tedious process. Fortunately, there is an easier way.

Navigating with the Time Display

When you need to move the playhead to a specific measure, beat, or click within a beat in the Timeline, you can simply change the information in the Time Display. By changing the numbers in the Time Display, you are actually using the Time Display for navigation.

There are two ways to change the numbers in the Time Display. You can double-click the number you want to change, and type a new number, or you can just click-drag the number you want to change up or down. Our goal is to send the playhead directly to 17.4.4.049.

1   Press the left arrow key twice to move the playhead two full measures to the left in the Timeline.

    NOTE ▶ You can also use the left and right arrow keys to move the playhead one measure at a time to the left or right.

2   Click-drag the measures portion of the Time Display up slightly to change the measure to 17.

3   Click-drag the beats number upward to change the beat from 1 to 4.

4   Double-click the ticks number, which is the number to the right of beats followed by a decimal point and three digits.

The number flashes.

5   Type *4* and press Return to change to the 4th tick in the 4th beat of the 17th measure.

Why do we need such a specific number? Because the space where you need to split this track is very, very specific. And when you're splitting a track, sometimes thousandths of a beat can count.

6   Notice the current playhead position on Track 1 in the Timeline. Don't move the playhead.

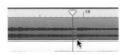

If you look at the waveform in Track 1, you can see that we are near a change in the music, but not quite there.

7   Double-click the last set of numbers in the Time Display. These numbers represent thousandths of a beat within the measure.

8   Type *049* and press Return.

Finally, the playhead is exactly in position to split the track.

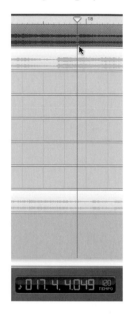

9   Click the region in Track 1 to select it, if it isn't already selected.

10   Press Cmd-T to split the track at the playhead position.

Notice that the title of each split region has a number after its name.

This number indicates a new copy of the original region. Each time you split the track, you create a new copy of the original region. This copy could be extended back to the full original recording or left as a smaller section.

11   Press Ctrl–left arrow several times until you can see all three regions in Track 1.

Evaluating the New Split Regions

Now that you have split the original track into three pieces, let's see how well the split regions work on their own. In a real recording situation, you might record a long region like this many times, then split the takes into smaller regions. You can then pick the best take of each section of the song to work with.

To evaluate the split regions, let's separate them in the Timeline and hear how cleanly they start and stop.

1   Click-drag the third region in Track 1 and move it to the right, leaving a gap between the last two regions.

2   Click-drag the second region and move it to the right to separate it from the first.

Once the regions are separated, you can hear how they sound and judge whether they start or stop abruptly.

3   Move the playhead to the beginning of the 9th measure.

4   Click Play and listen to the end of the first region and the beginning of the next.

How did it sound? To me, it sounds like both parts were cut off. It would be difficult to make a smooth transition between either of these and another take.

5   Move the playhead toward the end of the second region and listen to the end of the second and beginning of the third regions.

What did you think this time? These were better, but they're still rough. It's not your fault. It was the way that the regions were recorded. Remember, this performance was played like a live performance—one take, no pauses, sustain pedal used the entire time. It is nearly impossible to split a track cleanly under these circumstances.

Working with an Edit-Friendly Long Take

When you're recording long takes, consider creating edit-friendly moments within the take by inserting a brief pause and releasing the sustain pedal. This will produce a clean break in the waveform, and you will be able to try different takes and build a better song. (Obviously you wouldn't do this in a live performance, or if the song requires a solid single take.)

Let's work with the edit-friendly version of the same piano part—the version on Track 2. Note that this technique works not just for piano but for all the other instruments as well, including vocals.

1 Click Track 2 to select that track in the Timeline.

2 Click the Solo button on Track 1 to turn solo off on that track.

3 Click the Solo button on Track 2 to turn solo on for that track.

4 Double-click the Edit Friendly Piano region in Track 2 to open it in the Track Editor.

Make sure the Playhead Lock button is set so that the Timeline and the Track Editor playheads are ganged (locked together).

5 Play the region and watch it play in both the Timeline and Track Editor at the same time. When you get to the first break in the song (around the 10th measure), stop playback.

Did you find it on your own? The first break should be very obvious because there is a brief instant of silence between parts. This is also easy to identify by the flat line—no waveform—during the silence. Remember, when you're recording, you have to release the sustain pedal to get a clean break between musical phrases or parts.

6 Move the playhead to 10.3.1.001, which is the nearest beat to the break in the song.

Remember, when you are splitting or trimming a region you may use for a loop, it's important that the region ends on a beat. In this case, the split is on the 3rd beat in the 10th measure.

7 Press Cmd-T to split the track at the playhead position.

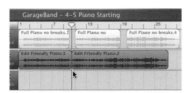

Project Tasks

It's your turn to find the second break to split the track. It isn't a big break, so you'll need to zoom in to the Track Editor to see it. As long as the playheads are locked, wherever you place the playhead in the Track Editor, the playhead in the Timeline will follow.

1   Zoom in to the region in the Track Editor for a closer view (and to see more grid lines).

2   Play the rest of the track and find the next break (18.3.1.089) in the song.

3   Split the track at (18.3.1.089).

4   Close the Track Editor.

5   Separate the three regions in Track 2 and listen to the start and stop of each one to hear if it's cleaner than the regions in Track 1.

Separating the Regions onto Different Tracks

Now that you have split up an edit-friendly region into usable parts, you can layer them on different tracks. Why different tracks? Because sometimes you need to overlap regions to get the timing just right between the last note of one region and the first of another.

The first region is fine where it is. In this exercise, you'll move the second region to Track 3 and the third region to Track 4. Then you'll zoom in to the track for more grid lines to align the different regions. When you're finished, nobody will ever know this piano part came from three separate regions—or possibly different takes from different performances.

1   Click-drag the second Edit Friendly Piano region from Track 2 to Track 3.

2   Click-drag the last region on Track 2 and move it to Track 4.

3   Move the playhead between the first region on Track 2 and the region on Track 3.

When you zoom in to a track, the playhead always stays visible. Since the playhead is between the two regions, you will zoom in to the space between them to make alignment easier.

4   Press Ctrl–right arrow to zoom into the Timeline until you have a clear view of the end of the region on Track 2 and the beginning of the region on Track 3.

You should have at least three or four grid lines between the regions.

If your grid ruler is still set to automatic (which it should be), then the more you zoom in, the more options you have to snap your region to. You don't necessarily have to align a region with a grid line. If you are zoomed in, you can also align to the tick marks in the ruler between grid lines.

5 Click-drag the region on Track 3 and move it so it overlaps the end of the region on Track 2.

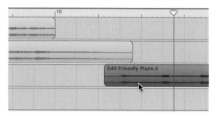

6 Click the Solo buttons on Tracks 2, 3, and 4 to solo the audio for those tracks.

7 Use the left or right arrows to move the playhead to the beginning of the 9th measure.

Because this is a full measure before the overlap, you'll be able to clearly hear the transition between the two regions.

8 Press the spacebar to start playback and listen to the pacing between the two regions.

It's OK if there is a slight beat between parts. Songs breathe, and musical instruments pause briefly and naturally as they move into a new part of the song.

If you hear a stagnant pause between the two regions, you need to move the region on Track 3 to the left to tighten the timing between them. But if the notes are stepping on each other from one region to the next, they are too close, and you need to move the lower region to the right.

9 Keep adjusting the region on Track 3 until the timing sounds right.

How do you know when it sounds right? You know. Trust your instincts. If you're unsure, it's not right. If you have to think about it, it's not right. Remember, the goal is to make it sound seamless between the regions, as if they came from a single live performance.

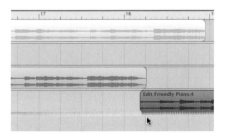

TIP ▶ Sometimes it helps to get your musical timing by turning on the metronome during playback. If you're having trouble aligning the different regions, stop playback and press Cmd-U to start the metronome during playback. Use the audible clicks to get a feel for the song and for when the next region should start. If you want to turn the metronome off, stop playback again and press Cmd-U to turn it off.

10 Click-drag the region on Track 4 and align it with the end of the region on Track 3.

11 Play the two regions to see how they sound together.

Work with the two regions until they sound right. The following screen shows what the last overlapping regions look like up close.

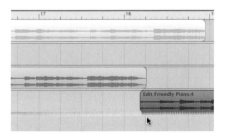

NOTE ▶ If you think you're tone deaf or rhythmically challenged, and you need to see and hear the finished part to make it work, save your project and open the project **4-6 Piano Finished** in the Lesson_04 folder and play the final edit of Tracks 2, 3 and 4.

12 When you finish, press Cmd-S to save your project.

13 Press Ctrl–left arrow to zoom out of the Timeline until you can see all of the regions in the lower tracks.

Editing and Arranging Small Takes to Build a Song

In the last exercise, you worked with long recorded regions and cut them up into smaller pieces. Another very useful recording technique is to start with small pieces and build the song up. In other words, break the song into the basic parts and record each one separately. Record several takes until you get what you want, then delete the unwanted takes and keep the best parts to arrange your song.

The main difference between working with short recorded regions and longer chopped-up ones is that the short regions can't be extended. The edited long regions still retain the information of the full recording. You can go back and extend those regions to bring back part of the region you trimmed previously.

For the following exercise, I recorded several takes of the beginning (intro), middle, and end of the song. I selected the best takes, which are the regions on Tracks 5, 7, and 9.

Before you arrange the song one last time using the smaller recorded regions, you need to duplicate the Piano Intro on Track 5.

There are two methods you have already worked with that you could try. First, you could trim any silence from the beginning and end of the region and loop it to double the length and the part. Second, you could Option-drag it to the lower track and overlap the two parts.

The trimming/looping method wouldn't be my first choice for this song or this part. That method is great if you created a part that was meant to be looped and repeated. Here, you want this piano part to sound more natural and less loopy.

1   Click the Solo buttons on Tracks 2, 3, and 4 to turn solo off on those tracks.

2   Click the Solo buttons on Tracks 5 and 6 to hear only the tracks we are working on. (Tracks 5 and 6 should be the only soloed tracks.)

3   Option-drag the Piano Intro region from Track 5 to Track 6 to duplicate it.

4   Drag the region on Track 6 so that it starts after the region on Track 5.

You can overlap them a bit if you wish.

5   Zoom into the Timeline and align the lower intro region so the two regions sound seamless.

Project Tasks

Now it's your turn to put it all together and finish arranging the different parts of this song. Arranging isn't easy, and making parts that were recorded separately sound like one continuous recording takes practice and patience.

1   Click the Solo button on Track 8 to unsolo the track.

2   Click-drag the Piano Middle section on Track 7 and move it to the right to align it with the end of the Piano Intro region on Track 6.

3   Zoom into the Timeline for more control as you fine-tune the placement of the region.

4   When the Piano Middle region is in place, click the Solo button on Track 8 to solo the track again with the other piano tracks.

5   Move the Piano Ending region on Track 8 until it starts right after the Piano Middle section.

6   Play your arrangement on Tracks 5 through 8 from start to finish to hear how the whole thing sounds together.

7   Save and close the project.

If you want to compare your finished project with mine, open **4-6 Piano Finished** in the Lesson_04 folder and play the finished arrangement.

You now have a foundation for recording Real Instrument tracks, testing different instrument sounds, and then looping, trimming, splitting, and arranging the recorded regions.

What You've Learned

- Real Instrument regions are digital recordings of actual instrument performances. You can't transpose, change the tempo, or edit individual notes in a Real Instrument region as you can with Software Instruments.

- You can connect real instruments to the computer through the audio-in port or an audio interface like an Mbox or PCR-A30 MIDI Keyboard Controller/USB Audio Interface.

- You can record a Real Instrument as a stereo or mono recording. Stereo uses two channels (Channel 1 and Channel 2); mono uses one (either Channel 1 or Channel 2).

- CD-quality stereo audio uses around 10 MB of disk space per minute.

- You can resize a Real Instrument region by click-dragging the lower-right or lower-left corner of the region. You can loop a region by click-dragging the upper-right corner.

- Monitoring input means that you can hear the instrument you're playing before and during recording.

- Recording a Real Instrument using a cycle region will only record during the first pass. The second pass of the playhead in the cycle region will play back the newly recorded region.

- You can add effects to a track before or after recording by using the Details portion of the Track Info window.

- You can hear different effects as you apply them to a track by playing the track in the Timeline and changing the instrument or effects in the Track Info window while the track is playing.

- You can save your effects settings and use them again on different tracks or projects.

- Grid lines are used to restrict the movement and placement of musical elements in a project in order to keep them in time (musical time). To override the grid restrictions, turn Snap to Grid off by pressing Cmd-G.

- The more you zoom in to a track, the more grid lines and detailed control you will have to move and trim regions in the Timeline.

- You can use the Time Display for navigation by double-clicking the number you want to change and typing in a new number and pressing Return. The playhead will go to whatever numbers you type into the Time Display.

- You can split a selected region at the playhead position by pressing Cmd-T or by choosing Edit > Split.

5

Lesson Files	Lessons > Lesson_05 > 5-1 LoopsTest Starting; 5-2 IvoryGroove Finished
Time	This lesson takes approximately 60 minutes to complete.
Goals	Understand the rules for combining Real Instrument and Software Instrument regions and loops
	Resize the Loop Browser
	Move keyword buttons to a different position in the Loop Browser
	Change the keyword on a keyword button
	Mark favorite loops
	Duplicate, resize, split, and extend loops to build a song
	Adjust the position of loops in the Timeline to make a song work
	Reset the Loop Browser to its default settings

Working with Apple Loops

Apple Loops are prerecorded music files that are designed to repeat (loop) over and over seamlessly as a pattern. Loops are commonly used for drum beats, rhythm parts, and other repeating musical sections within a song. GarageBand comes with over 1,000 prerecorded Apple Loops.

Apple Loops are incredibly flexible instrument regions that can be cut, copied, pasted, edited, transposed, and repeated to create a song or enhance your recorded tracks.

To extend your loop library, you can also add third-party loops, as well as Apple Loops from Soundtrack or the Jam Pack expansion for GarageBand. You will learn more about adding additional loops to your Loop Browser in Lesson 9.

In this lesson, you will learn how to customize the Loop Browser, mark and find favorite loops, and build a song from scratch using Apple Loops.

Preparing the Project

Open **5-1 LoopsTest Starting** from the Lesson_05 file in the Lessons folder. You will start with a project that has two empty tracks.

Understanding Apple Loops

As you have learned so far, Apple Loops come in different shapes, sizes, instruments, and colors. Before you build a song, let's examine some of the unique characteristics of the prerecorded Apple Loops that come with GarageBand.

In the previous lessons, you discovered that the green loops are Software Instrument loops and can be edited just like any Software Instrument region; you can even edit individual notes. Likewise, the blue loops are Real Instrument loops that can be edited like any Real Instrument region.

What happens if you place a Real Instrument loop into a Software Instrument region? Let's try it and find out. The first track in the current project is a Software Instrument track. The second track is a Real Instrument track.

1   Click the Loop Browser button to open the Loop Browser.

2   Click the Button View button in the lower-left corner of the Loop Browser (if it is not already in Button view). Then click the Reset button to clear any current results in the browser.

3   Click the Guitars button to show the Guitars loops in the results list.

The Acoustic Noodling guitar loops should be at the top of your results list. If you've installed the Jam Pack expansion or other additional loops, the

Acoustic Noodling loops may be further down in the results list. Notice that all the Acoustic Noodling loops are blue and have a waveform icon in the Loop Type column, indicating that they are all Real Instrument loops.

4   Click-drag the Acoustic Noodling 02 loop from the Loop Browser to the Grand Piano (top track) in the Timeline and release the mouse.

The track remains empty after you release the mouse because you can't put a Real Instrument region in a Software Instrument track. Software Instrument tracks can only play regions recorded using MIDI samples and note events.

5   Click-drag the Acoustic Noodling 02 loop from the Loop Browser to the 1st measure of the second track in the Timeline.

A green circle with a plus (+) symbol appears if the track will accept the loop. If you don't see the green plus sign, you will not be able to place the loop in that track.

This time it worked because the Acoustic Noodling 02 loop is a Real Instrument recording, the same as the track.

6   Click the top of the Loop Type column in the results list to move the Software Instrument loops to the top of the list.

▼	Name
🎵	Southern Rock Guitar 05
🎵	Southern Rock Guitar 04
🎵	Southern Rock Guitar 03
🎵	Southern Rock Guitar 02
🎵	Southern Rock Guitar 01
🎵	Dreamy Guitar Pattern 02
🎵	Dreamy Guitar Pattern 01

7   Click-drag the Southern Rock Guitar 05 loop from the browser to the 1st measure of the top track in the Timeline.

The Southern Rock Guitar 05 loop region appears in the top track as a green Software Instrument region. This is predictable since all you did is put a loop in the appropriate type of track.

OK, so this all seems like old news, right? Well, we're not quite done with our loop experiment.

What if you put a Software Instrument region in a Real Instrument track?

8   Click-drag the Southern Rock Guitar 05 loop from the browser and place it in the second track next to the Acoustic Noodling 02 region.

The Software Instrument loop transforms into a Real Instrument region.

As a Real Instrument loop, the Southern Rock Guitar region now shows waveforms in the Timeline instead of MIDI information.

9   Click the Acoustic Noodling 02 region in the second track to select the region.

10   Press the Delete key to delete the region from the Timeline.

11   Play the Timeline to hear the two Southern Rock Guitar 05 regions.

Were you expecting the Southern Rock Guitar to sound like a grand piano?

This is just a reminder that Software Instrument regions will always sound like the track instrument, regardless of the instrument sound used in the original recording. On the other hand, Real Instrument regions will always sound like the instrument that originally recorded the region, regardless of the track instrument. You can add effects to a Real Instrument track, but you can't change the instrument for a region by changing the track instrument, as you can with Software Instruments.

The Guitar region in the Real Instrument track sounds like a guitar because that is the MIDI instrument sound that originally recorded it. The fact that the track is named No Effects, implying that there are no effects on the track, has no effect (pun intended) on the instrument sound for the region in that track.

12 Double-click the Grand Piano track header to open the Software Instrument Track Info window.

13 Select Guitars > Steel String Acoustic for the track instrument, and then close the Track Info window.

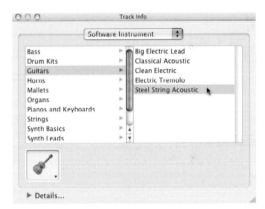

The instrument track header changes to Steel String Acoustic Guitar.

14 Play the region in the top track to hear the instrument change.

15 Double-click the No Effects track header to open the Real Instrument Track Info window.

16 Select Vocals > Female Basic to change the effects on the track, and then close the Track Info window.

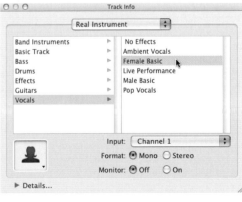

Before you click Play, see if you can predict the outcome of your actions. Will the Southern Rock Guitar loop sound like a female vocalist?

Will it still sound like a guitar? Perhaps it will sound like a southern female rock vocalist?

17 Play the region to hear the Southern Rock Guitar in the Female Basic track.

You probably guessed it. It still sounds like a guitar (although I have to admit I was curious to hear some of the other alternatives). All you changed was the preset effects or amplifier sounds to enhance Real Instrument recordings. If you are planning to record a basic female vocal part, this might be a terrific choice for your Real Instrument track.

18 Press Cmd-Delete twice to delete both tracks from the project.

19 Press Cmd-S to save the changes to the project.

So now that you have reviewed these loop basics, let's get ready to compose a new song.

Listening to the Finished Song

Before you start the next series of exercises, it's good to know what you're aiming for. Follow these steps to hear the finished song you will be creating from scratch using Apple Loops.

The song you'll create is called **IvoryGroove** and is based on a short theme song I composed for a production company. The production company used it with their animated logo at the beginning of their film and television productions. Since the process to develop the story for a film is similar to developing a song, I used the creative energy of a live music jam session as a template for the music.

In the many jam sessions I've experienced over the years, somebody in the band has an idea for a riff, and in a matter of seconds, other musicians catch the groove and join in. In **IvoryGroove**, as you'll hear in a moment, something similar happens. The piano comes in, then the strings double-up on the melody, then the bass and drums/percussion come in, and finally the song ends with a cymbal crash.

Keep in mind, a jam session is live musicians joining in to play an unrehearsed piece of music and to see where it goes. In some ways, writing a song in GarageBand is the opposite of a jam session because you have to think and plan each part to add it to the Timeline. On the other hand, since your musical choices in GarageBand are unlimited, the essence of a jam session lives on.

1 Choose File > Open and select **5-2 IvoryGroove Finished** from the Lesson_05 folder to open the song.

The project **5-2 IvoryGroove Finished** opens in the Timeline.

2 Press the Home key then press the spacebar to play the song from the beginning of the Timeline.

NOTE ▶ If you are running a slower computer and are having trouble playing this song, try muting the Electric Bass track.

3 Choose File > New to open a new song.

4 Name the song *IvoryGroove* and save it to your GarageBand Songs folder.

Customizing the Loop Browser

The Loop Browser is a complex organizational tool that goes beyond buttons and columns. There are many hidden features that you can use to customize the Loop Browser. Let's explore some of these features while we build the simple song using Apple Loops.

Resizing and Rearranging Columns in the Results List

A good place to start customizing your Loop Browser is in the results list. The results list has six different columns.

Loop Type column

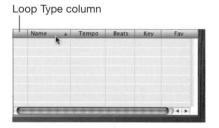

To view additional columns, you can click-drag the horizontal scroller below the results list.

1   Press Cmd-L or click the Loop Browser button to open the Loop Browser.

2   Click-drag the scroller toward the right to see the last columns in the results list.

    These columns contain information about the individual loops and can be used to sort the loops within the results list.

    All the columns can be moved or resized except for the Loop Type column, which always stays on the far left.

    To move a column, you simply click-drag the column header.

3   Locate the favorites column, which is labeled "Fav."

4   Click-drag the Fav column header toward the left and release it before the Name column.

You can also resize the columns by click-dragging the right edge of the column header.

5   Move your pointer to the right edge of the Name column header until it becomes a resize pointer.

6   Click-drag the right edge of the Name column to extend the column to the edge of the results list.

Extending the Name column makes it easier to read the names of the loops in the results list.

The Fav column does not need to be very wide because it isn't used for text.

Selecting Favorite Loops

With over 1,000 loops to choose from, sometimes it's a good idea to mark your favorites or the loops you plan to use for a specific song. That way, when you are ready to start building the song, you won't have to break your creative flow to go hunting for loops. Instead, they will all be located in one category—favorites. Any loop that is marked as a favorite can be located easily with the Favorites button in Button view or in the Favorites column in Column view.

1   Click the Reset button to reset (deselect) any buttons in the Loop Browser.

Loops						Fav ▾	Name
Reset ▸⊗	Drums	Piano	Rock/Blues	Single	Piano		
Favorites ⚑	Drum Kit	Elec Piano	Urban	Clean	Distorted		
Bass	Beats	Organ	World	Acoustic	Electric		
Guitars	Percussion	Synths	Electronic	Relaxed	Intense		
Strings	Shaker	Horn	Country	Cheerful	Dark		

The song is based around a piano melody, so let's start with the piano.

2 Click the Piano keyword button to select the piano loops.

3 Select 70s Ballad Piano 01 in the search results to preview the loop.

This loop is perfect for the song. All you have to do now is mark it as a favorite so you can look for other loops that may go well with this melody.

4 Click the box in the Fav column next to the 70s Ballad Piano 01 loop.

The Favorites button is no longer grayed out, indicating that you now have at least one loop marked as a favorite.

5 Click the Piano button to deselect the button and empty the search results list.

6 Click the Favorites button to view the loop you marked as a favorite in the list.

7 Click the Column View button to change the Loop Browser to Column view.

Notice the Favorites option in the Loops column.

8 Click Favorites in the Loops column, then Piano in the Favorites column.

Notice that the Piano descriptors all have one selection.

9 Click any of descriptors in the Piano column to select a favorite loop.

These descriptors apply to the loop you selected as a favorite, and include all the categories you could use to search for the 70s Ballad Piano 01 loop in the Loop Browser. Later in this lesson, you'll see that there are keyword buttons for each of these descriptors that you can use with the Loop Browser in Button view.

10 Click the Button View button again to return to the Button view.

Now that you have searched for a loop, marked it as a favorite, and found it in the Loop Browser using Button view and Column view, it's time to find and mark the rest of the loops for the song.

Moving Keyboard Buttons

Keyword buttons are not only easy to use, but also easy to move. To move a button, all you have to do is click-drag the button to a different button location. The button you move will swap places with the button in the current location. The only buttons that cannot be moved are Reset and Favorites.

Why would you want to move a button? Good question. Since you know that you want certain instruments for the song, it is useful to group all of the instrument buttons together near a common descriptor so you can spend less time searching for buttons and more time searching for loops.

For this song, you'll need a piano part (which you've already marked as a favorite), a bass, and some drums, so let's group them all together with the common descriptor Rock/Blues.

Let's start by moving the Rock/Blues button closer to the results list for easier access.

1   Locate the Rock/Blues button in the Loop Browser.

2   Click-drag the Rock/Blues button and move it on top of the Ensemble button, located at the top right of the keyword buttons.

The Ensemble button highlights when you move the other button over it to show that you are moving the new button to that location.

3   Release the mouse to complete the button move.

Loops					
Reset ⊗	Drums	Piano	Ensemble	Single	Rock/Blues
Favorites 🪈	Drum Kit	Elec Piano	Urban	Clean	Distorted
Bass	Beats	Organ	World	Acoustic	Electric
Guitars	Percussion	Synths	Electronic	Relaxed	Intense
Strings	Shaker	Horn	Country	Cheerful	Dark

Scale: Any   🔍   0 items

The Rock/Blues button is now in the upper-right corner, and the Ensemble button has moved to the old Rock/Blues position.

Let's move the other main instrument keyword buttons we need to the button positions below the Rock/Blues button.

4   Locate the Bass button and move it to the position directly below the Rock/Blues button.

5   Locate the Drums button and move it to the position below the Bass button.

Now that the buttons are in place, let's hunt for some more loops to use for the song.

6   Click the Rock/Blues button to select it (if it is not already selected).

7 Click the Bass button to narrow the search to Bass loops that are also classified as Rock/Blues loops.

8 Click-drag the scroller to scroll down through the results list until you locate Muted Rock Bass 01.

9 Click the Muted Rock Bass 01 loop to preview it in the results list.

10 Click again to stop the preview.

11 Mark the Muted Rock Bass 01 as a favorite.

12 Click the Bass keyword button to deselect it.

The Rock/Blues button remains selected.

13 Click the Drums button to search for Rock/Blues Drums loops.

14 Locate Relaxed Drum Groove 01 from the results list and mark it as a favorite.

15 Click the Drums button again to deselect it.

16 Click the Favorites button to view your current favorites.

You now have three loops in your favorites list.

17 Click the Favorites button again to deselect it.

Showing More Keyword Buttons

By default, the Loop Browser shows 35 buttons (including the Reset and Favorites buttons). You can easily increase the size of the Loop Browser to show up to 63 buttons.

Why would you want to see that many buttons? If you're just starting a song, you might not know exactly what type of loop you want. Some of the Genre or Mood buttons, like Cinematic, Experimental, Grooving, or Melodic, that are normally hidden from view might inspire you. If 35 buttons are a nice salad-bar-sized selection to choose from, 63 buttons are the full-blown keyword button buffet.

To resize the Loop Browser, you click-drag between the Record button and the Track Editor button.

Let's resize the Loop Browser to see more buttons.

1   Move your pointer over the empty gray space to the left of the Record button to change the pointer to a Hand tool.

2   Click-drag up the Loop Browser until all of the buttons are showing.

Notice all of the new buttons from which to choose. The Part button will be perfect for the cymbal crash part that we need for the end of the song.

3   Locate the Part button and swap it with the Intense button.

When you release the Part button over the Intense button, they will swap positions, leaving the Part button below the Drums.

Having all these buttons at your fingertips is great for browsing through loops and finding favorite loops to use later. Unfortunately, the expanded browser doesn't leave much room in the Timeline for arranging your song.

Now that you've seen the full button spread and have rearranged the buttons you need, it's time to resize the Loop Browser back to the more compact Timeline-friendly default size.

4   Click-drag the Loop Browser to resize it back to the normal size.

NOTE ▶ Enlarging the Loop Browser can be very useful when you are searching for loops and marking them as favorites. However, a larger Loop Browser isn't recommended while you are working in the Timeline because it takes up too much of the Timeline workspace.

Changing a Keyword Button

Now that you have resized the Loop Browser, you have seen some of the additional keyword button choices that are available for you to use.

Instead of dragging buttons to a more convenient location, you can simply change a keyword button to a new keyword.

1   Locate the Dark button at the bottom of the right column of keyword buttons.

2   Ctrl-click the Dark button to open a contextual menu of keyword choices.

The contextual menu has three submenus of keyword choices: Genre, Instruments, and Descriptors.

3   Choose Instruments > Percussion > Tambourine from the contextual menu.

NOTE ▶ Your contextual menu layout may differ from the picture depending on your screen resolution and the location of the contextual menu on your screen.

The Dark keyword changes to Tambourine in the Loop Browser.

4   Click the Reset button to make all the visible keyword buttons active in the Loop Browser.

Now that you know how to customize your Loop Browser, let's find the rest of the loops for the song.

Finishing the Loop Search

There are three loops left to find and mark as favorites. Let's start with the tambourine parts.

1   Click the Tambourine button to view the different choices in the results list.

2   Mark Tambourine 01 as a favorite.

3   Mark Tambourine 07 as a favorite.

4   Click the Tambourine button again to deselect it.

The last loop we need to find for the song is the cymbal crash. The easiest way to find it will be to simply type *cymbal* in the Search text field.

5   Type *cymbal* in the Search text field at the bottom of the Loop Browser and press Return.

6   Mark the Long Crash Cymbal 01 loop as a favorite.

You'll use this loop as the finale at the end of the song.

7   Click the Favorites button to view all of the favorite loops.

All of the loops you need to build the song **IvoryGroove** are now collected as favorites.

	Fav	Name
♪	☑	70s Ballad Piano 01
♫	☑	Long Crash Cymbal 01
♪	☑	Muted Rock Bass 01
♪	☑	Relaxed Drum Groove 01
♫	☑	Tambourine 01
♫	☑	Tambourine 07

8   Press Cmd-S to save your work.

Building a Song with Apple Loops

Now that you have collected all of the musical parts, it's time to build the song. Along the way you'll learn a few new tricks of the trade, like doubling a part with another instrument and transposing a region a full octave.

Starting with the Melody

There are different ways to begin a song. Many songs are built on a rhythm foundation. For this piece, you will start with the piano melody because it also has a solid rhythm, and all of the other parts work off the piano.

1 Click-drag the 70s Ballad Piano 01 loop from the Loop Browser to the 1st measure of the Grand Piano track in the Timeline.

2 Press the spacebar to listen to the first track in the Timeline.

When you hear this piano melody, does it make you want to pick up an instrument and play along? Which instrument? Bass? Drums? Guitar? Whichever instrument you imagined, I strongly encourage you to try this exercise again later and record the part you imagine with your instrument of choice. For this exercise, we'll pretend it's a keyboard player who joins in with some strings.

Strings? Don't worry if you didn't select any string parts in your loop favorites. Many string parts mirror the lead instrument. That's exactly what you are going to do here. There are three ways to double this track to create a strings track that mirrors the piano part.

- Create a new Software Instrument track, make the track instrument Strings, and duplicate the region from the Piano track into the new track.

- Create a new Software instrument track, make the new track Piano, duplicate the region from the original Piano track to the new track, and change the original track to Strings.

- Click-drag the 70s Ballad Piano 01 loop from the browser to the empty space below the first track to create a new Software Instrument Piano track. Change one of the two Piano tracks to Strings.

Since this is a lesson about working with Apple Loops, let's use the third method and create a new Software Instrument track by dragging the loop to the Timeline.

3 Click-drag the 70s Ballad Piano 01 loop from the browser to the 1st measure of the empty space below the first track.

A new Piano Software Instrument track appears below the top track in the Timeline.

4 Double-click the Grand Piano track header (the top track) to open the Track Info window.

5 Select Strings > Hollywood Strings. Then close the Track Info window.

The track name changes to Hollywood Strings.

The region is still named 70s Ballad Piano 01.

6 Double-click the region on the Hollywood Strings track to open it in the Track Editor.

7 Type *strings* in the Name field to change the name of the region in the Timeline.

8 Click the Loop Browser button to close the Track Editor and open the Loop Browser.

9 Play the doubled piano and strings part in the Timeline to hear how they sound together.

I think they sound pretty good. As I mentioned before, many string parts mirror the lead instrument melody. When you are working with Software Instruments in GarageBand, it's easy to double your lead part with strings.

Splitting a Software Instrument Region

Now that you've doubled the piano part with strings, there's a slight problem. If this song is really supposed to resemble a jam session, the strings can't start with the piano. The strings have to join in, after a few measures. All you need to do is cut off the first half of the strings region.

So how do you go about cutting off the first half of the Software Instrument region you want to trim?

You can't click and drag the beginning of the region (the left edge) to shorten it because Software Instrument regions like to maintain the integrity of the beginning of the region. You can only shorten a prerecorded Software Instrument region from the right side.

1   Click-drag the lower-right corner of the strings region in the top track to the left until it ends at the 3rd measure.

The region is now half the length, but it's the first half of the region instead of the second half. Chances are if you try to use the first half of the region with the second half, it will not sound very good. Let's try it anyway.

2   Click-drag the resized strings region to the right so it begins at the 3rd measure.

3   Play the song in the Timeline to hear how it sounds.

Yikes. It's worse than I expected. Remember, if your strings section is going to mirror the lead instrument, it needs to play the same notes at the same time. Let's extend the region again and do it the right way.

4 Move the full strings region back so that it lines up with the beginning of the piano region.

It's a good idea to zoom in to the Timeline a bit for a better view.

5 Press Ctrl–right arrow once to zoom in.

> **NOTE ▶** If you need to zoom in further to see the region better in the Timeline, press Ctrl–right arrow again. If you were already zoomed in to the Timeline, you may not need to zoom in further. Just make sure you have a clear view of the regions.

6 Click-drag the lower-right edge of the strings region to extend it back to the original full region.

7 Move your playhead to the beginning of the 3rd measure.

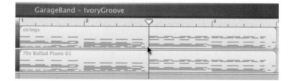

Notice the break in the note events that happens in the middle of the region at the beginning of the 3rd measure. That is where you will split the region.

8 Click the strings region to select it in the Timeline.

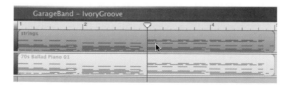

9 Press Cmd-T to split the selected region.

The original region splits into two separate regions. The first is the first half of the loop. The second is the second half of the loop.

10 Press Ctrl–left arrow to zoom out of the Timeline.

11 Click the empty track space on the strings track to deselect the regions in that track.

12 Click the first strings region to select it.

13 Press Delete to delete the region from the Timeline.

14 Listen to the edited section in the Timeline.

Mission accomplished! The piano section and strings will work perfectly for the beginning of the song.

Now that you have the piano and strings, let's continue building the song.

Extending Edited Software Regions

The first part of the song works great. The next step is to loop the melody regions to play a second time. Remember, to loop a region, you need to extend the loop from the upper-right corner.

1   Click-drag the upper-right corner of the piano region to loop the entire region once.

The loop ends at the beginning of the 9th measure.

2   Click-drag the upper-right corner of the strings region on the top track to loop the region once.

Why is the loop so short? Looping basically clones or duplicates whatever you click and drag with your loop pointer. If the region has been edited, the loops will be identical. The easiest way to get the full loop back is to just get the original loop from the Loop Browser and reinsert it in the Timeline.

3   Press Cmd-Z to undo the loop.

4   Click-drag the 70s Ballad Piano 01 loop from the browser to the Timeline and place it at the beginning of the 5th measure, next to the strings region on the top track.

NOTE ▶ Since the Software Instrument for the track is Hollywood Strings, any Software Instrument loop you add will automatically be assigned the Hollywood Strings as its instrument, regardless of the original Software Instrument assigned to the loop—in this case, a piano.

5   Press Cmd-S to save your work.

Adding the Rest of the Tracks

Now that you've built the melody, it's time to add the other tracks and finish the song. To continue the jam session theme, the drums and the bass will join the song at the end of the first full piano loop.

This exercise will help you review many of your new GarageBand skills.

1   Move your playhead to the beginning of the 5th measure.

2   Click-drag the Muted Rock Bass 01 loop from the Loop Browser to the playhead position below the second track in the Timeline.

    A new track appears in the Timeline with the muted bass region at the playhead position.

3   Click-drag the Relaxed Drum Groove 01 loop from the Loop Browser to the playhead position below the Electric Bass track.

4   Click-drag the upper-right corner of the drum region to loop it until it ends at the beginning of the 10th measure in the Timeline.

5   Loop the Muted Rock Bass 01 region until it ends on the 3rd beat of the 9th measure (halfway between the 9th and 10th measures).

NOTE ▶ Remember, each measure has four beats because this project is in 4/4 time. The more you zoom in to the Timeline, the more details you will see in the Beat Ruler. In the previous picture, you see four lines in each measure, representing each of the four beats. Each measure starts on the first beat.

6 Loop the second region in the strings track so it ends on the 3rd beat of the 9th measure (the same as the bass loop).

7 Click-drag the Tambourine 07 loop from the browser to the empty space below the bottom track and release it at the beginning of the 7th measure.

8 Press Ctrl–right arrow to zoom in to the Timeline one level.

This will allow you to place the following loops in the Timeline more precisely.

9 Click-drag the Tambourine 01 loop from the browser to the empty space below the bottom track and release it at the beginning of the 8th measure.

10 Click-drag the Long Crash Cymbal 01 loop to the empty space below the bottom track and release it at the beginning of the 10th measure.

11 Press Ctrl–right arrow several times to zoom in to the Timeline until you see each beat of each measure in the Beat Ruler.

There are four beats in each measure.

12 Click-drag the Long Crash Cymbal 01 loop toward the left to the 4th beat of the 9th measure.

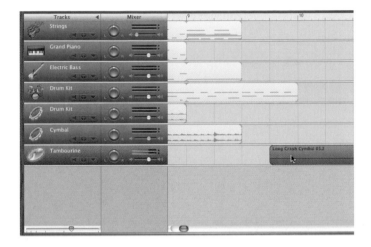

The cymbal needs to be precisely placed as the finale of the song. Next you need extend the lower Tambourine region so it ends at the same time as the other tambourine part.

16 Click-drag the lower-right corner of the Tambourine 01 region (the lower tambourine track) to resize it so that it ends at the beginning of the 9th measure.

Notice that the Tambourine regions are blue, which means they are Real Instrument regions.

17 Press Cmd-S to save the finished song.

18 Play the finished song to hear how it sounds.

Now that you've finished the song, you can reset the Loop Browser.

Resetting the Keywords in the Loop Browser

You can reset the keyword buttons in the Loop Browser by clicking the Reset button in the GarageBand General Preferences window.

1   Choose GarageBand > Preferences to open the General Preferences window.

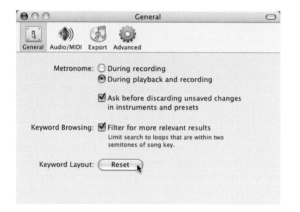

2   Click the Reset button to reset the keyword buttons in the Loop Browser back to the GarageBand default settings.

A dialog box will ask you if you are sure you want to reset the keyword buttons to the default settings.

3   Click Yes to reset the keyword layout.

The Reset button in the Loop Browser will clear any selected buttons, and clear the results list. The Reset button in the General Preferences window resets all of the keyword buttons to their original names and locations in the Loop Browser.

4   Close the General Preferences window.

What You've Learned

- Software Instrument loops can be converted to Real Instrument loops in the Timeline by adding them to a Real Instrument track.

- You can only shorten a Software Instrument loop from the lower-right edge of the loop region. You can't shorten a Software Instrument loop from the left edge.

- You can split a region at the playhead position by selecting the region and pressing Cmd-T.

- Looping a region by click-dragging the upper-right corner will only loop the current region. If you have edited a region in the Timeline, the loop pointer will allow you to loop only the edited portion of the region.

- You can rearrange the columns in the results list of the Loop Browser by dragging the column header. You can resize columns by dragging the right edge of the column header.

- You can move a keyword button to a new position in the Loop Browser by click-dragging the button to the new position.

- You can change a keyword by Ctrl-clicking a keyword button and selecting a new keyword from the contextual menu.

- To resize the Loop Browser, click-drag the empty gray space to the left of the Record button in the transport controls.

- To reset the keyword buttons in the Loop Browser to their original names and locations, click the Reset button in the GarageBand General Preferences window.

6

Lesson Files	Lesson > Lesson_06 > 6-1 Techno80s Starting; 6-2 Techno80s Finished
Time	This lesson takes approximately 60 minutes to complete.
Goals	Understand the difference between melody and rhythm
	Search for loops that fit the project
	Evaluate a monotonous arrangement
	Solo, mute, and change tracks using keyboard shortcuts
	Move a region out of time with snapping off
	Split a repetitive region
	Arrange the beginning, middle, and end of a song
	Create a drum turnaround
	Double a track with mixed instruments
	Preview and audition loops
	Move and resize a cycle region
	Copy, paste, and duplicate multiple regions in the Timeline

Arranging Music with GarageBand

Now that you've learned how to work with all of the different types of regions and tracks in GarageBand, it's time to start putting them all together to arrange a song.

Arranging is the art of putting musical parts together to build a song. There are many different styles and techniques for arranging music. In this lesson, you'll learn about the building blocks of a song, plus basic and advanced techniques for arranging music in the Timeline.

Clarifying Your Musical Goals

Where do you start when you're ready to create a song from scratch? The answer depends on the song, what you need to arrange, and whatever inspires you the most for that song.

Answering a few fundamental questions might help point you in the right direction:

- Why are you writing this song?
- Do you have lyrics you need to put to music?
- Do you already have a melody or music riff in your head that you want to start with?
- Will your song be melody-driven or rhythm-driven?

Let's start with the first question: Why are you writing this song? If your goal is simply to practice writing music, then whatever you come up with will work. But if you have a specific musical goal in mind, it's important to stay focused on that goal as you work. Setting a musical goal and following through may seem like a basic concept, but it's easy to get distracted when you're writing music. Before you know it, the sentimental tear jerker instrumental piece you were writing for your mother's birthday turns into a heavy metal, nosebleed-inducing ode to the electric guitar.

The first part of this lesson also has a goal. You're going to arrange a song that captures the essence of techno 80s music. In fact, the song title will be simply **Techno80s**.

The answer to the second question is that this song has no lyrics, but you're welcome to write some and record them after the lesson.

For the purposes of this lesson, the answer to question three is that we're not starting with a melody or riff in mind. However, when you are working on your own, you might want to look for a loop in the Loop Browser to start with. If you do have a preconceived melody, that's always a good place to start.

Finally, the last question: Will the song be melody-driven or rhythm-driven? For the **Techno80s** song, let's make it melody-driven.

Understanding Melody and Rhythm

What's the difference between melody and rhythm?

Melody is the plot, or story, of a song. It's the memorable part that you hum to yourself when you think of the song, and it's the part other people will remember as well. If you think of the theme song to your favorite movie, you are thinking of the melody. Melody is usually played by the lead instrument, or lead vocal, just as the lead storyline of a movie is played by the lead characters.

A melody-driven song means you write the melody first, then add other tracks that work well with the melody. Songs with lyrics usually use the vocals as the melody line. Most of today's popular music is melody-driven.

The song **Homecoming**, which you worked on in Lesson 2, was melody-based. I wrote and recorded the piano melody first, then added the other instrument parts.

Rhythm is the pulse or heartbeat of the song. Rhythm can be played by one instrument or many different instruments. Rhythm is felt as much as it is heard, and it dictates the pacing of the different instrument parts. Rhythm is usually set by the drums and followed by the other rhythm instruments, such as bass, rhythm guitar, and keyboards. The rhythm of a song may be faster or slower depending on the song's tempo. A slow tempo song might be a ballad with a slow and easy rhythm. A fast tempo song might be a rock song with a driving beat.

A rhythm-driven song means you write the beats, percussion, or rhythm parts first, then add other instrument parts that fit well with the rhythm. Rhythm-driven songs are often used to score movie trailers (previews), and fast-paced promos or commercials. Rap music is often rhythm-based, but it depends on the song.

The songs **Eyewitness** and **SciFiShow**, which you worked on in Lessons 1, 2, and 3, were rhythm-driven. In both cases, I wrote and recorded the rhythm tracks first, then came up with a melody to fit.

Now that you understand some of the basics of melody and rhythm and the need to start a song with one or the other, let's explore some of the fundamentals of music arranging.

Preparing the Project

Open the project **6-1 Techno80s Starting** located in the Lesson_06 folder.

Working with Basic Music Arrangement Techniques

Consider this section your basic training for song arrangement, before you dive into the battlefield of a full song. Throughout this lesson, I'll throw in some basic songwriting rules I've come up with over the years. Keep in mind that rules are meant to be broken, and that music is very subjective, so there are no absolutes. The "rules" of songwriting are more like guidelines to keep you and your music on track (pun intended).

Rule #1: Decide what type of song you are going to write, and choose instruments and parts that will work for that song.

This seems like a basic and obvious concept, but it's often overlooked, especially by new songwriters. Along with the power of GarageBand comes the temptation to try everything at once. There are so many different instruments and so many prerecorded loops to choose from that you might get caught up in the search and forget the song.

Think of songwriting like cooking. If you're baking a cake, you use the ingredients for cake. If you're making meatloaf, you use the meatloaf ingredients. If you mix the cake ingredients into the meatloaf, you get meatcake surprise, which probably tastes as bad as it sounds and is probably not what you were going for when you started.

Searching for Loops That Fit

Remember your goal! The song you are arranging is called **Techno80s**, so in theory it should consist of instruments that were used during that era. During the 1980s, electronic drum kits and digital keyboards infiltrated popular music. Some bands played all electronic techno instruments, for a total techno sound. Others bands had rock-and-roll roots and blended techno sounds with their classic rock instruments. The GarageBand loop library comes with some excellent examples of 80s music loops, which have all been conveniently named after the era "80s."

Let's look at some of the 80s loops available in the GarageBand loop library.

1   Click the Loop Browser button to show the Loop Browser.

2   Type *80s* in the Search text field and press Return to view all of the 80s loops.

3 Click the first loop, 80s Dance Bass Synth 01, to preview it.

Notice the familiar techno sound.

4 Press the down arrow to preview the next loop in the list.

5 Continue pressing the down arrow until you have previewed all 18 of the 80s loops in the results list.

> **NOTE ▶** If you have installed the Jam Pack expansion for GarageBand, or added additional third-party loops to the browser, you may have more than 18 different 80s loops. If so, preview some of them, but you don't have to listen to all of them at this time.

As you can see, you have all the ingredients you need for a basic techno 80s song.

Of course, you aren't limited to only regions marked 80s. These are just a good place to start.

6 Click the Loop Browser button to close the Loop Browser.

Evaluating a Monotonous Arrangement

Now that you've heard some of the building blocks for the song, let's evaluate a very basic arrangement in the Timeline.

There are currently three basic tracks with music in the Timeline: a synthesizer track, synthetic bass track, and drum kit. These are the basic ingredients of a song. All three tracks utilize the prerecorded 80s loops from the Loop Browser. Let's listen to hear how it sounds.

1   Play the song in the Timeline and listen to the tracks.

What do you think? I think the different parts work well together. They definitely have an 80s sound, and I think they could work as part of a song. So what's wrong with this arrangement? For starters, there is no beginning, no middle, and no end. Just the same thing repeated over and over from start to finish.

2   Press the Home key to move the playhead to the beginning of the Timeline.

3   Click the Cycle button and create a cycle region over the regions in the Timeline.

Using Shortcuts to Solo and Mute Tracks

Now that you have heard all three tracks together, let's see how it sounds if we listen to just one or two tracks at a time. You already know how to click the Solo and Mute buttons to listen to specific tracks. For this exercise, you'll learn some new keyboard shortcuts.

The keyboard shortcut for Solo is S. The keyboard shortcut for Mute is M. In addition, you can use your up and down arrows to change the selected track in the Timeline.

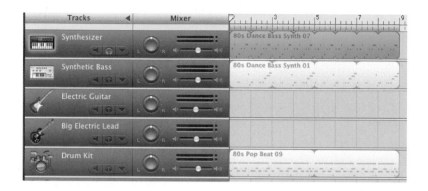

1   Click the track header for the top track in the Timeline to select that track.

2   Press the down arrow to select the next track down in the Timeline.

3   Press the up arrow to select the track above the current selected track.

    The top track should now be selected.

4   Press S to solo the top track.

5   Press the spacebar to start playback and listen to only the top track.

    After you've heard the first measure or so, move on to the next step. Keep playback going.

6   While the playhead is moving, press the down arrow to select the second track from the top.

7   Press S to solo that track with the first.

8   Press the up arrow to select the track above.

9   Press M to mute the top track.

10 Press the down arrow four times to select the first Drum Kit track.

11 Press S to solo the Drum Kit track with the Synthetic Bass track.

12 Experiment with different combinations of the tracks to see how they sound together.

13 Press the spacebar to stop playback.

14 Click the Cycle button to close the cycle region.

What did you think this time? I think it is much more interesting when you hear one part alone, then add other parts over time, instead of all of them at once. Why is it better that way? Because when you have only one instrument, then start adding new instruments, it feels like the beginning of a song instead of just a lot of repeating loops.

This leads me to another rule of songwriting.

Rule #2: Make sure your song has a beginning, middle, and end.

Again, this seems simple, and it is. Most songs have a defined beginning, which leads to a middle, and then eventually it ends. Remember, songs are like stories, which also have a defined beginning, middle, and end. I'm not saying that you should make every song start and end the same way. I'm saying that you should define the start and end with something special.

Evaluating a Region That Is Out of Time with the Rest of the Project

Have you heard the musical term "off beat?" Off beat is an expression for a musical part that is out of time with the other music. Sometimes recording a musical part that is played outside the main rhythmic pulses (beats) of a song is intentional—it's a way to make the part stand out from the rest of the song. When you play a part off beat intentionally, it is often referred to as playing the *backbeat* of a song. Most of the time, you want to keep all of your musical parts in time. For this exercise, we'll focus on the negative effects of accidentally making your regions out of time.

There are three ways you can make regions out of time or off beat:

- You move a region while snapping is off.

- Your performance is not in time with the music when you record a region. If your music is out of time when you record it, it'll be out of time when you play it back in the Timeline.

- You change the project tempo in a song with recorded Real Instrument regions. The Real Instrument regions you record will not change tempo along with the rest of the song, so they will be out of time with the other regions that do change tempo.

To get a feel for why this is important, let's demonstrate what it sounds like when musical parts are out of time with one another.

1   Click-drag the region in the Drum Kit track to the beginning of the 3rd measure.

NOTE ▸ If your Time Display is showing actual time, click the lower-left corner of the display to switch back to musical time.

2   Play the Timeline from the beginning and listen to the regions together.

All of the regions work together with the rhythm (time) of the song.

3   Press Cmd-G to turn snapping off in the Timeline.

For a review of GarageBand's Snap to Grid feature, see Lesson 4.

4   Click-drag the same region to the left a little bit (not a full beat).

5   Play the Timeline from the beginning and listen to the timing of the regions.

How does it sound? If it sounds pretty chaotic and doesn't fit the groove of the other regions, that's because you moved it out of time or off beat.

If you got lucky and it still sounds good, move it a little more. Chances are if you move it again, it'll be out of time with the other regions.

6   Press Cmd-G to turn snapping back on.

7   Click-drag the region in the Drum Kit track to the beginning of the 2nd measure.

8   Play the Timeline again and listen to the difference when the drum beat is in time with the other regions.

NOTE ▶   A region does not have to start at the beginning of a measure to be in time with the other regions. When snapping is on, you can snap a region to different beats or ticks within beats, depending on the settings you have for Snap to Grid. When the grid is set to automatic, it will adjust the snap-to value of the grid as you zoom in or out of the Timeline.

Arranging the Beginning of the Song

Now it's time to liven up the opening of this song. Remember how much better it sounded when you experimented with the Solo and Mute buttons to bring the different instruments into the song? Let's arrange the regions in the Timeline to create that same effect. This will become the opening of the **Techno80s** song.

1   Click-drag the region in the Synthetic Bass track so that it starts at the beginning of the 2nd measure.

2   Click-drag the region in the Drum Kit track so that it starts at the beginning of the 5th measure.

3   Play the new opening to hear how it sounds.

The beginning of the song is better, but the synthesizer riff on the top track is starting to get annoying. It's a cool and catchy synthesizer riff, but too much of any repetitive musical part can become a distraction in your song.

That reminds me of another songwriting rule.

Rule #3: Sprinkle your music with catchy, stand-out riffs to liven up the song, but don't flood your song with these riffs, or you'll drown the other tracks.

In other words, less is more. It's common to use a catchy riff several times in a song, perhaps near the beginning, middle, and end. By spreading them out, you leave the audience wanting more instead of wanting it to end.

Think of your song as an action movie. In most action movies, the crashes, chases, and explosions are separated by story. If you went to an action movie that was just a series of explosions over and over, you'd probably be tired of them in a few minutes. The same thing goes for musical explosions—or cool musical riffs or parts—that you add to your song to make it more interesting.

Splitting a Repetitive Region

Let's split the region in the Synthesizer track so that it comes in and out of the song instead of playing continuously.

1 Select the 80s Dance Bass Synth 07 region in the top track.

2 Move your playhead to the beginning of the 3rd measure.

3 Press Cmd-T to split the region at the playhead position.

The region splits into two separate regions.

4 Move the playhead to the beginning of the 7th measure.

5 Press Cmd-T to split the region again at the playhead position.

6 Click the empty track space after the last region in the top track to deselect the regions in that track.

NOTE ▶ You can click the empty space on any track to deselect a region or regions.

7 Click the middle 80s Dance Bass Synth 07 region in the top track to select that region.

8   Press Delete to delete the middle region from the Timeline.

There are now two short regions in the Synthesizer track.

9   Play the Timeline from the beginning to hear the new opening.

Notice how the different parts take turns. The synthesizer part is no longer distracting you from hearing the rest of the tracks.

Finishing the Beginning of the Song

The beginning of the song is almost finished. All you need to do is trim the region in the Synthetic Bass track and make one modification to the second Synthesizer region.

1   Press Ctrl–right arrow to zoom in to the Timeline.

2   Move the playhead to the 3rd beat of the 7th measure (halfway between the 7th and 8th measures).

Check the Time Display to confirm that the playhead is in the correct position.

3   Click-drag the upper-right corner of the region in the Synthetic Bass track and shorten the region until it ends at the playhead position.

The 80s Dance Bass Synth 01 region should now end halfway between the 7th and 8th measures.

4 Click-drag the upper-right corner of the second region in the Synthesizer track and shorten it by one full loop segment.

The remaining loop region should start at the beginning of the 7th measure and end at the beginning of the 8th measure.

Now that you've shortened the second synth part, let's add another synth loop to keep things interesting.

5 Click the Loop Browser button to open the Loop Browser (if it's not already open).

6 Click the 80s Dance Bass Synth 06 loop in the results list to hear the loop.

7 Click again to stop previewing the loop in the results list.

	Fav	Name	
♪	☐	80s Dance Bass Synth 01	
♪	☐	80s Dance Bass Synth 02	
♪	☐	80s Dance Bass Synth 03	
♪	☐	80s Dance Bass Synth 04	
♪	☐	80s Dance Bass Synth 05	
◀)	■	80s Dance Bass Synth 06	▲
♪	☐	80s Dance Bass Synth 07	▼

8 Click-drag the 80s Dance Bass Synth 06 loop from the browser and drop it in the top track at the beginning of the 6th measure.

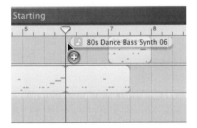

The new loop region appears in the track right before the original loop region.

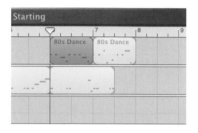

9   Press the spacebar to hear the new region in the Timeline.

The two synthesizer loops work well together and sound as if they were meant to play together.

10   Press Shift-Cmd-S to open the Save As window.

11   Change the name of the project to *Techno80s* and save it in your GarageBand Songs folder on the Desktop.

That's it. You've arranged the beginning of the song using basic arranging techniques. Basic arranging techniques include finding loops, adding them to the Timeline, and arranging the regions so they start at different times. You also split and resized regions to make them less repetitive.

Knowing how to physically move regions in the Timeline is the physical act of arranging music. But keep in mind that your overall goal is to build a great song. Always think about *why* you are arranging the song in a particular way, and make sure it sounds good. If it doesn't sound good to you, it probably won't sound good to anyone else. If you're not sure if you like a part, change it. When the part is right, you know immediately.

Listening to the Finished Song

Let's listen to the finished song so you'll have a better understanding of the middle and end of the song.

1   Choose File > Open and select **6-2 Techno80s Finished** from the Lesson_06 folder.

2   Click Open to open the song.

   The song **Techno80s Finished** opens.

3   Play the Timeline and listen to the complete song.

   As the song plays, see if you notice the song change as it goes from the beginning to the middle to the end.

   Now let's isolate the melody tracks so we can focus on finishing them.

4   Click the Solo buttons on the top four tracks, the melody tracks for this song.

5   Play the song again to hear only the melody tracks.

Keep in mind that the melody is the most memorable part of the song. Melody varies greatly, depending on the type of song you are writing.

6   Choose File > Open Recent and select **Techno80s** from the list of recent files.

7   Click the Don't Save button so that you don't save changes to the finished song.

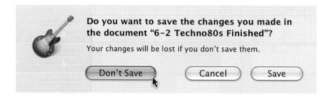

The **Techno80s** song in progress opens in GarageBand.

Working with Advanced Music Arrangement Techniques

Now that you understand basic arranging, let's use some more advanced techniques as you finish the song.

Doubling a Track with Mixed Instruments

The next section of your **Techno80s** song is an example of blending both techno and classic rock instruments to double a track.

In the last lesson, you doubled a piano track with a strings track to mirror the melody. In this exercise, you'll use two different electric guitar sounds to add some classic rock instrumentation to this techno song.

Doubling a track is an advanced arranging technique that is used to make a musical part stronger. Doubling is also called *fattening* a track.

1   Press Cmd-L to open the Loop Browser (if it is not already open).

> **NOTE** ▶ The Loop Browser will no longer show your 80s search results because you closed the project.

2   Click the Guitars keyword button to search for guitar loops.

3   Locate the Ambient Guitar 01 loop in the results list.

4   Click the Ambient Guitar 01 loop in the results list to preview the loop.

5   Click again to stop previewing the loop.

Now that you've previewed the loop, you are ready to add it to the Timeline.

6   Select the Electric Guitar track (third track from the top) in the Timeline.

7 Click-drag the Ambient Guitar 01 loop from the browser to the beginning of the 9th measure in the Electric Guitar track.

The Ambient Guitar 01 region appears in the track between the 9th and 11th measures.

Since the Ambient Guitar 01 loop is a Software Instrument region, you can change the sound by changing the instrument for the track.

8 Option-drag the Ambient Guitar 01 region to the track below (the Big Electric Lead track) to double the region.

You should now have two identical Ambient Guitar 01 regions in the electric guitar tracks.

9 Play the doubled guitar tracks to hear how they sound together.

They sound good, but let's make it sound like the Electric Guitar starts the riff, then the Big Electric Lead guitar joins in.

10 Move the playhead to the beginning of the 13th measure.

11 Click-drag the upper-right corner of the region in the Electric Guitar track to extend (loop) the region to the playhead position (end of the 12th measure).

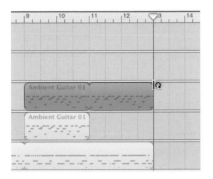

12 Select the region in the Big Electric Lead track and move it until it ends at the playhead position.

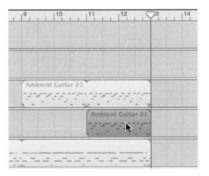

Now both guitar regions end at the end of the 12th measure.

13 Press the left arrow key five times to move the playhead back five measures in the Timeline.

Notice how it sounds like two separate guitar players playing the same part. This is because you had one start before the other joined in.

14 Press Cmd-S to save your progress.

15 Play the song from the transition at the beginning to the guitar section.

If this was a song with lyrics, the first part of the song would be the first verse, and the guitar part would be the chorus or pre-chorus.

When you played the song again, did you notice the musical gap between the synthesizer and guitar parts? The gap is there by design to let the song breathe. That's right. Breathe.

Rule #4: Add a few breaks in the music so your song can breathe.

Musical parts all playing together at full throttle for an extended period of time can be exhausting for both the musicians and the listener. If you build in a few breaks for changes or transitions in the song, you give the instrument parts a chance to take turns, and the song a chance to change.

Songs with vocal lyrics have built-in breaks between the verses and chorus because the vocalist needs to take a breath from time to time. When you take instrument breaks in the song as you transition from one section to the next, you keep the audience in suspense as to what they will hear next. Will it be a bass? Will it be another synthesizer riff? Perhaps a cowbell?

Previewing vs. Auditioning Loops

Now that you know that the break in music between the synths and guitars is intentional, let's introduce another classic rock instrument: the electric bass. Instead of previewing the different bass selections in the browser, you will audition the loops with the rest of the song.

What's the difference between previewing and auditioning loops? It's simple. Previewing a loop means that you play it in the Loop Browser to hear what it sounds like. Auditioning a loop means that you are listening to it in the browser while the song is playing in the Timeline. Previewing loops is great for finding loops you like, and adding basic tracks to the Timeline. Auditioning loops is important when you need to find loops that fit well with a song, or partial song, that is already in the Timeline.

Before you start auditioning loops, it's a good idea to set a cycle region for the part of the song you want to audition.

1   Click the Cycle button to view the cycle region.

2   Click-drag the middle of the existing cycle region (yellow bar) and slide it to the right until it ends at the beginning of the 13th measure.

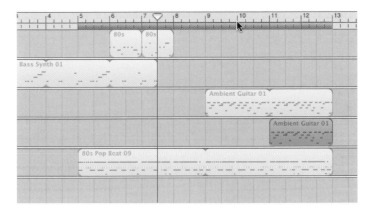

NOTE ▶ If you accidentally clear your cycle region instead of moving it, just click-drag your pointer in the Cycle Region Ruler to draw a new region.

3   Click-drag the left edge of the cycle region until it starts at the beginning of the 7th measure.

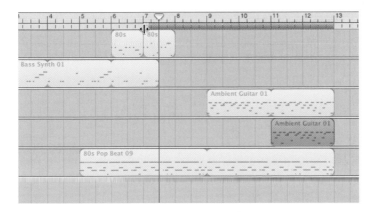

Now that the cycle region is in place, you're ready to audition some bass loops to find one that works with this song.

4   Click the Reset button in the Loop Browser to clear the search results and deselect the Guitars button.

5   Click the Bass button to search for bass loops.

6   Type *slap* in the Search field and press Return to narrow the list to Slap Bass loops.

The list now shows seven different Slap Bass choices to audition.

NOTE ▶ If you are working with Jam Pack or additional loops, your list may be different than the picture, and you may have more than seven Slap Bass choices.

Remember, as you audition loops, you are looking for a bass loop that sounds good in the gap between synths and guitars. It also needs to sound good with the guitar part. This bass loop is the transition instrument that leads the song from the techno into the classic rock guitar section.

7   Click the Play button in the transport controls to start playing the cycle region in the Timeline.

8   Click the first bass loop in the search results to hear it with the cycle region.

9   Press the down arrow to move to the next loop down in the list.

If you need to raise or lower the volume of the loops you are auditioning, you can use adjust the Preview Volume slider located at the bottom of the Loop Browser.

10 Use the up and down arrows to audition the different loops until you find one that has the right classic rock bass guitar sound.

> **NOTE** ▶ If you are working with with a slower computer and have trouble processing the song with the loops you are auditioning, you can skip this step.

11 Press the spacebar to stop playback.

Which bass loop did you like best? I like the Electric Slap 09 loop, because it's edgy and fits with the groove of the whole song. Let's try using the Electric Slap 09 bass in the song. If you want to try a different bass part, you can after this lesson.

12 Press C to close the cycle region.

13 Move the playhead to the beginning of the 8th measure, which is also the beginning of the gap or break between instrument parts.

14 Click the scroller on the right side of the window and drag it down to view the lower tracks in the Timeline.

15 Locate the Electric Bass track, which is the second track from the bottom.

16 Click-drag the Electric Slap 09 region from the Loop Browser to the play-head position on the Electric Bass track.

The Electric Slap 09 region appears in the Electric Bass track in the Timeline.

17 Click-drag the upper-right corner of the Electric Slap 09 region to extend it to the end of the 12th measure.

The extended region will be five full loop segments in length.

18 Press Cmd-L to close the Loop Browser.

19 Press Cmd-S to save your progress.

20 Play the entire song in the Timeline to hear the new bass part in context with the rest of the song.

Creating a Turnaround with the Drum Tracks

Another advanced music arranging technique is creating a drum turnaround. You could easily use the same drum region for an entire song, but it will sound repetitive and won't be very interesting or dynamic. Instead, let's create a turnaround with the drum tracks.

What's a turnaround? A turnaround is when a part changes either to lead the song in a new direction or to turn the song back around to a familiar part, like chorus or verse. Turnarounds can also be used to lead the song to the big finish or ending.

There are many techniques for creating turnarounds. One method is to add a different drum part to the existing drum tracks. Another method is to double an existing drum part on another track and offset the second part so it starts on a different beat. The result is an enhanced drum part that feels like the drummer just kicked it up a notch to lead the song in a new direction.

To create the turnaround, you'll start by extending the existing drum part.

1 Select the 80s Pop Beat 09 region in the Timeline.

2   Click-drag the upper-right corner of the 80s Pop Beat 09 region and extend it to the beginning of the 29th measure.

Now that you have extended the drum beat, you can split the track and use part of it for the turnaround. You'll split the second-to-last loop segment of the drum region.

3   Click the empty track space next to the 80s Pop Beat 09 region to deselect all regions in the Timeline.

4   Click the 80s Pop Beat 09 region to select the region, and only that region.

5   Move the playhead to the beginning of the 21st measure.

> **NOTE ▶** When you split a track, it will split all the selected regions at the playhead position. For this reason, it's important to make sure only the track or tracks you want to split are selected.

6   Press Cmd-T to split the track at the playhead position.

7   Press the right arrow key four times to move the playhead to the beginning of the 25th measure.

8   Press Cmd-T to split the track at the playhead position.

You now have three separate drum regions in the top Drum Kit track.

9 Press the down arrow to select the second Drum Kit track.

Next you are going to move the middle drum region one track lower than the others.

10 Click-drag the middle 80s Pop Beat 09 region from the Drum Kit track above and move it to the track that is below the top Drum Kit track.

11 Press Ctrl–right arrow to zoom into the Timeline until you can read each measure number in the Beat Ruler.

12 Click-drag the scroller at the bottom of the Timeline until you can view the Timeline between the 17th and 25th measures.

It's OK if you see more of the Timeline than the 17th to the 25th measures.

13 Move the playhead to the 2nd beat of the 18th measure.

14 Click-drag the drum region in the lower Drum Kit track to the left until it starts at the playhead position.

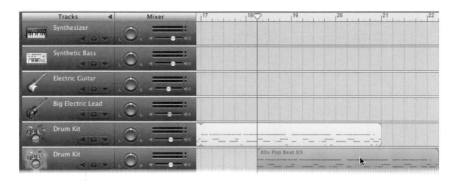

15 Press the left arrow twice to move the playhead two measures to the left.

16 Play the doubled-offset drum tracks to hear how they sound together.

Notice how it sounds like the drummer did something different—a turn-around—and the drum part turns around back to the original beat. This technique works with most steady drum beats.

Finishing the Turnaround

The final step in the drum turnaround is to add another percussion loop at the end. Instead of the turnaround leading the song back to a familiar sound, it will lead to a new sound that kicks off the end of the song.

1 Locate the third Drum Kit track (the lowest Drum Kit track) in the Timeline.

2 Move the playhead to the beginning of the 22nd measure.

This is where you will place the new drum part.

3 Press Cmd-L to open the Loop Browser and click the Reset button to deselect any keywords.

4 Type *Pop Beat* in the Search text field and press Return.

5 Click-drag the 80s Pop Beat 07 loop from the browser to the playhead position on the lowest Drum Kit track.

6 Press the left arrow key several times to move the playhead before the drum turnaround.

7 Listen to the finished turnaround.

Building the Song with Established Parts

Most songs contain two or three sections that repeat several times, such as the verses or chorus.

Now that you've introduced the main instrument parts for the song and arranged them in the Timeline, you can copy and paste them in the Timeline. Once you've repeated a section of the song, you can make subtle changes to keep the parts from getting stale.

There are different ways to copy and paste regions in the Timeline. Let's review the different methods as you duplicate some of the existing parts of the song.

1   Press Ctrl–left arrow to zoom out of the Timeline until you can clearly see the bass region and the drum turnaround section in the Timeline.

2   Move the playhead to the beginning of the 22nd measure.

3   Option-drag the Electric Slap 09 bass region and move the duplicate region so it starts at the playhead position (beginning of the 22nd measure).

4   Click-drag the upper-right corner of the duplicated bass region and
extend it one loop segment.

The extended region should end at the beginning of the 28th measure.

Now let's copy and paste the doubled guitar section.

5   Move the playhead to the beginning of the 25th measure.

6   Click-drag the empty track space to the left of the top guitar region and
move the mouse to the right and down to lasso (select) both guitar regions.

The lasso needs to start in the blank track space of the highest or lowest
track.

7   Option-drag either selected region and drag the duplicate so that it starts
at the playhead position (beginning of the 25th measure).

Next, you'll copy and paste the region on the Synthetic Bass track.

8   Click the 80s Dance Bass Synth 01 region in the Synthetic Bass track to select the region.

9   Press Cmd-C to copy the selected region.

10 Press the left arrow key to move the playhead to the beginning of the 16th measure.

The left arrow key only moves the playhead one measure at a time, so you will need to press the left arrow several times.

11 Press Cmd-V to paste the copied region at the playhead position.

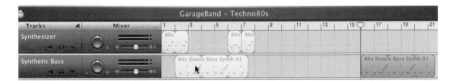

For this copy and paste maneuver, you will select two regions in the same track and paste both at the same time.

12 Shift-click the first and third regions in the Synthesizer track to select both regions.

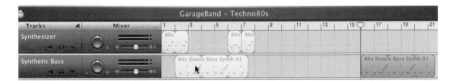

13 Press Cmd-C to copy both regions.

14 Move the playhead to the beginning of the 14th measure.

15 Press Cmd-V to paste both regions starting at the 14th measure.

Both pasted regions appear in the track. Now let's duplicate the region in the lowest Drum Kit track.

16 Move the playhead to the beginning of the 27th measure.

17 Option-drag the region in the lowest Drum Kit track to the playhead position to duplicate the region so it starts at the beginning of the 27th measure.

18 Press Cmd-S to save your work.

As you can see, copy, paste, and duplicate are very useful tools for arranging a song once you have the main parts in the Timeline. Now you know how to create the sections of a song, such as a verse and chorus, and then copy and paste those sections to repeat them later in the song.

Finishing the Song

The song is nearly finished. Now all you need to do is clean up a few sections and select a couple of new loops to fill in the gaps.

Let's start by cleaning up the second section on the Synthesizer track to make room for some new loops.

1 Click-drag the upper-right corner of the last region in the Synthetic Bass track and extend the last looped segment so it ends at the start of the 22nd measure.

2 Select the last region in the Synthesizer track and move it to the right so that it ends at the same time as the region on the track below.

Both regions should end at the beginning of the 22nd measure.

3 Press Cmd-L to open the Loop Browser, if it is not already open.

4 Type *80s* in the Search text field and press Return.

5   Click-drag the 80s Dance Bass Synth 09 loop from the browser to the top track in the Timeline and place it at the beginning of the 17th measure.

6   Option-drag the new region in the top track and drag the duplicate to the empty space on the right between the 19th and 21st measures.

> **NOTE ▶** You could have extended this region instead of duplicating it. However, you'll be transposing this region in the Track Editor shortly. Duplicating a region makes it easier to change only the duplicated portion. Otherwise you would need to split the region when you are ready to transpose it.

You still need a transition piece to lead the song from the classic rock instrument section back to the techno sound. Let's add another Synth Bass loop.

7   Click-drag the 80s Dance Bass Synth 05 loop from the browser to the Synthetic Bass track and place it at the beginning of the 13th measure.

8   Press Cmd-L to close the Loop Browser.

9   Move the playhead to the beginning of the 23rd measure.

10 Option-drag the new region you just placed in the Synthetic Bass track and drag the duplicate so it starts at the playhead position.

11 Play the Timeline from the 13th to the 23rd measure to hear the second techno section of the song.

Notice that using a variety of techno synth parts in combination keeps it interesting, yet you still hear the familiar synth riff that plays at the beginning of the song.

Let's transpose one of the regions to make it a full octave lower.

12 Locate the 80s Dance Bass Synth 09 region that starts at the beginning of the 19th measure in the Synthesizer track.

13 Double-click the region to open it in the Track Editor.

14 Type *–12* in the Transpose field in the Track Editor to transpose the region one octave lower and press Return.

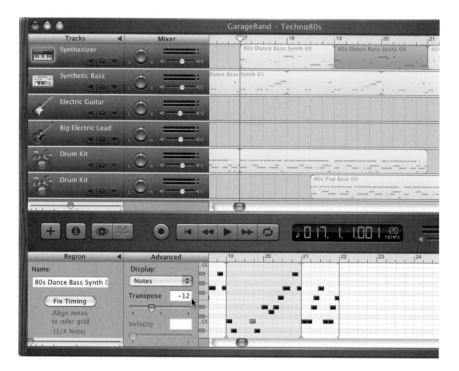

15 Press Cmd-E to close the Track Editor.

16 Press the left arrow several times to back up the playhead a few measures.

17 Press the spacebar to play the revised techno section of the song.

The last task in finishing this song arrangement is to edit the final doubled guitar part so that instead of overlapping, they take turns playing one after the other.

18 Locate the Ambient Guitar 01 region that starts at the 25th measure on the third track from the top (Electric Guitar track).

19 Click-drag the upper-right corner of the Ambient Guitar 01 region to the left to shorten the entire region by one full looped segment.

20 Press Cmd-S to save your work.

21 Listen to the entire song to hear your finished arrangement.

Congratulations! You just arranged an entire song from scratch using basic and advanced song-arranging techniques.

Remember, a page full of words does not make a story, just like a lot of notes played together doesn't make a song. Plan your songs as you arrange them. They should have parts that repeat, such as the verse and chorus, and subtle variations between the repetitive parts to keep them interesting.

In the next lesson, you'll learn about mixing your song and using advanced editing techniques in the Track Editor.

Project Tasks

Since you did such a great job arranging this song, you and the song both deserve some hearty applause.

1   Open the Loop Browser and find the loop called Crowd Applause 01.

2   Place it on the lowest track starting at the beginning of the 27th measure.

3   Play your song one more time with the applause.

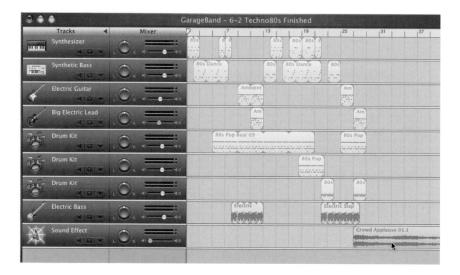

What You've Learned

- Arranging music means putting all of the different pieces together to build a finished song. This includes selecting the instruments and the instrument parts that work best for the song.

- Melody is the memorable part of a song that you can hum to yourself and is usually performed by the lead vocals or lead instrument.

- Rhythm is the heartbeat or pulse of a song and is usually performed by the drums and additional instruments like rhythm guitar.

- The up and down arrows can be used to change which track is selected in the Timeline. The up arrow selects the track above the current selected track. The down arrow selects the next track below the current select track.

- S and M are the shortcut keys for soloing and muting the selected track.

- When the timing of a region doesn't match the rest of the song, it is off beat, or out of time. This can happen if you move a region in the Timeline while snapping is turned off. To fix the timing, turn snapping on and move the region again to snap it to the Timeline grid.

- Spreading out regions so the different instruments start one after another instead of all at once is a common technique for building the beginning of a song.

- Basic arranging techniques include adding regions to the Timeline, and moving, extending, and splitting regions.

- Previewing a loop in the Loop Brower means that you listen to the loop by itself. Auditioning a loop means that you are listening to a loop in the browser while the song is playing in the Timeline. Auditioning is a process of evaluating how something sounds in context with the song.

- To double a track, you place the identical region in the same location on two separate tracks with similar or complementary instruments, such as two different electric guitar tracks.

- A drum turnaround is a change in the drum track that leads the song in a new direction, or turns the song back around to a familiar established musical part.

- Once you've established the main sections of the song (intro, verse, chorus, and so on), you can copy and paste or Option-drag the different sections to repeat them later in the song.

- To select regions in different consecutive tracks, you can click-drag a lasso over the clips. The lasso needs to start in the blank track space of the highest or lowest track. Shift-click to select multiple regions that are on different tracks, or are not consecutive.

7

Lesson Files   Lessons > Lesson_07 > 7-1 Highway Bound unmxd; 7–2 Highway
                             Bound mixed

Time   This lesson takes approximately 60 minutes to complete.

Goals   Understand basic mixing

Work with the Track Mixer

Set volume levels for each track

Set pan position for each track

Join two separate regions

Fix the timing of a Software Instrument region

Change the velocity for an entire region

Add effects to a track

Show a track's Volume curve

Add control points to the Volume curve

Show the Master track

Add control points and effects to the Master track

Adjust the master output volume levels to avoid clipping

Mixing and Effects

With GarageBand, you have the ability to record and create professional-quality music. However, to make your finished songs actually sound professional, you need to understand the fine art of mixing music.

Fortunately, GarageBand's interface includes an easy-to-use Track Mixer with controls for volume level and pan position.

In the last lesson, you arranged a song in the Timeline using basic and advanced music arrangement techniques. Your goal in this lesson is to take an arranged song to the next level to make it sound like a professional composition. To accomplish this, you'll need to apply professional mixing techniques, including balancing volume, panning, fixing timing, changing velocity, and adding effects.

Understanding Basic Mixing

Mixing a song is the art of carefully blending all of the different sounds and musical textures into one cohesive, balanced piece of music. Arranging regions in separate tracks is easy once you get the hang of it—in fact, you've been arranging songs since you started this book. Mixing takes a little more practice. It also takes some ear training.

Ear training means being able to listen beyond the basic music to analyze the full panoramic scope of a song. Chefs train their pallets so they can taste food beyond the basics. For instance, an Italian chef can taste the full array of spices in a marinara sauce, from oregano to fresh ground pepper. Some chefs can even tell you what type of tomato was used and how ripe it was. It's great to be able to taste the spaghetti sauce and know whether you like it not. It's even better if you know why.

Throughout this lesson, you'll be training your ear, so that by the end of the exercises, you too will be able to hear beyond the music and notice the subtle elements within the mix of a song.

Let's start by listening to the finished song titled **Highway Bound**.

1   Open **7-2 Highway Bound mixed** from the Lesson_07 folder.

    This finished song includes 11 tracks plus an empty track at the bottom for you to record your own track after the lesson.

2   Press the spacebar to play the finished song.

    I wrote this song about a nomadic Southern rock band that lives on the road traveling from gig to gig. They're always the opening act, never the headliner, and they never play in the same town twice. Might make for an interesting documentary, and if so, this would be the opening title music.

    Now that you've heard the finished piece, let's compare it to the unmixed song.

3   Choose File > Open and select **7-1 Highway Bound unmxd** from the Lesson_07 folder.

4   Play the entire unmixed song and listen for anything that stands out, in either a good or bad way.

As you play the song, listen for the following:

- Are some parts difficult to hear?

- Do some parts seem too loud?

- Does the song sound and feel finished?

- Is the overall volume of the song even?

- Does it sound like something you'd buy, or does it sound more like something homemade?

What was your impression of unmixed song? My impression is that all of the musical elements (instruments and parts) are there, but the levels are all over the place. The unmixed song doesn't sound or feel very professional.

Now that you've listened to the unmixed song, let's save it in your folder so you'll be able to compare your work to the unmixed version.

5   Press Shift-Cmd-S to open the Save As window.

6   Change the name to *Highway Bound* and save it to your GarageBand Songs folder.

Working with the Track Mixer

The first step to mixing a song in GarageBand is a basic understanding of the Track Mixer.

The Track Mixer is located between the track header and the Timeline. You can hide or show the Track Mixer by clicking the triangle next to the word "Tracks" at the top of the window.

1 Locate the triangle next to the word "Tracks" at the top of the window.

2 Click the triangle to show the Track Mixer.

The Track Mixer appears between the track headers and the Timeline.

The Track Mixer contains three separate tools: the Volume slider, the Pan wheel, and the Level meters.

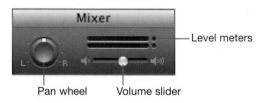

Let's start with the Volume slider.

Adjusting Levels with the Volume Slider

The Volume slider allows you to adjust the volume levels for an individual track. The overall goal is to blend the different levels of all the tracks so that all the instruments can be heard, but the emphasis is on the right tracks.

By default, the Volume slider is set to 0 dB (decibels) for all tracks. You click-drag the slider to the right to raise the volume level and to the left to lower the volume level. You can adjust the volume for an individual track while the play-head is static or while you are playing the song.

Let's start by adjusting the volume level on the first Drum Kit track. There are three different Drum Kit tracks. You'll be starting on the highest one. You'll need to solo the track so you can hear the level change without the other tracks.

1 Click the highest Drum Kit track to select it in the Timeline.

   The track turns brighter green to indicate it has been selected.

2 Press S or click the Solo button to solo the track.

3 Click-drag the Volume slider all the way to the left.

   The slider turns blue when you click it to indicate it has been selected.

   The track is silent when the Volume slider is in the far-left position.

   Next, you'll raise the volume while the track is playing.

4 Press the Home key, and then press the spacebar to start playback at the beginning of the song.

5 Click-drag the Volume slider to the right to raise the volume level while the track is playing.

6 Release the slider when you think you've reached a good volume level.

   How do you know if you're volume level is good? You can look at the Level meters.

Using the Level Meters

The Level meters use colored bars to visually represent the volume level for the track.

The lower the volume, the shorter the solid colored bars. If the color is green, the level is within a safe range and isn't too loud. If the color turns from green to yellow, that means caution—your sound is bordering on being too loud. If it turns red, you need to stop and turn the volume down immediately. The two squares at the end of the Level meters are the clipping indicators. Clipping means your music is not only too loud, but it could be distorted.

The Level meters in GarageBand are "sticky," which means a single line of the colored bar will stick to the highest position on the meter while the average levels continue to change. The average volume level is marked by the solid colored bar, and the peaks are marked with the vertical line.

Let's create a cycle region and take a look at the Level meters in action.

1   Press the left arrow to move your playhead back to the beginning of the Timeline.

    You may have to press it several times, depending on the current playhead position.

2   Press C to open the cycle region.

3   Click-drag the ends of the yellow cycle region bar to resize the cycle region until it is approximately the length of the first region in the selected track.

4   Press the spacebar to play the drum region.

5   As the region plays, watch the average levels and the peak levels in the meter.

If any of the levels in the meter turn yellow or red, lower the volume for the track. You'll know your level is acceptable when the average and peaks are within the green "safe" region of the meter.

Keep in mind that you can use the Level meters to see the levels, but the only way to make sure the levels are right for the song is to hear the track with the rest of the song.

Using the Pan Wheel

The Pan wheel controls the left-to-right placement of a track within the stereo field. The "Pan" in Pan wheel stands for "panoramic." A panoramic photograph is an image that includes your full visual spectrum from the far left to the far right. In other words, it's everything you can see without turning your head. A stereo field is everything you can hear from the far left to the far right, without turning your head.

Imagine a panoramic photograph of the Rocky Mountains with a train cutting through the far-left side of the image. Visually, you place the train on the left side of your field of view. You would also place the sound of the train on the far-left side of the stereo field.

By default, all of the tracks in GarageBand start with the pan position set to the center. With center pan position, the sound is heard

equally out of both speakers—it sounds like it is directly in front of you in the center of the audio space.

To adjust the pan position of a track, click the small white dots on the Pan wheel. Let's adjust the pan position of the selected track.

This exercise works best if you are listening through headphones, so take a minute and put on your headset before you start. Make sure your headphones have the right speaker (R) on the right ear and the left speaker (L) on the left ear.

1   Click the dot next to the L on the lower-left side of the Pan wheel to change the pan position to the far left of the stereo field.

2   Press the spacebar to listen to the cycle region.

Notice that the drums sound like they are coming from the far left.

NOTE ▶ If you hear the drums coming from the far right, you probably have your headphones on backwards.

3   Click the dot next to the R on the lower-right side of the Pan wheel to change the pan position to the far right of the stereo field.

Notice that the sound of the drums jumps to the far-right side.

4   Click the dot on the middle-right side between the center position and the far-right position.

If the Pan wheel were a clock, the dot would be at 2:00.

Notice that the drums still sound like they are on the right, but closer to the middle of the stereo field.

5   Press the spacebar to stop playback.

6   Press C to close the cycle region.

7   Press S to unsolo the track.

Resetting the Volume and Pan Controls

If you want to quickly reset the volume or pan controls to the default position, all you need to do is Option-click the control.

Let's reset the levels for the selected track.

1   Option-click the Pan wheel to reset the track's pan position to center.

The Pan wheel resets to the default center position.

2   Option-click the Volume slider to reset it to the default position.

Now that you have a better understanding of the Track Mixer and how to use it, let's start mixing the song.

Creating a Rough Mix

There are different stages to mixing. You start with a rough mix, then fine-tune the mix, and finally polish the mix in the final master. There are five basic steps for creating the final mix:

- Step 1: Adjust the volume levels of the individual tracks to balance the sound of the different instruments.

- Step 2: Adjust the pan positions of the individual tracks to place them in the correct location in the stereo field.

- Step 3: Find and fix any musical imperfections like timing, velocity, or performance. (This may require editing in the Track Editor, or re-recording a section of the song.)

- Step 4: Add and adjust effects to enhance the sound of individual tracks, or the whole song.

- Step 5: Create dynamic volume changes over time using the Volume curves on individual tracks and the Master track.

Let's start with step 1, adjusting the volume levels of the different tracks.

As you can imagine, there are hundreds of combinations of volume levels you could try on this song. Instead of experimenting, let's use logic and come up with a plan.

Planning Your Volume Mix

To mix the volume levels, you need to know what type of sound you are going for in your song. What style of music is this song? A vocal ballad might favor the vocal tracks and the lead instruments, and keep the drums low in the mix. A club song might favor the drums and synth bass tracks and bury the supporting tracks in the mix. Rock songs often favor the lead guitar and vocals and keep the drums about midlevel in the mix. Every song is different, every style is different, and every mix is different.

As I mentioned before, this song is about a nomadic Southern rock band, and I want the style to feel like a live performance. The guitars are the lead instruments and should be played higher (louder) in the mix. The shaker, tambourine, and strings are supporting instruments that should be lower (quieter) in the overall mix.

Mixing Volume Levels for Individual Tracks

The first step is to adjust the volume levels to balance the song. Let's start by listening to the first half of the unmixed song to get a feel for the current volume levels.

1   Press the Home key to move the playhead to the beginning.

2   Press the spacebar to play the first half of the song.

    As you listen to the tracks, notice the levels of the guitars, shaker, and tambourine.

3   Press the spacebar again to stop playback.

    The default volume level is a good starting point for your lead instruments.

    Instead of raising the guitar volume to make it louder, let's lower the other tracks accordingly.

NOTE ▶ Adjusting track volume is like adjusting water temperature in a sink with separate cold and hot controls. If you are running both hot and cold water, and you want to make the overall temperature hotter, you can just turn down the cold instead of turning up the hot. The same goes for volume—instead of making a track louder to hear it better, you might need to turn the other tracks down a bit.

Let's start with the shaker and tambourine tracks. They both seem about twice as loud as they need to be, so let's lower them to half of their current volume.

4   Click-drag the Volume slider on the Tambourine track to the left, so that you lower it by half the distance to the left.

The new Volume slider position should be about one-third from the left edge of the Volume slider.

5   Repeat step 4, only this time adjust the volume of the Shaker track.

6   Move the playhead to the beginning of the 7th measure and listen to the mix with the new shaker and tambourine levels.

Both the shaker and tambourine are now at a more natural level in the song.

7   Move the playhead back to the beginning and listen to the first half of the song again.

As you listen, try to figure out which tracks are still too loud.

Did you hear anything that stood out as too loud? How about the third Drum Kit track? It seems too loud to me, and it's drowning out the guitars. The nice thing about drums is that they don't have to be loud to be appreciated.

Let's lower the Drum Kit tracks. Since they are all different drum parts, the tracks will need to be different levels. The first (highest) Drum Kit track sounds OK at the default level.

8   Click-drag the Volume slider on the second Drum Kit track to a little bit below half on the Volume slider.

9   Click-drag the Volume slider on the third Drum Kit track to the middle position on the slider.

10   Click-drag the Volume slider on the 4th Drum Kit track to the middle position on the slider.

11   Listen to the first half of the song to hear the Drum Kit tracks at their new levels in the mix.

Notice the difference in the overall song now that the drums, shaker, and tambourine are lower in the mix.

When you are doing a rough mix, you need to adjust only the levels of the instruments that seem too loud or out of place. The additional tracks, like the Bass and Hollywood Strings, will be adjusted as needed after the tracks are panned.

Panning the Individual Tracks

Now it's time to place the individual tracks in their proper position within the stereo field. There are many different styles for panning the tracks. The important thing is to spread the tracks out within the stereo field. Remember the panoramic photo of the Rocky Mountains? Imagine a beautiful panoramic picture with mountains spread from the left to right side of the frame, birds in the air, a stream in the foreground, a grove of trees on the right side, and a train cutting through the lower left of the frame. The photographer utilized the full stereo field when composing the picture.

Now imagine the same photo taken from the top of a mountain looking directly at another mountain. All you see is a mountain peak in the middle of the frame and empty sky on either side. This photographer didn't utilize the full stereo field when composing the picture.

Right now your song has all of the tracks panned to the center. To re-create that onstage in the real world, all of the musicians would have to line up one behind the other in the center of the stage. That wouldn't look very natural, and it doesn't sound natural either. Your ears, trained or untrained, are accustomed to hearing *where* a sound is coming from, as well as hearing the sound itself.

Let's use the pan controls to place the different musicians where they would be if they were performing this song on stage.

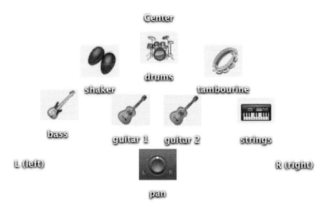

The illustration shows the relative position of the musicians performing **Highway Bound** on stage. The drums are in the middle of the stage (center pan position). The tambourine and shaker are performed by the backup singers on the left and right of the drums. The two guitars are next to each other, just to the left and right of center stage. The bass is on the left side of the stage, and the keyboard (which plays the strings) is on the right.

To set the panning control for each instrument, simply adjust the Pan wheel so it is pointing in the direction of the instrument in the panoramic field of the stage.

Let's start with the guitars.

1   Locate the Acoustic Guitar 1 track.

2   Click the first dot to the left of center on the Pan wheel to place the sound of that track just to the left of center.

Now let's pan the second guitar track to just to the right of center.

3   Locate the Acoustic Guitar 2 track and click the first dot to the right of center on the Pan wheel to place the sound.

If you compare the pan positions of the two guitar tracks to the picture of the band, you'll see that the controls for each track point to the actual instrument.

Using the picture as a guide, let's set the panning controls for the rest of the tracks.

4   Pan the Tambourine track to the second dot to the right of center.

5   Pan the Shaker track to the second dot to the left of center.

6   Pan the Hollywood Strings track to the third dot to the right.

7   Pan the Electric Bass track to the third dot to the left.

8 Play the first half of the song from the beginning to hear the rough mix.

So, what did you hear this time? Did it sound like the same old song, or did you hear the different instruments (tracks) performing from different places in the stereo field?

Take a closer look at the guitar tracks for a moment. You're probably wondering why I doubled some of the regions but not all of them. I was going for a live performance feel, where one guitar starts, the other joins in, and they mirror each other (not easy to do live). Then the first guitar drops out to let the second lead, and then they play together again, alternating from time to time. The idea is to give the feeling that this was performed by two real guitar players playing on separate tracks from different locations on stage, instead of sounding like a bunch of Software Instrument loops on tracks in the Timeline.

9 Play the entire song from the beginning and listen with your trained ear to the different guitar tracks as well as the other tracks.

Did you notice that the bass seems out of place so far to the left? Some ears are more sensitive to bass than others. However, anytime you pan the bass too far from center, it has a tendency to sound a little strange. Low, bassy sounds feel better if they are closer to the center of the mix, regardless of where they might be on the stage.

10 Change the pan position for the Electric Bass track to one click to the left of center.

11 Press Cmd-S to save your rough mix.

Congratulations! You just completed your rough mix of the song. You're ready to proceed to the next steps.

Fixing the Timing and Velocity of a Software Region

The next step toward creating the final mix is to fix any problems in the recordings or tracks. Now that you've mixed the volume and pan levels for the song, it'll be easier to hear any mistakes and take care of them.

There are no glaring mistakes, but when I listen to the song, I notice that the timing of some of the notes in the Strings track seems a little off.

These notes are off because that's how I recorded them. Fortunately, you can fix the timing of the notes in any Software Instrument region.

Evaluating Timing in the Track Editor

To appreciate timing that is not right, it's a good idea to look at an example of timing that is perfect.

Let's examine one of the drum regions in the Track Editor. This is a prerecorded Apple Loop, and it has perfect timing. Then we'll take a look at a Hollywood Strings region where the timing is a little off.

1   Double-click the first region in the first (highest) Drum Kit track to open it in the Track Editor.

Let's resize the Track Editor for a larger view of the Southern Rock Drums region. You can resize the Track Editor the same way you resize the Loop Browser.

2   Click-drag the gray space to the left of the Record button and drag upward to make the Track Editor larger.

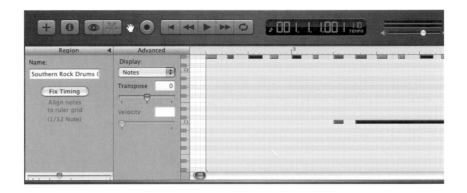

3   Click-drag the scroller on the right side of the Track Editor to move the note events into view.

Each MIDI note event in the Track Editor is perfectly aligned to the grid. Let's take a closer look at the grid.

4   Click-drag the Track Editor's Zoom slider all the way to the left of the slider control.

The note events in the Track Editor move closer together.

5   Locate the grid timing information above the Track Editor's Zoom slider.

The ruler and grid are currently set at 1/4 notes.

6   Click-drag the Track Editor's Zoom slider to the right until the grid is set to 1/32 notes.

When you have zoomed in to the Track Editor, the Region section of the Track Editor will indicate that the ruler grid is at 1/32. Notice how detailed

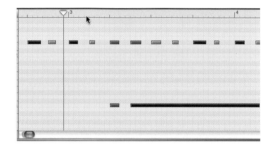

the grid is at that level, and how many lines there are in the ruler for one measure.

Each note event is lined up perfectly on a grid line. This means that each note is perfectly in time with the grid and the song.

Now let's evaluate the timing of the first Hollywood Strings region.

7   Double-click the first Hollywood Strings region in the Hollywood Strings track to open it in the Track Editor.

8   Click-drag the scroller at the bottom of the Track Editor to view the note at the beginning of the 9th measure.

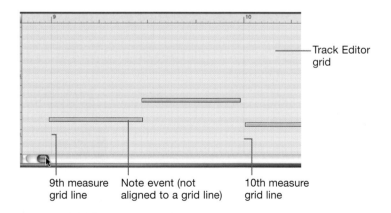

Track Editor grid

9th measure grid line   Note event (not aligned to a grid line)   10th measure grid line

Notice that the note doesn't start exactly on the grid line.

If you use the scroller to view some of the other notes in the region, you notice the same thing. Many of them are close to the grid lines, but most of them are slightly off.

Fixing the Timing of a Note

Now that you know how to use the Track Editor to tell if the timing is off, it's time to fix it. To fix the timing of a note, all you need to do is click-drag the note to the nearest gridline. Let's fix the note at the beginning of the 9th measure.

1 Click-drag the scroller in the Track Editor to view the 9th measure in the Track Editor.

2 Move your playhead to the beginning of the 9th measure to use as a guide for aligning the note.

3 Click-drag the note event to the right so it lines up with the playhead and the grid line at the start of the 9th measure.

As you can see, to adjust the timing of a single note in a Software Instrument region, all you have to do is move the note.

Instead of manually adjusting every note in both Hollywood Strings regions, wouldn't it be nice if you could do it all automatically? Well, you can. First, let's turn the two Hollywood Strings regions into one long region.

Joining Regions

Sometimes you split a region into smaller segments as you arrange a song. The Hollywood Strings regions in this song were once part of one long region that was split into two regions. Anytime you split a region, you can join that region back to its original parts again. Keep in mind you can only join a region back to its original parts, and not to another region.

To rejoin separate regions, all you need to do is select the two regions (they must be touching) and then press Cmd-J (for Join).

Let's try it.

1 Shift-click the second Hollywood Strings region in the Timeline to select it.

Both of the Hollywood Strings regions should be selected. If not, Shift-click the one that is not selected to select it.

2 Press Cmd-J to join the two regions into one long region.

There is now only one long Hollywood Strings region.

3 Press Cmd-S to save your work.

Fixing the Timing of an Entire Region

Now that you've joined the two separate Hollywood Strings regions, you can fix the timing for all of the notes at one time.

Keep in mind that very few people (if any) can play an instrument in perfect time. So you probably wouldn't want to do this on a lead guitar region or on other instrument that was played with feeling. The music will sound like it was performed by a computer.

To fix the timing of an entire region, you must first load the region into the Track Editor.

1 Double-click the Hollywood Strings region to load it into the Track Editor.

2 Click the region in the Track Editor to select it.

The Track Editor turns green when the Software Instrument region is selected.

3   Locate the Fix Timing button to the left of the Track Editor, and make sure the grid is set to 1/32 Note.

4   Drag the scroller in the Track Editor to the right to view the 14th measure.

Notice that the note at the beginning of the 14th measure is not aligned with the grid. The note at the beginning of the 15th measure is off as well.

5   Click the Fix Timing button to fix all of the notes in the entire region.

Notice that the notes at the beginning of the 14th and 15th measures are now both aligned to the grid.

The Fix Timing button will align the beginning of every note in the region to the nearest grid line. When you set up the grid to 32nd notes, the grid is at the finest level of detail, with the most lines per measure, and the notes will move the shortest distance to the nearest grid line. If you moved to the nearest 16th note, the notes that are off would have to move farther to a grid line. This, in turn, would move them farther from the original place in the song at which you wanted them to play.

The moral here is that you need to be careful when you use the Fix Timing button. If you move the notes too far when you are adjusting the timing, they will play at the wrong time in the song, and it will sound terrible even if they are aligned to the grid.

Changing Velocity for an Entire Region

Now that the timing is right for the Hollywood Strings region, I noticed that the notes are a very light shade of gray. This means that they were recorded at a very low velocity. Just as you adjust the timing of note events, you can change the velocity for one note or all of them at once.

In Lesson 1, you changed the velocity of one note in a region by clicking the note event to select it and then dragging the Velocity slider. To change all of the notes at once, you first need to select them all.

1   Move the scroller in the Track Editor until you can see the 15th measure.

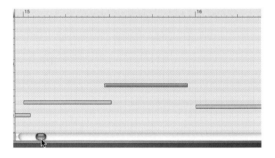

Notice that the different note events are different shades of gray.

2   Click the first note event in the 15th measure to hear it, and check the velocity in the Velocity field in the Track Editor.

The velocity of the note is 16. That's pretty low considering that 0 is the lowest and 127 is the highest.

3   Click the 2nd note in the 15th measure to check the velocity.

The velocity is 41. This note is definitely played with more intensity than the first note, but it's still relatively low.

Let's raise the velocity for all of the notes in this region simultaneously.

4   Press Cmd-A to select all the notes in the region.

All the notes turn green to indicate that they have been selected.

The Velocity field shows the level of the note event with the lowest velocity in the entire region. That level is 4. With all of the note events selected, you will raise the velocity of each note by the same relative amount when you raise the lowest velocity. Let's raise the lowest velocity from 4 to 24. This will also raise the velocity of every note in the region by the same relative amount (in this case 20.

5   Type 24 in the Velocity field and press Return.

The velocity of each note in the region has been raised by 20.

6   Click the empty track space above a note in the Track Editor to deselect all of the notes.

7   Click the 2nd note in the 15th measure.

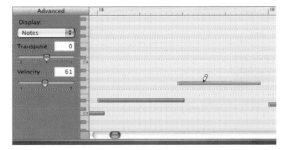

The velocity of this note had been 41 and was raised by 20. The velocity is now 61.

8   Press Cmd-E to close the Track Editor, then press Cmd-S to save the project.

9   Listen to the first half of the song to hear the new and improved Hollywood Strings in the mix.

You've fixed various problems in the timing and note velocity for the song, and in doing so, you have just completed the third step in the mixing process. Now you can move on to the next step—adding effects.

Adding Effects to a Track

Effects enhance the sound of the overall song. Each Real Instrument and Software Instrument comes with a set of professional-quality effects.

Each different effect has a slider or pop-up menu you can use to adjust the parameters of the effect. In Lesson 4, you learned how to add effects to a Real Instrument track. You use the same method to add effects to a Software Instrument track in the Timeline.

Let's add some Echo, Reverb, and EQ to the Hollywood Strings track. You'll start by soloing the track and creating a cycle region so you can hear how the track sounds before and after we adjust the effects.

1   Select the Hollywood Strings track and press S to solo the track.

2   Press C to open the cycle region.

3   Create a cycle region over the first part of the Hollywood Strings track (approximately the 8th to the 18th measures).

4   Press the spacebar to start playing the cycle region of the Hollywood Strings track.

    Listen to how the track sounds before we adjust the effects.

5   Double-click the Hollywood Strings track header to open the Track Info window.

6 Click the Details triangle to reveal the details portion of the Track Info window.

Notice the blue checked boxes for Equalizer, Echo, and Reverb. Those boxes show which effects are being applied to the track. Let's adjust all three of those effects.

7 Click-drag the Echo slider to around 25 on the slider.

The slider starts with 0 and ends at 100. So 25 will be about one-quarter of the distance from the left edge of the slider.

8 Click-drag the Reverb slider to around 33, one-third of the distance from the left edge of the slider.

Both the Reverb and Echo effects use sliders. Now let's try the Equalizer, which has a pop-up menu of preset sounds.

TIP Make sure that you like the way an effect sounds on a soloed track before you add it to the mix. Also, keep in mind that a little echo and reverb go a long way, so use them sparingly.

9   Click the pop-up menu to the right of the Equalizer and choose Add Brightness to listen to this setting.

Add Brightness is one of the preset EQ settings.

NOTE ▸ You may see a dialog box asking if you want to save the instrument settings. Don't save the settings for this exercise. When you are working on your own, and want to save your effects settings, by all means save all the effects settings you want.

10   Repeat step 9 but select a different EQ setting.

11   Try all of the different settings to hear how they sound.

Notice that some settings make a difference you can hear, and some do not. These presets are made for a variety of different instruments, so not all the settings will be noticeable with the strings sound.

12   Choose Brighten Strings from the Equalizer pop-up menu.

13   Close the Track Info window and stop playback.

14   Press C to close the cycle region.

15   Press S to unsolo the selected track.

16   Press Cmd-S to save your work.

Manually Adjusting the EQ for a Track

Now that you've added effects to the Hollywood Strings track, let's add effects to the Acoustic Guitar 2 track. Our goal is to make it sound slightly different from the Acoustic Guitar 1 track.

To accomplish this, you'll add Reverb and manually adjust the EQ. Just to keep things interesting, let's use keyboard shortcuts to select the track and open the Track Info window.

1   Press the down arrow six times until the Acoustic Guitar 2 track is selected.

2   Press Cmd-I to open the Track Info window for the selected track.

3   Click the Details triangle to reveal the effects settings, if they are not already showing.

4   Click-drag the Reverb effect to around 25 on the Reverb slider.

5   Check the Equalizer box to enable the Equalizer effect.

6   Click the Edit button.

The Edit button is the button that looks like a pencil, to the right of the Equalizer pop-up menu. The pop-up is automatically set to Manual to allow you to manually adjust your Equalizer settings.

The manual Equalizer settings window opens with all parameters set to Neutral.

7   Press S to solo the Acoustic Guitar 2 track.

8 Press C to turn on the cycle region.

9 Listen to the soloed track.

10 Experiment with the different EQ sliders to manually adjust the EQ.

11 Click the EQ pop-up menu at the top of the Equalizer window to choose a different EQ preset.

A dialog box opens to ask if you want to save the file (effect setting) before changing effects.

12 Click Don't Save.

As you can see, you can save any of your effects settings as presets. For now, let's stick with a built-in preset.

13 Choose Bass Boost from the pop-up menu.

This EQ setting boosts the bass end of the selected track.

14 Close the Track Info window.

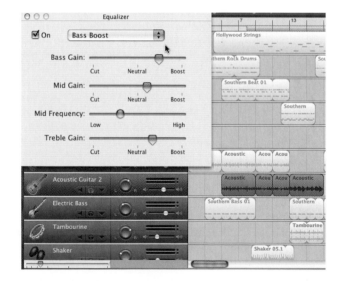

The Equalizer window stays open in case you want to adjust the EQ with the Track Info window closed.

15 Close the Equalizer window.

16 Press the spacebar to play the cycle region.

17 Press the up arrow to select the track above (the Acoustic Guitar 1 track).

18 Press S to solo the selected track.

Now you hear both guitar tracks together.

19 Press the spacebar to stop playback.

20 Press C to turn off the cycle region.

21 Unsolo both the guitar tracks.

22 Press Cmd-S to save your progress.

Mission accomplished. You've added effects to the Acoustic Guitar 2 track to make it sound slightly different than the Acoustic Guitar 1 track.

That's the end of the fourth step in creating a final mix—adding and adjusting effects. Now it's on to the last step, creating dynamic volume changes over time using Volume curves.

Working with Volume Curves

So far, you have adjusted the different track volume levels for each individual track using the Volume slider in the Track Mixer. This method is great for setting one volume level for an entire track. But what if you need the volume level to change during the song?

This next series of exercises will show you how to change the volume within a track by setting control points along the Volume curve. To make changes to a track's Volume curve, you first need to show the Volume curve in the Timeline.

Showing Volume Curves

There are two ways to show the Volume curve for a track:

- Press A (for Audio) to show the Volume curve for the selected track.
- In the track header, click the triangle to the right of the Solo button.

Our goal in the next two exercises is to show the Volume curve and then set control points on the Volume curve to fade the volume of the Hollywood Strings track up and down during the song.

First, you need to show the Volume curve.

1 Select the Hollywood Strings track.

2 Click the triangle next to the Solo button to show the track's Volume curve.

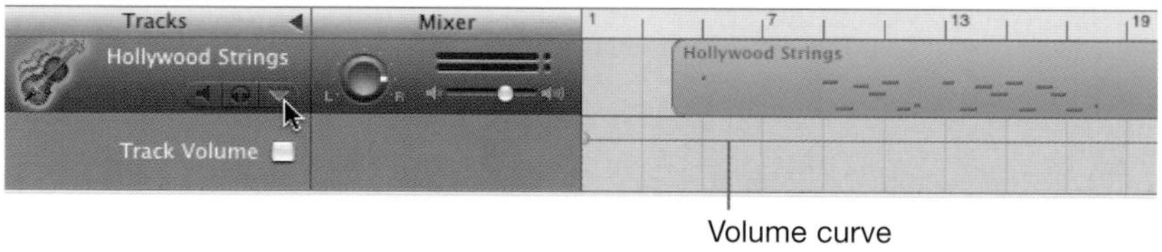

Volume curve

The Volume curve appears below the Hollywood Strings track.

In this case, the Volume curve isn't actually a curve. It's a straight line that represents the steady volume of the track.

3 Click-drag the Hollywood Strings track Volume slider all the way to the left and watch the movement of the Volume curve.

As you can see, the Volume slider moves the Volume curve.

4 Option-click the Hollywood Strings track Volume slider to move the slider back to the default position.

If the Volume curve does not move to the default position, click the Hollywood Strings track Volume slider once to apply the new position to the Volume curve.

Adding and Adjusting Control Points

Now that you can see the Volume curve, you can make adjustments to it using control points. Control points set a fixed volume level on the Volume curve at a specific point along the Timeline. Changing the position of a control point allows you to bend the Volume curve, which raises or lowers the volume between the control points.

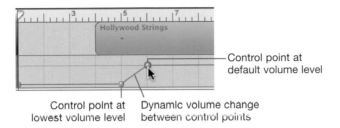

Control point at default volume level

Control point at lowest volume level

Dynamic volume change between control points

You need two control points to change the volume dynamically. The first control point is for the starting volume level. The second control point is for the new volume level.

You can move a control point by click-dragging the point. You can add a new control point by clicking the Volume curve. Control points are often used to fade music in or fade music out. In a movie theater, the lights slowly fade down before the movie starts, then fade back up after the movie. With music, when you slowly fade the volume of a song up from silence or slowly fade the music down to silence, this is *fading in* or *fading out* the music. Let's add some control points to fade in the Hollywood Strings track.

1   Locate the large green point on the far left of the Volume curve.

This control point sets the volume for the overall track.

2 Click-drag the control point at the beginning of the Volume curve and drag it down to the bottom of the track to lower the volume of the track to the lowest possible volume (silence).

Notice the gray horizontal line above the current Volume curve position. This line indicates the default volume level.

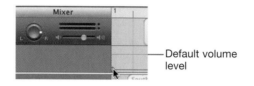

— Default volume
level

3 Move the playhead to the beginning of the 5th measure.

NOTE ▶ You may wish to zoom in to the track one or two levels (Ctrl–right arrow) to see the numbered measures you are looking for in the Beat Ruler.

4 Click the Volume curve at the playhead position to set a control point where the first note is played in the Hollywood Strings region.

A new control point appears in the Volume curve at the playhead position. This control point has a value that is the same as the lowest volume level.

Notice that the Track Volume box is checked, which indicates that the track volume curve is active. The Track Volume box automatically becomes checked whenever you click a control point in the volume curve.

5 Move your playhead to the beginning of the 6th measure.

6 Click the Volume curve at the playhead position to set a new point at that position.

Let's change the value of the new control point so that it is the same as the default volume level for the track.

7   Click-drag the new control point (at the 6th measure) up to the horizontal gray default volume line.

The volume of the track gradually changes between the 5th and 7th measures to fade the volume of the track up from silence.

8   Press the Home key to move the playhead to the beginning of the track.

9   Press S to solo the track, then play the first part of the song and listen to the Hollywood Strings track fade in.

10 Press S to unsolo the track and play the beginning of the song again to hear the fade-in mixed with the rest of the tracks.

Now that you've added control points to the Volume curve for the Hollywood Strings track, let's hide the Volume curve.

11 Press A to hide the Volume curve on the Hollywood Strings track.

12 Press the Home key to move the playhead back to the beginning of the Timeline.

Notice that the Volume slider for the Hollywood Strings track is at the lowest volume position. That's because the Volume curve is now at its lowest position, which is at the beginning of the Timeline.

10 Try to click-drag the Volume slider on the Hollywood Strings track.

The Volume slider is disabled because the Volume curve has been changed. Once you add the first control point, the Volume slider becomes disabled.

14 Press the spacebar to play the beginning of the song. Watch the Volume slider in the Hollywood Strings track as the song plays.

The Volume slider moves to reflect the value of the Volume curve. By setting the control points, you have automated the Volume slider.

15 Press Cmd-S to save your work.

Now that you know how to add control points to dynamically change the volume of an individual track, it's time to move on to the Master track.

Working with the Master Track

Throughout this lesson, you have been mixing the song by adjusting the individual tracks. The song has come a long way since the arrangement you started with, and the mix is almost finished.

There's one thing left to work with, and that is the Master track. Unlike individual tracks, the Master track controls the entire song. In the next series of exercises, you'll work with the Master track to change the volume and effects for the overall song.

There are two ways to show the Master track:

• Choose Track > Show Master Track.

• Press Cmd-B.

Let's try it now.

1 Choose Track > Show Master Track.

The Master track appears at the bottom of the Timeline.

2 Press Cmd-B to hide the Master track.

Understanding the Different Volume Controls

There are four different volume controls to consider as you finish your song. Each volume control adjusts a particular level.

Track Volume

Track volume is the volume level of an individual track. You adjust it using either the track's Volume slider or the track's Volume curve. The purpose of adjusting the track volume is to balance the levels of the different tracks in order to make them higher or lower in the overall mix.

Master Track Volume

To dynamically adjust the volume levels of the overall song, you adjust the volume of the Master track, which is a combination of all the mixed individual tracks. To change Master track volume, you adjust the control points in the Master track's Volume curve. The time to adjust Master track volume is after you have balanced the levels of all the individual tracks.

Master Output Volume

It is important to understand the difference between the overall song volume, which you control through the Master track, and the master output volume. The *master output volume* is the volume level that goes out of GarageBand to the computer. This output level determines the level your song will have when it is exported—for example, when it is ouput from GarageBand to iTunes.

You can control the master output volume of the song by using the Master Output Volume slider, located in the lower-right corner of the window.

This slider should only be adjusted after you have mixed the levels of the individual tracks and then adjusted the Master track volume. Once the overall song is mixed, you use the Master Output Volume slider to raise or lower the output level. This step ensures that you avoid clipping and that the export volume of the finished song is not too low.

Computer Output Volume

The computer output volume is how loud you hear your GarageBand project through your headphones or computer speakers. You should always use volume controls for your computer to adjust the loudness in your headphones and speakers. You should not use the Master Output Volume slider in GarageBand for this purpose. Adjusting your computer's output volume level lets you listen to your GarageBand music as loudly or quietly as you like without changing the output level of the actual project so that it exports too loudly or too quietly.

> **NOTE** ▶ The volume controls for your computer can be accessed through the speaker icon in the menu at the top of the screen or in the Sound pane of your System Preferences window.

Now that you understand the difference between the different volume controls, let's focus on the Master track volume and the master output volume.

Adding Control Points to the Master Track

One of the most important features of the Master track is that it can be used to dynamically change the Volume curve of the overall song. Let's add control points to the Master track Volume curve to fade out the end of the song.

1 Press Cmd-B to show the Master track.

2 Move the playhead to the beginning of the 29th measure.

3 Play the end of the song and listen to the way it sounds.

   Did you notice that the strings keep going long after the last bass note? Let's fade out the Master track after the last note in the Electric Bass track.

4 Move the playhead to the beginning of the 31st measure.

5 Click the Master track Volume curve at the beginning of the 31st measure to add a control point.

NOTE ▶ When you use the playhead as a guide for placing control points, you may have trouble clicking exactly on the Volume curve at the playhead position. If necessary, move the playhead out of the way so you can set your control point exactly where you want to.

6   Click the Master track Volume curve at the beginning of the 32nd measure to add a control point.

7   Click-drag the control point at the playhead position down to the lowest volume level.

8   Press the left arrow five times to move the playhead back five measures.

9   Play the end of the song and listen to the Master track volume fade out at the end.

Now the song has a nice clean fade after the last note.

Adding Effects to the Overall Song

To add an effect to an individual track, you used the Track Info window for the track. The Master track also has a Track Info window that allows you to make changes to the overall song.

There are two ways to open the Master Track Info window:

· Select the Master track and press Cmd-I.

· Choose Track > Show Track Info.

Let's open the Master Track Info window and add an effect to the entire song.

1   Press Cmd-I to open the Master Track Info window.

The Master Track Info window opens.

2   Select Rock from the effects presets list.

3   Select Rock Basic from the list of specific presets on the right.

You may see a dialog box that asks if you want to save the file before opening a new one. Click Don't Save.

You just added a Rock Basic preset to the overall song. Let's listen to the song to hear how it sounds.

4   Press the Home key and then the spacebar to play the song from the beginning.

5   While the song is playing, press the down arrow to hear the other Rock preset effects applied to the song. Stop playback when you have selected an effect.

Did you find a favorite preset? I like the way the LA Rock preset sounds. You can select whichever you like best.

6   Click the Details triangle to view the other effects options for the Master track.

At the bottom right of the Track Info window for the Master track are the Tempo, Time signature, and Key controls for the entire song. The other controls work the same way they do for the individual track effects. You can even save master effects settings to create your own presets.

7   Click the Details triangle again to close the details portion of the window, and then close the Master Track Info window.

8   Press Cmd-B to hide the Master track.

Now that you've added control points and effects to the Master track, it's time to check the output level for clipping. This is the last thing you do to your final mix to prepare the song for export.

Checking for Clipping

You've finished your final mix, adjusted all of the track levels individually, and made adjustments to the overall song. The last thing you need to do is play the song from the beginning and watch the Master Output Volume meters to make sure the song output levels are good, and not clipping.

The yellow and red indicate that the output level is clipping.

Good output level

When the output level is good, the average volume levels (solid green bars) move as high as the middle or upper third of the meters, and the peaks (green lines) never turn yellow or red.

To change the output volume for the song, you click-drag the Master Output Volume slider.

Let's raise the master output volume to illustrate clipping.

1   Click-drag the Master Output Volume slider to the right so that it is near the highest level.

It doesn't need to be at the highest level to cause clipping.

NOTE ▶ You may wish to take a moment to lower the volume of your computer because the playback will now be louder than normal.

2   Press the Home key and then the spacebar to play the song from the beginning.

As the song plays, watch the Master Output Volume meters for any signs of clipping. If the clipping indicators turn red, press the spacebar to stop playback.

3   Click the red clipping indicators to reset them.

4   Click-drag the Master Output Volume slider to the left to lower the output volume of the song.

5   Repeat steps 2 through 4 until you find a good level for the Master track volume.

Make sure your output level isn't too low. Try to set the output level as loud as you can safely, without the meters reaching the yellow or the red clipping range.

6   Press Cmd-S to save the finished mix.

Testing Your Trained Ear

Now that you understand how to mix a song in GarageBand, let's put your ear to the test. In this exercise, you'll listen to the original, unmixed song, then the mixed song. See if you hear the difference in the two versions.

1   Choose File > Open Recent > **7-1 Highway Bound unmxd** to open the original unmixed version.

2   Play the first half of the song.

3   Choose File > Open Recent > Highway Bound to open your finished mix.

4   Play the finished mix.

As the song plays, ask yourself the following questions:

- Does the mixed version of the song sound better than the unmixed version?

- Do you notice the left-to-right placement of the different tracks in the stereo field?

- Do you notice the overall balance of the volume between the tracks?

- Can you hear that the lead instruments (guitars) are louder in the mix than the supporting instruments?

If you heard any or all of these things, you've trained your ear to hear beyond the basic song.

Congratulations! Now you know how to mix your songs to make them sound professional.

What You've Learned

- The Track Mixer includes a Volume slider, Pan wheel, and Level meters for each track.
- You use the controls in the Track Mixer to adjust the levels of an individual track.
- When the levels in the Level meter turn red, that means the volume is too loud. This is also known as clipping.
- Changing the pan position of a track changes the placement of that track to a different location in the left-to-right stereo field.
- Option-clicking the track controls will reset the Volume slider or Pan wheel.
- You can add or change the effects on a track in the Track Info window.
- You can add or change the effects for the overall song in the Master Track Info window.
- You can dynamically change the volume of a track or the song over time by adding control points to the Volume curve.
- You can add control points to the Volume curve by clicking the Volume curve.
- You can move a control point by dragging it.
- The Master track Volume curve is for dynamically adjusting the volume of the overall song in the Timeline.
- The master output volume is the output level of the finished song that will be used when you export the song.
- You can use the Master Output Volume slider to adjust the master output volume.
- To change the volume of your playback in your headphones or speakers, use the volume controls for the computer, not the Master Output Volume slider.

8

Lesson Files	Lessons > Lesson_08 > Eyewitness; Highway Bound; SciFiShow; IvoryGroove; Techno80s; Homecoming
Time	This lesson takes approximately 45 minutes to complete.
Goals	Set GarageBand export preferences
	Evaluate a song's output levels
	Export an entire song to iTunes
	Export selected tracks to iTunes
	Export using a cycle region
	Use your playlist of GarageBand songs with an iPhoto slideshow
	Use your GarageBand songs with iMovie
	Use your GarageBand songs with iDVD
	Convert your playlist songs from AIFF format to MP3

Lesson 8
Sharing Your Finished Songs

Now that you know how to record, arrange, and mix your songs in GarageBand, it's time to learn how to export your songs to iTunes so that you can share them with other iLife applications, download them onto your iPod, and even burn them to a CD.

The capability to share your GarageBand songs with the other iLife applications is one of the greatest features of the entire iLife suite. All of the iLife applications, including GarageBand, are designed to work together seamlessly. This means you can write music in GarageBand, export your songs to iTunes, and use your custom music in your iPhoto slideshows, in iMovie videos, and in iDVD, either as background music for your DVD menu or as part of your DVD movies and slideshows.

The focus of this lesson is learning how to prepare your GarageBand projects for exporting to iTunes. You'll also export your projects to a playlist in iTunes and learn how to use your new GarageBand playlist in iPhoto, iMovie, and iDVD.

Exporting to iTunes

Exporting to iTunes is as simple as choosing File > Export to iTunes. Before you begin exporting, however, there are a few things you'll need to do to prepare your songs.

In the next series of exercises, you'll set your GarageBand preferences to create a playlist in iTunes. Then you'll evaluate each song to make sure that you are exporting the whole song, and you'll check the output levels for clipping. Finally, you'll export your songs to a new playlist in iTunes.

Since you'll be working with the finished mixed songs from the other lessons, this is a great time to practice your ear training so that you can hear beyond the basic music. As you play the different songs, listen for the levels and placement of the tracks in the stereo field, and see if you notice any of the arrangement rules and techniques you learned in Lessons 6 and 7.

Let's take a moment to review the song arrangement rules from Lesson 6. Here's a summary of these rules:

* Rule #1: Decide what type of song you are going to write, and choose instruments and parts that will work for that song.

* Rule #2: Make sure your song has a beginning, middle, and end.

* Rule #3: Sprinkle your music with catchy, stand-out riffs to liven up the song, but don't flood your song with these riffs, or you'll drown the other tracks.

* Rule #4: Add a few breaks in the music so your song can breathe.

Setting GarageBand Preferences for iTunes

The first step in preparing a song to export to iTunes is to set your song and playlist information in the Export pane of the GarageBand preferences.

Let's open the first song and set up the song and playlist information.

1   Choose File > Open and select **Eyewitness** from the Lesson_08 folder.

2   Choose GarageBand > Preferences to open the General Preferences window.

3   Click the Export button at the top of the General Preferences window to open the Export pane.

The Export pane opens within the General Preferences window.

Next, you'll need to name your iTunes playlist and album. By default, GarageBand names the playlist and album after the registered user of the computer.

4   Type *Lesson08* in the iTunes Playlist field.

5   Type *GarageBand Lessons Album* in the Album Name field.

Song and Playlist Information

GarageBand will use this as the default information when exporting your songs.

iTunes Playlist:	Lesson08
Composer Name:	Mary Plummer
Album Name:	GarageBand Lessons Album

6   Close the General Preferences window.

Now that you've set up the export information, iTunes will automatically create a playlist titled Lesson08 and include the composer's name as well as the album name information in the playlist.

Evaluating the Song's Output Level

Once you've set your export preferences, it's time to check the output levels for the song to make sure that it isn't clipping. Remember, the Master Output Volume meters are located in the lower-right corner of the GarageBand window. You can use the Master Output Volume slider to raise or lower the output level as needed.

Also, since training your ears takes practice, remember to listen beyond the basic song for the left-to-right placement of the different instruments in the stereo field, as well as the balance between the volume levels of the different tracks.

Let's play the song and check the output levels. If the levels are too high, you'll need to lower the output. If the levels are too low, you'll need to raise the output.

1   Press the spacebar to begin playback. As the song plays, watch the Master Output Volume meters for signs of clipping.

If you see any clipping (red) in the meters, stop playback.

You should discover clipping around the 15th, 20th, and 25th measures.

2   Click the clipping indicators (red dots) to reset them.

3   Click-drag the Master Output Volume slider to lower the output volume to just above halfway on the slider.

4   Press the left arrow key several times to back up the playhead a few measures.

5   Play the rest of the song to check the new output levels.

If your levels are still clipping, use the Master Volume Output slider to lower them again. But be careful not to set your levels too low. Ideally, your levels should peak in the highest green to yellow portion of the meter.

6   Press Cmd-S to save your project with the new corrected levels.

TIP It's a good idea to always save your project with the corrected levels before outputting to iTunes. That way, if you decide to output the song again, or go back to work on the song later, the levels will be correct.

Exporting a Song

Files are exported to iTunes in AIFF (Audio Interchange File Format) at 44.1 kHz (kilohertz). This is an audio file format the can be exported to an audio CD. Your songs can then be burned to an audio CD, downloaded to an iPod, or converted to another format, such as MP3, from within iTunes.

When you export a song to iTunes, the entire song, from the beginning of the first measure to the end of the last region, is exported.

Let's export the song **Eyewitness** to iTunes.

1   Choose File > Export to iTunes to export the song.

GarageBand begins to mix down your song.

The mixdown process means that all of the different tracks are mixed (at the current levels) into one stereo pair (left and right) for iTunes.

File	Edit	Track	Con
New			⌘N
Open...			⌘O
Open Recent			▶
Close			⌘W
Save			⌘S
Save As...			⇧⌘S
Revert to Saved			
Export to iTunes			

Creating mixdown   (Cancel)

A mixdown window shows the progress of the mixdown. You can cancel the export process during mixdown by clicking Cancel.

When mixdown is complete, iTunes launches with your song in the new playlist. If your iTunes window does not open, click the iTunes icon in the Dock.

NOTE ▶ If you have more than one version of iTunes on your computer (for example, OS 9 and OS X versions), GarageBand may export to the older version of iTunes. Launch the most recent version of iTunes before you export.

2   Click the playlist you created, Lesson08, to open the new playlist (if it is not already open).

NOTE ▶ If the playlist appears with your name (user name) instead of Lesson08, change the playlist name in the GarageBand preferences and export again.

3   Select **Eyewitness** in the playlist to select the song.

4   Press the spacebar to play the song in iTunes.

    You don't have to listen to the whole song.

5   Press the spacebar to stop playing the song.

    Let's leave iTunes open so we can export a few more songs.

6   Press Cmd-H to hide iTunes.

7   Click the GarageBand icon in your Dock to return to GarageBand.

Exporting Selected Tracks

Now that you know how easy it is to export a complete song, let's look at exporting selected tracks. Sometimes you want to export only specific tracks. Perhaps you recorded a rough lead vocal track, and you want to practice singing (Karaoke style) to the song without hearing the rough lead vocal track. In that case, you would simply mute the vocal track in the Timeline, and then export the song. Any track that is muted in the Timeline will not be exported.

This method works great if you are the lead singer and want to practice your vocals when you're at home, in the car, wherever. You can simply mute the vocal track, export the song to iTunes, and then burn it to a CD or download it to your iPod.

Also, coordinating a time and place to rehearse can be one of the most challenging things for a band. You can use GarageBand to export custom mixes of your original songs so that you can practice even if you can't all be at the same place at the same time.

Let's open the finished mix of **Highway Bound** and export several different versions that would be good for rehearsing.

1   Choose File > Open and select **Highway Bound** from the Lesson_08 folder.

First, you'll export the finished mix. You don't have to check the levels on this one, though it's a good habit if you want to for practice.

2   Choose File > Export to iTunes to export the song.

Now, let's create rehearsal versions for the first guitar player who plays the Acoustic Guitar 1 track. The first version will be just the Acoustic Guitar 1 track soloed so the guitarist can practice along with the sound of the finished part. The second version will be the finished song with the Acoustic Guitar 1 track muted so the guitarist can practice playing along with the other band members without hearing the guitar part already recorded in the song.

Before you export a new version of the song, you'll want to save the project and rename it accordingly.

3   Press Shift-Cmd-S to open the Save As window.

4   Name the project *Highway Bound Guitar1 only* and save it to your
   GarageBand Songs folder.

5   Click the Solo button on the Acoustic Guitar 1 track to solo the track.

The Acoustic Guitar 1 track solos and all of the other tracks and regions
turn gray to indicate they have been muted.

6   Choose File > Export to iTunes to export the guitars-only version of
   the song.

The new version of the song is exported to iTunes.

Now you'll export a version of the song with the Acoustic Guitar 1
track muted.

7   Press Shift-Cmd-S to open the Save As window.

8   Name the new version of the song *Highway Bound -Guitar1*, and
   click Save.

9   Click the Mute button on the Acoustic Guitar 1 track to mute the track,
   and press Cmd-S to save the song with the muted track.

This time, the Acoustic Guitar 1 track and regions are gray to indicate
they have been muted.

10 Choose File > Export to iTunes to export this version of the song.

11 Click the iTunes icon in your Dock to see your playlist with all three versions of the song **Highway Bound**.

12 Double-click each of the **Highway Bound** versions and listen to the first few seconds to make sure you exported it correctly.

Here's what you should have:

- **Highway Bound**: Full song with all tracks
- **Highway Bound Guitar1 only**: Full song with Acoustic Guitar 1 track only
- **Highway Bound -Guitar1**: Full song minus the Acoustic Guitar 1 track

Exporting with a Cycle Region

Sometimes you may only want to export part of a song, or you may want the song to export beyond the end of the last region in the Timeline. When you add effects to a song, like echo or reverb, the final notes continue beyond the last region. If you export the entire song normally, the last notes will cut off abruptly at the end because export just includes the song up to the end of the last region.

To extend a song beyond the end of the last region, you can create a cycle region and extend it until the last note with effects ends in the Timeline. Exporting with a cycle region will export a song from the beginning to the end of the region.

Let's open the **SciFiShow** and try exporting the song without a cycle region. Then we'll export it again with a cycle region in order to preserve the sustained final notes.

1   Click the GarageBand icon in the Dock, and then choose File > Open and select **SciFiShow** from the Lesson_08 folder.

2   Play the song once to hear the final mix, and listen carefully to the ending.

As you listen to the ending, watch the playhead to hear when the last note actually ends.

Let's export the song as-is to see what happens to the ending when it is exported.

3   Choose File > Export to iTunes to export the song.

4   Click your iTunes icon in the Dock to see the updated playlist.

5   Double-click **SciFiShow** in the iTunes playlist to listen to the exported mix.

Did you notice the abrupt ending? It sounds like the song was cut off, which is definitely not the lasting impression you want to leave someone who hears your song for the first time.

Let's create a cycle region over the entire song, including an extra measure for the last notes to trail off. Then we'll export the new version to iTunes.

6   Click the GarageBand icon in the Dock to return to GarageBand.

7 Press Shift-Cmd-S to open the Save As window.

8 Change the name of the song to *SciFiShow extended* and save it to your GarageBand Songs folder.

9 Press C to turn on the cycle region.

10 Press Ctrl–right arrow to zoom in to the Timeline several levels.

11 Click-drag the right edge of the cycle region to extend it to the beginning of the 27th measure (one full measure longer than the end of the last region).

The left edge of the cycle region (yellow bar) should start at the beginning of the song.

12 Press Cmd-S to save the new version of the song.

13 Choose File > Export to iTunes to export the extended song.

14 Click the iTunes icon in the Dock to see the updated playlist.

Notice that the length of the extended version is 52 seconds long, and the original **SciFiShow** is only 50 seconds.

15 Listen to each version of the song in iTunes to hear the difference.

To listen to the song, double-click the song in the playlist, or select the song in the playlist and click the Play button at the top of the window.

Project Tasks

Now that you understand the different ways to export a song from GarageBand to iTunes, it's your turn to finish the playlist. There are three songs left to export: **IvoryGroove**, **Homecoming**, and **Techno80s**. Open each song, check the output levels, and export the entire song to iTunes. Be sure to save each song before you move on to the next one. For the song **Techno 80s**, you'll need to add a cycle region to be sure the end of the song gets exported.

1   Open **IvoryGroove** from the Lesson_08 folder.

2   Listen to the song, watching the output levels and paying special attention to the ending.

    Notice that I used control points to fade in and out the Hollywood Strings track. You'll work more with control points in the next lesson.

3   Export the song to iTunes.

4   Open **Homecoming**, listen to the song, and check the levels and the ending. Make any necessary adjustments to the output levels.

5   Export the song to iTunes.

6   Open the song **Techno80s**.

    Notice the control points that were used to fade in and out the Crowd Applause 01 region. The song actually ends before the end of the last region.

7   Create a cycle region that starts at the beginning of the 1st measure and ends at the beginning of the 33rd measure.

    This is also the position of the last control point on the Sound Effect Volume curve.

8   Export the song with the cycle region to end the song when the applause fades out.

9   Click the iTunes icon and check each of the new songs to make sure they were exported properly.

Source			Song Name	Time
Library		▲	Song Name	Time
Radio	1	☑	Eyewitness	1:36
Music Store	2	☑	Highway Bound	1:09
60's Music	3	☑	Highway Bound Guitar1 only	1:09
My Top Rated	4	☑	Highway Bound –Guitar1	1:09
Recently Played	5	☑	SciFiShow	0:50
Top 25 Most Played	6	☑	SciFiShow extended	0:52
Lesson08	7	☑	IvoryGroove	0:22
	8	☑	Homecoming	1:55
	9 ◀)	☑	Techno80s	1:04

NOTE ▶ If you saved your GarageBand projects with the Hide Extension box unchecked, you will see a .band extension after the song name in iTunes.

Now that you've created your Lesson08 playlist, let's see how to use it with the other iLife applications.

Using Your Playlist with iLife

One of the many enhancements in the iLife '04 upgrade is the use of iTunes playlists. Previous versions of iPhoto, iMovie, and iDVD were limited to one song from iTunes.

Let's take a closer look at all three applications to see how to access your customized playlist of GarageBand songs. First, let's select only the songs you want to include in iTunes.

Disabling Playlist Songs in iTunes

Your playlist includes not only the finished mixes of your GarageBand songs, but also the guitar rehearsal versions of **Highway Bound**, and a bad version of **SciFiShow** where the last note is cut off too early. Let's disable these songs so they will not be included when the playlist is used by the other applications.

Active tracks all have a blue check box to the left of the song name. To disable a song in the playlist, simply uncheck the box next to the song name.

1   Click the box for **Highway Bound Guitar1 only** to disable that song.

2   Click the box for **Highway Bound -Guitar1** to disable that song.

3   Click the box for **SciFiShow** to disable that song.

	Song Name	Time
1	☑ Eyewitness	1:36
2	☑ Highway Bound	1:09
3	☐ Highway Bound Guitar1 only	1:09
4	☐ Highway Bound –Guitar1	1:09
5	☐ SciFiShow	0:50
6	☑ SciFiShow extended	0:52
7	☑ IvoryGroove	0:22
8	☑ Homecoming	1:55
9 ◀	☑ Techno80s	1:04

4   Double-click the first song in the playlist (**Eyewitness**) to play the song in iTunes.

5   Press the right arrow key to move to the next active song.

6   Press the right arrow key until you cycle through all of the active songs.

Notice that iTunes skips any song that is not active.

This method of unchecking the box works to disable a song for burning to a CD or playing in iTunes. However, you will need to move them out of the playlist to exclude them from playing in the other iLife applications.

7   Click the + button at the bottom left of the iTunes window to add a new playlist.

8   Double-click the new untitled playlist in the Source pane of iTunes, and change the name of the playlist to *practice songs*.

9   Click your Lesson08 playlist to select it and view the songs.

10   Click **Highway Bound Guitar1 only** to select that song.

11   Cmd-click **SciFiShow** and **Highway Bound -Guitar1** to select both songs.

You should now have all three songs selected.

Now let's drag these songs to the practice songs playlist.

12 Click-drag any of the selected songs to grab all three selections and drag them to the practice songs playlist.

The practice songs icon darkens when you drag the pointer with the selected songs over it. A green + appears to indicate that the songs will be added to the playlist.

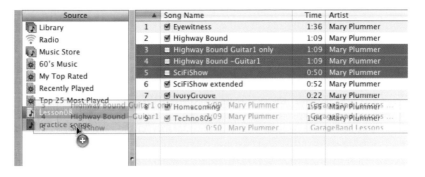

13 Press Delete to delete the selected regions in the Lesson08 playlist.

You may see a dialog box that asks if you are sure you want to remove the songs from the list. If so, click Yes in the dialog box.

The Lesson08 playlist now contains only the full songs, and the practice songs playlist contains the examples of incomplete songs.

Source		Song Name	Time
Library	1	☑ Eyewitness	1:36
Radio	2	☑ Highway Bound	1:09
Music Store	3	☑ SciFiShow extended	0:52
60's Music	4	☑ IvoryGroove	0:22
My Top Rated	5	☑ Homecoming	1:55
Recently Played	6	☑ Techno80s	1:04
Top 25 Most Played			
Lesson08			
practice songs			

Your playlist is now ready for action. At this time, you could burn it to a CD, convert the songs to MP3, or use the playlist with the other iLife applications.

Using Your Playlist for an iPhoto Slideshow

Let's see how to access the playlist for a slideshow in iPhoto.

One of the most frustrating things about the previous versions of iPhoto was the limitation of one song for a slideshow. Any song, no matter how good it is, can get old after a few plays, especially during a slideshow. Now you can use your entire playlist (or whichever songs are active in iTunes) for your iPhoto slideshow.

iPhoto now gives you a choice of either one song or an entire playlist. Let's create a slideshow and use your Lesson08 playlist for the music. You can use your own pictures for the slideshow.

1   Click the iPhoto icon in the Dock to launch iPhoto.

If you don't have iPhoto in your Dock, double-click the iPhoto icon in the Applications folder on your computer.

The iPhoto window opens.

2   Click the Slideshow button at the bottom left of the window.

The photos in my project are from a recent GarageBand recording session with guitarist William Whitacre, who specializes in bluegrass and classical guitar.

You will have access only to your own pictures on your computer. If you don't have any photos in your iPhoto library, you can still follow along with the steps so you will know how to add music to a future slideshow project.

3   Click the Music button at the top of the Slideshow window.

4   Click the Source pop-up menu to view your iTunes playlists.

5   Choose Lesson08 from the available playlists.

6   The Slideshow window indicates that you have selected the entire Lesson08 playlist.

If you prefer to play one song over and over during the slideshow, you can select a specific song from the playlist.

7   Click **Eyewitness** from the playlist to select that song.

The playlist information at the bottom of the Slideshow window changes to indicate that you have selected a song: **Eyewitness**.

To deselect a song, click the empty space below the list of songs. If no songs are selected, the entire playlist will be used for the slideshow.

8   Click the Save Settings button in the lower-left of the Slideshow music pane to save your music settings.

If you opened an active project, and don't want to save this playlist to the project, click the Cancel button instead.

9   Close the iPhoto window to quit iPhoto.

As you can see, it is very easy to use your GarageBand songs with iPhoto. Now let's see how to access the playlist in iMovie.

> **MORE INFO** ▶ *You can get more detailed information on the new features available in iPhoto '04, including adding audio to your iPhoto slideshows, in the iPhoto Help menu and iPhoto documentation that comes with the software.*

Using Your Playlist with iMovie

To use your GarageBand songs in iMovie, all you need to do is click the Audio button and select the song you want to use from the Lesson08 playlist in iTunes. You can import audio into iMovie in any format that works with QuickTime. Two of the most common formats are AIFF and MP3. Your songs were exported from GarageBand to iTunes in AIFF format.

1   Click the iMovie icon in your Dock to launch iMovie.

> **NOTE** ▶ You may see a dialog window asking if you want to create a new project or open an existing project. Either selection will work for this test.

2   Click the Audio button to view the Audio pane in the iMovie window.

3   Click the pop-up menu at the top of the Audio pane and select your Lesson08 playlist from iTunes.

Once your playlist is in the Audio pane, you can click-drag any of the songs from the playlist to the Timeline.

NOTE ▶ If you are working with an existing project and have video in the Timeline, you can add music below the video track. If you created a new project, you can simply add music to the audio track without any video or photos. The point of this exercise is to show you how to add music to your projects.

4   Click-drag **Homecoming** from the playlist to the beginning of the iMovie Timeline.

The song **Homecoming** becomes an audio track in the iMovie Timeline.

5   Close the iMovie window.

If you get a dialog box to save your iMovie project, you can decide if you'd like to save your playlist with the current project before you close the project.

Once again, you can see firsthand how easy it is to add your GarageBand songs to another iLife application, this time iMovie. The last iLife application to try is iDVD.

MORE INFO ▶ *You can get more detailed information on the new features available in iMovie '04, including adding audio to your iMovie projects, in the iMovie Help menu and iMovie documentation that comes with the software.*

Using Your Playlist Songs in iDVD

The seamless integration between all of the iLife applications includes iDVD, which has many new enhancements. The previous versions of iDVD were limited to 30 seconds of background music for your DVD menu, and only 3 minutes of music for a slideshow presentation. With iDVD '04, you can play 15 minutes of background music with your DVD menus and an entire playlist of songs for your slideshows.

iDVD supports MP3 and AIFF audio files, just like iMovie does.

To add a song or playlist to your DVD, you need to click the media panel in the Customize drawer, and then select your playlist or song. Let's walk through the process so you will be prepared to add music the next time you create a custom project in iDVD.

NOTE ► Keep in mind that iDVD uses terms unique to iDVD. Throughout this exercise I will use the official iDVD terms. However, I will also explain what they are in case you are new to iDVD.

1   Double-click the GarageBand_DVD project in the Lesson_08 folder on your computer to launch iDVD and open the sample project.

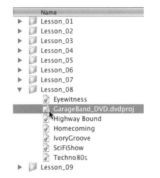

I built this sample project so you can add music to the menu, build a slideshow, and add your playlist to the slideshow.

2   Click the Customize button at the bottom of the iDVD window to open the Customize drawer.

The Customize drawer opens to the side of the iDVD window. The Customize drawer looks like a panel. It allows you to customize your DVD project.

3 Click the Media button at the top of the Customize drawer to access the media for your project.

4 Choose Audio from the pop-up menu (if it is not already selected) to view your iTunes playlists.

5 Click the Lesson08 playlist to select it.

Your playlist appears at the bottom of the Customize drawer.

6 Click the song **SciFiShow extended** to select it from the playlist.

7 Click Apply to apply that song to your background menu.

To add a song or playlist to your slideshow, you first need to create a slideshow.

8 Click the Slideshow button in the lower-left corner to create a slideshow.

My Slideshow appears on your menu to indicate that you have created a slideshow.

9 Double-click My Slideshow on your menu to open the Slideshow Editor in the iDVD window.

You will need to add photos from your iPhoto library. I did not include pictures with this project.

10 Select Photos in the media pop-up in the Customize drawer if it is not already selected.

Your iPhoto library and albums will appear below the pop-up menu. Select one of your albums to use for this example. If you don't have any photo albums, you can add random photos from your iPhoto library. You have to have photos in the slideshow before you will be able to add music.

11 Click-drag your iPhoto album from the Customize pane to the empty space in the GarageBand window that says "Drag photos here" and release your mouse.

A green circle with a + (plus sign) appears, indicating that you are adding the photos to your slideshow.

Your photos appear in the Slideshow window.

To add a song or playlist to your iDVD slideshow, you can simply select the entire playlist in the Audio pane of the Customize drawer and click the Apply button. You can also click-drag the playlist to the Audio well of your Slideshow Editor. Let's try the second method to keep things interesting.

12 Change the Media popup from Photos to Audio.

13 Locate the Audio well in the Slideshow editor near the bottom-right corner of the iDVD window.

The Audio well is labeled Audio and looks like a speaker (audio) icon inside of a box.

The well is where you place the songs that you wish to use with your slideshow. If you drag one song, or click the Apply button, the slideshow will only play that song. If you drag an entire playlist to the well, or click Apply with the playlist selected, the slideshow will play the entire playlist starting with the first song.

14 Click-drag the Lesson08 playlist from the Customize drawer to the Audio well in the Slideshow Editor.

A green circle with a + appears, indicating that you are adding the playlist songs to the Audio well.

A green iTunes song icon appears in the Audio well to show that you have
added iTunes songs to the slideshow.

The songs in the playlist play in the same order in which they appear in
your iTunes playlist.

15 Hold your pointer over the Audio well to show the name of the first song
in the playlist (Eyewitness) and the duration of the entire playlist, 6:59.

You can also drag a single song from your playlist to the well.

To empty the contents of the Audio well, simply click the file, drag it out
of the well, and release it anywhere outside of the well area.

NOTE ▸ When you add a playlist to the Audio well, the slide duration is
automatically set to "Fit to Audio." If you remove your songs from the
Audio well, the slide duration will return to the default duration.

16 Press Cmd-S to save your project, and then close the iDVD window to
quit iDVD.

MORE INFO ▸ *You can get more detailed information on the new features
available in iDVD '04, including adding audio to your iDVD projects, in the
iDVD Help menu and iDVD documentation that comes with the software.*

Converting AIFF Files to MP3

Now that you know how to export your GarageBand songs to iTunes and how
to use your custom music with the other iLife applications, let's look at how to
convert your AIFF files to MP3 in iTunes.

To convert files from one audio format to another in iTunes, you need to set
the conversion format in the iTunes preferences.

Understanding the Different Audio Formats

There are currently four different choices for importing or converting audio files in iTunes: MPEG-4 AAC, AIFF, MP3, and WAV.

MPEG-4 AAC (often referred to just as AAC) is a new compression format that rivals the sound quality of CDs (AIFF 44.1 kHz). The WAV and AIFF encoders do not compress the songs, so the songs are higher quality, and the files are several times larger than AAC and MP3 compressed files. The WAV encoder is used with Windows computers.

If you are using a Macintosh and QuickTime 6.2 or later or a Windows computer, the default encoding format is MPEG-4 AAC. If you are using an earlier version of QuickTime on your Mac, the default format is MP3 (or whatever you have set in the Importing Preferences).

How do you know which format to use? If you plan to use your music for video projects or to burn high-quality audio CDs, you should use AIFF encoding for the best results.

If you plan to store your music on a hard disk or iPod, the AAC setting creates files that are usually less than 1 MB for each minute of music and will sound as good or better than MP3 files encoded at the same bit rate. If you are using an earlier version of QuickTime or MP3 player, you can use the MP3 setting.

Let's change the preferences in iTunes to convert your songs to MP3 files.

1   Click the iTunes icon in your Dock to launch iTunes (if it is not already open).

2   Choose iTunes > Preferences to open the iTunes Preferences window.

3   Click the Importing button at the top of the iTunes Preferences window to view the Importing pane.

4   Click the Importing Using pop-up menu and choose MP3 Encoder from the file format options.

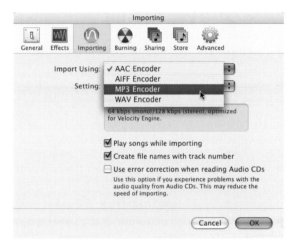

5   Click OK.

Changing the import format in iTunes will convert any imported files to the current format setting.

You can also convert existing files to a different format. Now that you've changed the import format, let's convert your existing playlist songs from AIFF to MP3. When you convert files, iTunes creates duplicates of the selected songs and changes the format of the duplicates.

6   Press Cmd-A to select all of the songs in your playlist (if they are not already selected).

7   Choose Advanced > Convert Selection to MP3 to begin the conversion process.

A playlist named Converting Songs appears while iTunes converts your songs.

When iTunes finishes, all of the songs in your playlist are still linked to the original AIFF files, and the new MP3 converted files are in the iTunes Library.

Your playlist is now ready to download to your iPod and can be shared with Mac OS X or Windows 2000 and Windows XP computers.

Viewing the iTunes Library in the Finder

The last stop on your iTunes file sharing and converting tour is to actually see the files in the iTunes Library in the Finder.

1   Press Cmd-Q to quit iTunes.

2   Double-click your hard drive icon to open your hard drive.

3   Click the Music button, located on the left of the Finder window, to open your Music folder.

4   Click the Column View button to view your Finder as columns.

5   Click the iTunes folder to open the contents, and then check the iTunes Music folder.

6   Click the folder with your name (or the user name), and then click the GarageBand Lessons Album folder to view the album contents.

Notice that you have two versions of each song. The songs with .aif extensions are the AIFF format files that were exported from GarageBand. The songs with .mp3 extensions are the files that were converted in iTunes.

You can preview (listen to) the song files in the Finder.

7   Click any of the song files to open them in the Preview column of the Finder.

The selected song file opens in the Preview column.

8   Click the Play button in the Preview controls to preview the song.

9   Click the MP3 version of the same song and listen to it in the Preview column.

Can you hear a difference in the sound quality? You may or may not hear a difference, depending on what type of speakers or headphones you are using. The .aif version is uncompressed and takes 16.1 MB of disk space, while the the .mp3 version is compressed and takes only 1.8 MB of disk space. You can use the compressed version for your iPod to maximize space, and the .aif version for your video presentations for better quality audio.

There you have it! You now know how to export your songs from GarageBand to iTunes, and from there, how to share your songs with the other iLife applications.

What You've Learned

- GarageBand exports songs to iTunes as 44.1 kHz AIFF files and places them in an iTunes playlist, as determined by the GarageBand export preferences.
- Exporting a song in GarageBand exports from the beginning of the first measure in the Timeline to the end of the last region in the Timeline.
- Exporting a song from GarageBand with your cycle region on will export only the part of the Timeline within the cycle region. This is very useful for projects where the final notes sustain longer than the end of the last region.
- GarageBand will not export tracks that are muted in the Timeline. Muting tracks before exporting allows you to export custom mixes of the songs.
- You can use your playlist of GarageBand songs with all of the iLife applications, including iPhoto, iMovie, and iDVD.
- You can convert your playlist from AIFF format to MP3 format files by changing the import format in the iTunes preferences, and then choosing Advanced > Convert Selection to MP3.
- Converting files in iTunes converts the file format of all selected files in your playlist. However, the original files remain in the iTunes Library in their original format.

9

Lesson **9**

Advanced GarageBand Tips and Techniques

At this point, if you've been following along with all of the lessons, you know how to create tracks, record Real Instruments and Software Instruments, arrange music, edit regions, add effects, mix, and export the finished song to iTunes. So what's left? Now that you understand the basic GarageBand features and techniques, there are some advanced features that may be useful as you create more complex compositions.

The goal in this lesson is to cover a lot of different advanced GarageBand features, functions, tips, and techniques. Note that some of the information in this lesson is not documented in the GarageBand Help, so be prepared to proceed into uncharted territories, and by all means do try these techniques at home.

Strategies for Minimizing the Load on Your Processor

Certain features in GarageBand are more processor-intensive than others. Whether you are working with a dual-processor G5 or a slower computer, it's a good idea to be aware of the things that are the most processor-intensive so you can use them sparingly and thereby get the most out of your GarageBand experience.

The most processor-intensive tracks are

- Software Instrument tracks

- Real Instrument tracks using amp simulators

- Tracks with a lot of effects

Also, remember that the more tracks you use in a song, the more demand on your processor.

If your processor is overloaded, try muting or deleting some tracks in the song or turning off some of the effects.

In the following exercises, you'll learn some additional techniques for monitoring and minimizing GarageBand's load on your computer's processor.

Monitoring the Processor with the Playhead

Did you know that the playhead changes color to indicate the level of demand on your computer's processor? The playhead turns from white to yellow to orange to red to indicate how processor-intensive the song is. White indicates the lowest processor load; red is the highest.

When the playhead turns dark orange to red, you are pushing the maximum load on the computer processor, and you could be overloading it. When the processor overloads, playback will be interrupted by a dialog that warns you that you are using too many tracks, effects, and notes.

Part of the song was not played

This song has too many tracks, effects, or notes to be played in real-time.
To maximize performance, look in GarageBand Help under Performance.

Continue

To see how the playhead helps you gauge the load on your processor, let's play the song SciFiShow in the Timeline.

1   Choose File > Open and select **9-1 SciFiShow** from the Lesson_09 folder.

2   Press the Home key to move the playhead to the beginning of the song, if it is not there already.

3   Play the song.

4   Watch the playhead change colors when you get to the middle of the song, where there are more Software Instrument regions.

Notice how the playhead changes to yellow in the 8th measure, when it goes from playing two Software Instrument tracks to three. When the processor must mix four to five Software Instrument tracks, around measure 11, it turns dark orange to red, depending on your processor.

5   Mute the two lowest tracks in the Timeline and play the song again.

Notice that the demands on the processor are less when you mute several tracks. That is because muting a track not only silences it, but also keeps it from being processed by the CPU. This in turn increases the processor's performance on the unmuted tracks.

6   Unmute the lower two tracks.

NOTE ▶ Muting tracks keeps them from being processed by the CPU. Soloing tracks, on the other hand, silences all the other tracks but does not stop the CPU from processing these tracks.

Now you know how to identify changes in the processor load by the color of the playhead. Remember, the next time your playhead turns red and you overload your processor, you can lighten the processor load by muting tracks, turning off effects, or deleting unnecessary tracks from the Timeline.

Setting GarageBand Preferences to Help Minimize Processor Load

There are several options in GarageBand's preferences that can also help mini-mize the load on your processor. Let's take a look at some of these options.

1 Choose GarageBand > Preferences to open the General Preferences window.

2 Click the Audio/MIDI button to view the Audio/MIDI pane.

3 Check the "Optimize for" section to see which option you have selected.

The option "Maximum number of simultaneous tracks" is recommended for slower computers. If your processor is overloading, or the playhead turns red often while playing your song, you may wish to click this option. If you are running a fast computer and haven't had any issues with performance, select "Minimum delay when playing instruments live."

NOTE ▶ The "Minimum delay" option is recommended to help reduce latency (delay) between when you play your Real Instrument and when you hear the sound. If you have a slower computer, you should use the "Minimum delay" option only while you are recording the Real Instrument tracks.

You can also lower the number of tracks and voices per instrument in the Advanced pane of the General Preferences window.

4   Click the Advanced tab at the top of the General Preferences window to view the Advanced pane.

There are three pop-up menus in the Advanced pane. The top two pop-up menus allow you to raise or lower the number of Real Instrument and Software Instrument tracks that you can play in real time.

5   Click the Real Instrument Tracks pop-up to see the minimum and maximum number of Real Instrument tracks available.

Notice that the minimum number is 8 and the maximum number is 255.

6   Click the Software Instrument Tracks pop-up to see the minimum and maximum number of Software Instrument tracks available.

Notice that the minimum number is 8 and the maximum number is 64. Software Instrument tracks are more processor-intensive than Real Instrument tracks, so the maximum is lower.

7   Click the "Voices per instrument" pop-up to view the minimum and maximum voices per instrument.

Voices refer to the number of Software Instrument notes that can be played at one time. The more Software Instrument notes (voices) you play at once, the more processor-intensive it is to play that region. The number is different for sampled instruments (including piano, drum, brass, bass, guitar, and woodwind instruments) than for other instruments (organ, electric piano, synthesizers, and clavinet instruments.) GarageBand automatically chooses the appropriate number for your computer's CPU. This is the Automatic setting in the pop-up menu.

8   Change all three pop-up menus to Automatic, if they are not already set that way.

If you are having trouble playing your Timeline, you can try setting the number of tracks in the pop-up menus to the lowest number. If you set the number of tracks higher than your computer can support, this can affect your computer's performance.

Exporting from GarageBand to iTunes and Back

If you are working with a slower computer, you have another option: you can mix down your basic tracks by exporting the song to iTunes, and then bring the mixed file back into GarageBand.

In the good ol' days of working with a 4-track recorder, you often needed to mix down your basic tracks to one track in order to add additional tracks to the song. By mixing down your tracks in GarageBand, you are essentially doing the same thing. Your mixed-down region from iTunes will demand a fraction of the processor load required by the original separate tracks.

This following exercise assumes that you are building a song with a lot of tracks, and you don't have the CPU to support it. You'll start mixing down the basic tracks (drums, percussion, bass, and rhythm tracks). Then you'll add additional instruments to these mixed-down tracks in the Timeline. Finally, you'll drag the mixed down files from iTunes back to the GarageBand Timeline in order to add more tracks and finish the song.

Let's start by setting the export preferences and mixing down the current song.

1   Choose GarageBand > Preferences to open the General Preferences window if it is not already open.

2   Click the Export button to open the Export pane.

3 Type *Mixdown Tracks* in the iTunes Playlist field, and press Return.

The Composer Name and Album Name should still be set from Lesson 8.

4 Close the Export Preferences window.

5 Create a cycle region from the beginning of the song to the 27th measure.

This will allow you to mix the entire song, plus the residual notes that sustain beyond the last region.

6 Choose File > Export to iTunes to export the project **9-1 SciFiShow** to iTunes.

GarageBand exports a mixed-down version of the project and places it in a new playlist in iTunes.

Now let's open a new project and add the mixed-down song from iTunes to the project.

7 Choose File > New to create a new project.

You don't need to save the other version of the song, so click Don't Save to the original version,

8 Name the new project *SciFiShow 2* and create it in your GarageBand Songs folder.

This song uses the default GarageBand settings, so you don't need to change any of the default settings for the new project.

The new project opens in GarageBand.

9 Press Cmd-Delete to delete the Grand Piano track from the new project.

Next, you'll need to move the GarageBand window so you can also see the iTunes window at the same time.

10 Click-drag the GarageBand window header (top of the window) down to move it to the lower half of your computer screen.

You should see the open iTunes window on the Desktop. If you don't see iTunes, click the iTunes icon in your Dock to open iTunes.

You'll also need to resize the iTunes window.

11 Click-drag the lower-right corner of the iTunes window upward until iTunes is only on the top half of your computer screen.

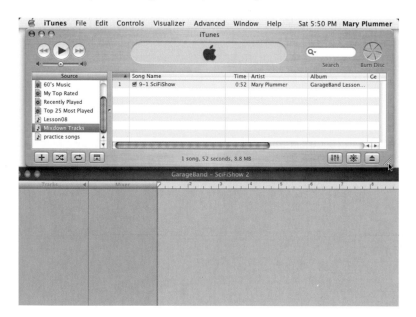

12 Click the Mixdown Tracks playlist in the iTunes Source list.

The mixed version of **9-1 SciFiShow** appears in the song list.

To add the mixed version of the song to GarageBand, all you need to do is click-drag the song from the playlist to the Timeline.

13 Click-drag the **9-1 SciFiShow** song from iTunes to the top left (1st measure) of the GarageBand Timeline.

A green circle with a plus (+) appears, indicating that you are adding a file to the Timeline.

14 Release the mouse to add the mixed song to the Timeline.

The mixed song appears in the Timeline as a recorded Real Instrument region titled 9-1 SciFiShow.

NOTE ▶ The number after the name of the region refers to how many copies there are of that particular file. If the number has a decimal point, the number after the decimal represents that version of the specific copy.

15 Close iTunes.

You could now add additional regions and tracks to the mixed-down version of the song.

The mixed-down version of the song is stored in the iTunes Library.

16 Press Cmd-S to save the project.

There you have it. If you play the mixed-down version of the song, the play-head remains white, indicating that the processor load is minimal.

This technique is terrific if you are working with a slower computer or a laptop and you want to build a song that requires a lot of CPU to play in the Timeline.

Remember, you can always go back to the original song to make adjustments to the basic tracks if you need to. Then you can mix them down again by exporting to iTunes.

Tips for Mixing Down Tracks to iTunes

- Be sure to mix the tracks before you export to iTunes. You won't be able to adjust the volume or panning levels of the individual tracks once they have been mixed down to one stereo file in iTunes.

- Export the basic tracks that don't need a lot of finessing once you've added them to the Timeline. If you have a track that you aren't sure about, don't include it with the mixdown to iTunes because if you change your mind, you'll have to export the tracks again.

- Change the name of the song after you mix down the tracks so you don't get confused about which version of the song you are working on.

- When you export a song to iTunes, any tracks that have been muted will not be included in the mixdown.

- If you have a song with dozens of tracks, you may want to mix down the tracks by instrument types. For example, export all of the percussion and drums tracks together. Then export the rhythm tracks. Finally, export the supporting tracks. Then drag all of the exported files from iTunes into a new project.

- Make sure you are recording and building your songs at the right tempo for the project. You won't be able to change tempos after you record or export the mixed-down tracks. Remember, if the project and the imported recording file are different tempos, they will not play in time, and as a result, they will sound awkward.

Adding an MP3 File to the Timeline

You can add files that are in AIFF, WAV, or MP3 format to the Timeline. If you add an MP3 file to the Timeline, GarageBand will automatically convert the MP3 file to AIFF format and make it a Real Instrument region.

Let's try adding an MP3 file to the current GarageBand project. This time we'll drag the song from the iTunes Library using the Finder.

1   Click the Finder icon in your Dock, or double-click your hard drive icon to open the Finder.

2   Click the Music tab in the Finder.

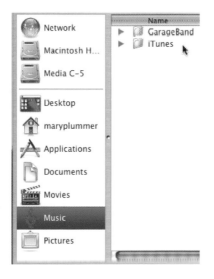

You'll see the GarageBand and the iTunes folders. The GarageBand folder is the default location for saved projects.

NOTE ► Keep in mind that every time you save a song with recorded Real Instrument regions or export a song to iTunes, it is going to require disk space. If you plan to do a lot of recording or exporting to iTunes, it's a good idea to save your GarageBand songs and iTunes Library to a hard drive that is separate from your boot drive. This will keep your boot drive from filling up with music files.

3   Open your iTunes folder, navigate to your GarageBand Lessons Album, and open the Lessons Album folder to reveal your exported songs.

4   Click-drag the lower-right corner of the Finder window so it fits in the upper half of your computer screen.

You should be able to see both windows at the same time.

5   Scroll through the songs in the GarageBand Lessons Album and locate the **Eyewitness.mp3** file you created in Lesson 8.

6   Click-drag the **Eyewitness.mp3** file from the Finder to the Timeline, below the first track. Release the mouse.

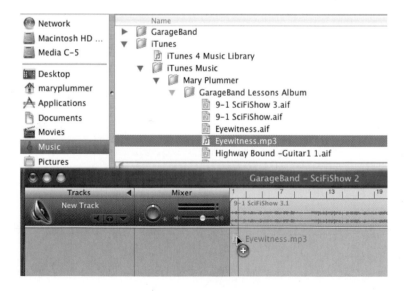

A converting window appears, which shows that GarageBand is converting the file from MP3 to AIFF. A new track appears in the Timeline with the converted **Eyewitness** song as a Real Instrument region.

You can use this technique to add MP3 files to your GarageBand projects. When you save your song, any files you have added to the song will be saved with the GarageBand project.

Now that you know how to add files to your projects, let's look at how Real Instrument recordings are stored on your computer. Keep your GarageBand window on the lower half of your screen and the Finder on the upper half of your screen for the next exercise.

Reusing Your Real Instrument Recordings

Have you ever wondered how Real Instrument recordings are stored on your computer? GarageBand stores all of the Real Instrument recordings in a media folder inside of your project. Understanding how your Real Instrument recordings are stored will enable you to find the recording files and reuse them in other projects.

In this exercise, you'll locate the Real Instrument recordings for the song **Eyewitness**, preview the recording files in the Finder, and then add the female vocal recording to the current GarageBand project.

First, let's change the Finder to Column view and locate the Lessons folder on you computer.

1   Click the Column View button in the Finder to change the Finder to Column view.

2   Locate and click your Lessons folder for this book to show the contents in the next column.

3 Click the Lesson_02 folder to show the Lesson_02 files in the next column.

Notice that there are four GarageBand projects.

OK, so you found the projects. Where are the Media folders for the projects? The Media folders are hidden within the Package Contents of each file. Let's locate and open the Media folder for the **2-2 Eyewitness Finished** project.

4 Ctrl-click the project **2-2 Eyewitness Finished** to open the contextual menu.

5 Choose Show Package Contents from the contextual menu.

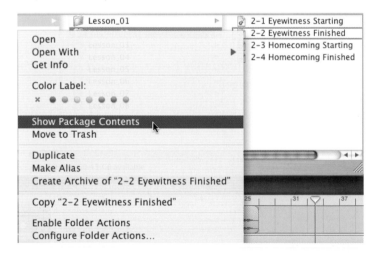

A new window opens that shows the contents of the **2-2 Eyewitness Finished** project. The contents include the project data and a Media folder.

6 Click the Column View button to view the new window as columns.

Now that you have located the Media folder and changed the view to columns, you can preview the recordings directly in the Finder. Remember, your goal is to locate the female vocal recording.

7 Click the Media folder to reveal the contents in the next column.

Five different recording files appear in the right column.

These recordings are numbered according to the recorded take that was saved in the finished project. The lowest recording number is 7, which means I recorded 6 takes that I didn't keep. The highest number is 37, which means that I recorded at least 37 different Real Instrument regions when I was creating this song. As you see, I kept only 5.

Let's preview the different takes to find the female vocal recording that I created with my synthesizer.

NOTE ▶ This was not an actual recording of a female voice. However, the region in the song **Eyewitness** was called Basic Famale Vocal because that was the GarageBand effects preset I used.

To preview the recording, click the recording to open it in the Preview column.

8 Click Recording#07.aif to open the file in the Preview column.

Recording#07.aif opens in the Preview window.

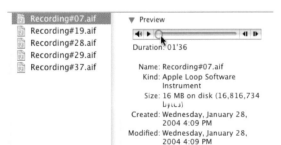

9   Click the Play button in the Preview window to preview (listen to) the file.

You may not hear audio right away, depending on when that actual sound starts after the beginning of the recording. Remember, Real Instrument recordings begin at the playhead position when you click Record, not when you play the first note.

Take a moment to preview the other recordings. You can press the down arrow to move down to the next recording.

Now that you've located the female vocal recording (Recording#07), you can add it to the current GarageBand project.

10   Click-drag the top of the Media window and drag it upward to the top of the screen, so you can see the GarageBand window.

You may need to resize the Media window to move it out of the way.

11   Click-drag Recording#07.aif from the Media window to the GarageBand window and release it below the lowest track in the Timeline.

A new track appears with Recording#07.1 as the name. "07.1" means that it is the first copy of the 07 file.

12   Press Cmd-S to save the project with the new files.

When you save a project, all of the Real Instrument recorded regions, which are purple, are saved to the Media folder of that project.

Project Tasks

Take a moment to locate the **SciFiShow 2** project file in your Finder, show the Package Contents, and view the contents of the Media folder.

1   Locate your GarageBand Songs folder.

2   Open the GarageBand Songs folder and Ctrl-click the **SciFiShow 2** project.

3   Choose Show Package Contents from the contextual menu.

4   Open the Media folder to view the recordings inside.

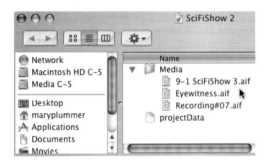

5   Close the Media folder, but keep the Finder open and the GarageBand window as is.

Now you know how to locate and reuse recordings from one song to another.

Archiving Your Recordings

You can archive your recordings by saving all of your best takes in one project. You'll then have your best recordings available to reuse for new projects.

The specific steps for archiving are simple. When you first record a project, save all of the best takes to that project and add the word "recordings" to the name of the project—for example, Eyewitness Recordings. Save this version of the song, then choose File > Save As and save the song again with just the song name (Eyewitness). For this version, you'll delete everything except the takes you want to use for the actual song. Resave the song when you finish deleting the unwanted recordings. The result will be two versions of your song—one version with all of the best recordings archived, and the other with just the best takes that you actually use in the finished song.

After the song is completed, you can always delete the recordings version of the song if you want to clear some disk space and don't think you'll ever need the other takes again.

Adding Loops to GarageBand

As you know, GarageBand comes with over 1,000 Apple Loops. You can add additional loops to GarageBand by dragging them to the Loop Browser.

Before you add loops, it's a good idea to know where the Apple Loops for GarageBand are stored and how they are organized. In the next series of exercises, you will locate the Apple Loops Library, add new loops through the Loop Browser, and search for them in the browser.

Preparing the Project

Before you begin the next exercise, let's open the next project for Lesson 9.

1 Open **9-2 Adding Loops** from the Lesson_09 folder.

   This project contains four Real Instrument recordings that I recorded in GarageBand and then turned into Apple Loops using the Soundtrack Loop Utility. The Soundtrack Loop Utility is companion software that comes with the Apple Soundtrack application.

2 Click the Loop Browser button to open the Loop Browser, if it is not already open.

3 Resize the GarageBand window again so that it fits in the lower half of the screen.

4 Open the Finder, if it is not already open, and resize it to fit in the upper half of your screen.

Exploring the Apple Loops Folder

When you originally installed GarageBand, an index was created for all the Apple Loops included with the program. The Loop Browser uses this index to find loops and show them in the results list.

Let's take a brief field trip to the Library to locate the Apple Loops that were originally installed with GarageBand.

1   Click the Column View button in the Finder to view your Finder in Column view, if it is not already.

2   Click to select the following in the Finder: Macintosh Hard Drive > Library > Application Support > GarageBand.

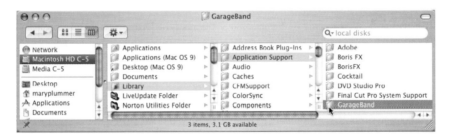

When you click GarageBand, you will reveal the three folders that were included with your original GarageBand installation: Apple Loops, Apple Loops Index, and Instrument Library.

Your Apple Loops are stored in the folder called Apple Loops. The Apple Loops index, stored in the Apple Loops Index folder, is updated each time you add loops to the Loop Browser. The Instrument Library folder is where the Software Instruments and effects are stored.

Let's take a look inside the Apple Loops folder.

3   Click to select the following: Apple Loops > Apple Loops for GarageBand.

When you click the Apple Loops for GarageBand folder, you reveal all of the Apple Loops that came with GarageBand.

You can scroll down through the different loops, and even preview them in the Preview column.

4   Click the first loop 70s Ballad Drums 01.aif to open it in the Preview column.

5   Click the Play button to listen to the loop.

When you preview a loop in the Finder, you will hear it in its native key and tempo. If you preview the same loop in the Loop Browser, it will always conform to the project key and tempo.

Now that you know where the loops are stored, let's add some to your collection.

To add loops to your collection, you don't drag them to the Apple Loops folder. Instead, you drag them to the Loop Browser in GarageBand.

Adding Loops to the Loop Browser

Whenever you add additional loops to your collection through the Loop Browser, they will be added to the index. To add loops, you simply drag and drop the individual loops—or folder of loops—to the Loop Browser.

> **NOTE ▶** You can add loops from other music software to the Loop Browser. If the loops are not Apple Loops, it is possible that they will not appear in the Loop Browser after they have been indexed. If that is the case, you may need to drag them into a song from the Finder. Loops that are dragged into the Timeline from the Finder will not appear in the Loop Browser. If they don't appear in the Loop Browser, you can still use them in the Timeline. You just won't be able to search for them using the Loop Browser keyword buttons or columns.

Let's drag a folder of loops to the Loop Browser to add them to your loop collection.

1   Locate your Lessons folder in the Finder.

2   Click the Lesson_09 folder to open it and select the Lesson_09 New Loops folder to reveal the contents.

3   Click the GarageBand window to make it active.

4   Click-drag the Lesson_09 New Loops folder from the Finder to the Loop Browser in the GarageBand window.

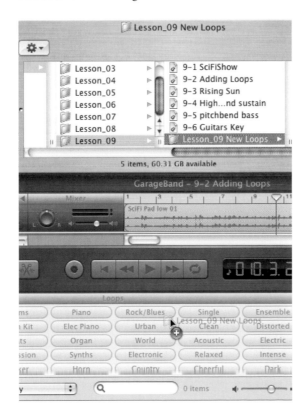

A green circle with a plus (+) appears, indicating that you are adding loops to the Loop Browser.

5   Release the mouse to add the loops.

A progress window appears, which shows that the new loops are being imported.

Let's search for the new SciFi Pad Low 01 and SciFi Pad 02 loops in the Loop Browser.

6   Click the Electronic button in the Loop Browser.

7   Scroll through the results to find the SciFi Pad loops.

8   Click the SciFi Pad 02 loop to preview it in the browser.

Project Tasks

Now that you know how to add loops to GarageBand through the Loop Browser, let's locate the new loops in the Finder.

1   Click your Macintosh hard drive in the Finder, and then choose the following: Library > Application Support > GarageBand Apple Loops.

2   Click the Lesson_09 New Loops folder in the Apple Loops folder to see the new imported loops.

3 Click the GarageBand window to make it active, and press Cmd-S to save your project.

As you can see, it is very easy to add loops to your collection through the Loop Browser.

If you install the Jam Pack expansion for GarageBand, it comes with over 2,000 new Apple Loops. You'll learn more about working with the Jam Pack in Appendix A.

Adding Loops from Other Applications

If you like working with loops, you can easily find tens of thousands of loops that will work with GarageBand. Keep in mind that these loops take space on the hard drive.

If you are using another music application like Soundtrack on the same computer, be careful not to double up your loops. Since Soundtrack and GarageBand can use the same Apple Loops, you can drag the entire Apple Loops folder installed with Soundtrack to the GarageBand Loop Browser to index them and also add them to GarageBand's Apple Loops folder in the Finder. This process will make a copy of all the new loops. Open Soundtrack and index the GarageBand Apple Loops folder in the Finder. Then you can delete the duplicate Apple Loops that were installed with Soundtrack.

Soundtrack can index loops located anywhere on the hard drive, GarageBand can only index loops that are added through the Loop Browser and automatically placed in GarageBand's Apple Loops folder.

> **MORE INFO** ▶ *For more information on indexing and moving the Soundtrack loop library, you can read the Soundtrack documentation or the book* Apple Pro Training Series: Soundtrack.

Working with Multiple Control Points in the Timeline

In Lesson 7, you added control points to the Volume curve to dynamically change the volume of a track or song. Adjusting control points can be a tedious job, especially if you have a lot of points that you need to raise or lower one at a time. Let's look at a few techniques to select a group of control points and move them together.

1   Open **9-1 SciFiShow** located in Lesson_09 in your Lessons folder.

2   Move the playhead to the beginning of the 10th measure.

3   Play the song from the 10th to the 15th measure and listen to the volume level of the Falling Star track.

   I think the Falling Star track sounds too low (quiet) in the mix.

4   Click the Volume slider on the Falling Star track and try to raise the volume of the track.

   The Volume slider doesn't respond, which means the track has active control points in the Volume curve.

5   Press A to show the Volume curve for the selected track.

   Notice the control points that have already been placed on the Falling Star Volume curve. These points were set to fade in and out the first region and also fade in the second region.

Now that you know that the track is too low in the mix, how do you go about raising the volume? You could click and drag each individual control point. However, your goal is to raise all of the control points at one time, while maintaining the relative position of each point in the Volume curve. To do this, you will need to select all of the points at one time.

One method of selecting a group of control points is to click-drag the pointer along the Volume curve in the empty space above or below the control points until they are all selected. Let's try it.

6   Click-drag your pointer from right to left starting above the last control point in the Falling Star Volume curve. Drag the pointer toward the left all the way to the beginning of the track to select all of the points, including the first control point. Release the mouse.

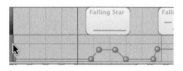

The Volume curve area turns green as you click-drag the pointer. When you release the mouse, all the points within the selected area are outlined with a darker green color to show that they have been selected.

To raise the relative volume of all of the points at one time, simply click-drag one of the control points upward. Since your goal is to raise the highest control points to the default volume level, let's click-drag one of the highest points to the gray line that marks the default level.

7   Click-drag the last control point in the track to the gray line that marks the default volume level.

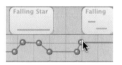

All of the points move at the same time, yet maintain their relative position to one another in the Volume curve.

Now let's lower just the four lowest control points to the lowest position on the Volume curve. To do that, you will first need to deselect the selected points.

8   Click anywhere in the empty Volume curve area to deselect the control points.

Click-dragging works great to select control points that are next to one another. What if you want to select random control points that aren't contiguous? You can select multiple, noncontiguous control points by Shift-clicking only the points you want.

9 Shift-click the four lowest points in the Volume curve. (Don't forget the first point in the track.)

The points look larger and are outlined with a darker color when they have been selected.

10 Click-drag one of the selected points downward to the lowest position on the Volume curve.

All four of the selected points move in unison to the lowest position.

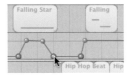

11 Listen to the song again from the 10th to the 17th measures.

Your Volume curve looks great but doesn't sound very good. I liked the track better without any control points. Fortunately, GarageBand makes it really easy to change your mind. To delete control points, you simply select them all and press Delete.

And what's the easiest way to select all of the control points on a track? You can select all of the control points in a track by clicking the Volume curve's header.

12 Click the Volume curve header on the Falling Star track to select all the control points.

Now you can delete them by pressing the Delete key.

13 Press Delete to delete all of the control points in the track.

14 Click the Track Volume box to turn off the Volume curve and return control of the track to the Volume slider.

> **NOTE ▶** You do not have to delete control points to turn off the Volume curve. Any time you uncheck the Track Volume box, the Volume curve becomes inactive and the Volume slider controls the track. Likewise, if you want to override the Volume slider with the Volume curve, simply check the Track Volume box.

15 Press A to hide the Volume curve, or click the triangle next to the Solo button on the track header.

16 Option-click the Volume slider to return it to the default position.

Remember:

- You can Shift-click to select multiple, noncontiguous control points.
- You can click-drag to select control points that are next to one another.
- You can click the Volume curve's header to select all the control points in the track at one time.

Advanced Track Editor Techniques

In the next series of exercises, you'll learn some advanced techniques for working with regions in the Track Editor. You'll split a region inside the Track Editor, and then loop and extend the split region to finish the song.

Preparing the Project

Before you begin the next exercise, let's do a little housekeeping and move the GarageBand window back into the full-screen position.

> **NOTE ▶** If you open another project in GarageBand, the new project window will automatically fit the full screen.

1 Click the green Zoom button in the upper-left corner of the GarageBand window to zoom the window to fit the screen.

2   Choose File > Open and open the project **9-3 Track Editor** from the Lesson_09 folder.

If you get a dialog box asking if you want to save the project, click Save to keep your changes.

The project opens with four guitar tracks. The lower tracks have been muted because they are the finished tracks. You'll be working with the top two tracks.

Splitting a Real Instrument Region in the Track Editor

In Lesson 4, you learned about recording, editing, and looping Real Instrument recorded regions. In this exercise, you'll take that knowledge to the next level. Instead of simply trimming the ends of a recording so they make a nice loop, you'll actually create a loop from within a recorded region.

This technique is very useful for songs with repetitive parts. It also allows you to extend the length of a song by extending a part by a few measures.

For this exercise, you'll be working with two Real Instrument guitar recordings of the traditional song "House of the Rising Sun." The two guitar parts for this project were performed by my friend William Whitacre.

> **TIP** ▶ Many traditional songs such as "House of the Rising Sun" are great for recording because they are in the public domain. When you use the basic melody and lyrics of a public domain composition, and not someone else's arrangement, you can record your own version without rights clearance issues. This tip is from entertainment attorney and music publisher William L. Whitacre.

Before you start editing the tracks, let's save the project to your GarageBand Songs folder.

1   Press Cmd-Shift-S to open the Save As window.

2   Choose your GarageBand Songs folder from the Where pop-up menu and click Save.

3   Play the tracks in the Timeline to hear the two different guitar parts played at the same time.

4   Drag the playhead to the end of the longest region in the second track to determine the length of the song in the Time Display.

The Time Display is currently set to actual time. As you see, the song ends at 1:44, which is 1 minute and 44 seconds.

Your goal in this exercise is to extend the song so that it lasts for at least two minutes. To do this, you'll select a section of the song in the Track Editor that you want to repeat, split the selected section, and then loop it.

Let's start with the top guitar track.

5   Double-click the Barre Rhythm track region in the top track to open that region in the Track Editor.

6   Press S to solo the selected track, then click the musical note button in the lower-left corner of the Time Display to change the display to musical time.

7   Click drag the Track Editor's Zoom slider all the way to the left (if it's not already there).

The section of the region you will select is from the 4th beat of the 12th measure to the 4th beat of the 21st measure. To select part of a region in the Track Editor, you need to use the crosshair.

8   Click-drag the scroller at the bottom of the Track Editor until you see the 22nd measure.

9   Movie the playhead to the 4th beat in the 21st measure on the Track Editor's Beat Ruler.

10   Move your pointer to the lower portion of the playhead below the waveform.

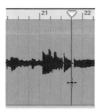

The pointer becomes a crosshair. If you don't see a crosshair, click your mouse once in the Track Editor at the playhead position.

11 Click-drag the crosshair toward the left starting at the 4th beat of the 21st measure and ending at the 4th beat of the 12th measure.

The selected section of the region turns blue as you drag the crosshair.

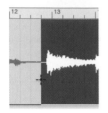

12 Click the blue selected section of the region in the Track Editor to split the region.

Notice the region is now split in the Timeline and selected for easy delete or Option-drag maneuvers.

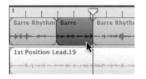

13 Press the down arrow to select the second track in the Timeline.

14 Press S to solo the second track along with the first.

15 Click the 1st Position Lead region in the second track to open it in the Track Editor.

16 Repeat steps 9 through 12 to split the second track the same as the first.

Now that you've split both tracks, it's time to loop the region in the middle to extend the song.

17 Click the last region on the first track to select the last half of the song.

18 Shift-click the last region on the second track to select it along with the first.

19 Click-drag either of the selected regions toward the right (around the 41st measure) to move them out of the way.

20 Click-drag the upper-right corner of the middle region on the top track and extend it by one full loop segment.

The new looped segment should end on the 4th beat of the 30th measure.

21 Press Ctrl–right arrow to zoom in to the extended loop so you can see where it ends.

If you see a small loop segment at the end, click-drag the upper-right corner to the left until it ends on the 4th beat of the 30th measure.

In the next exercise, you'll see how to put the pieces back together to finish the song.

Moving Regions in the Track Editor

Now it's time to move the last region on the top track back into position. The best way to do this is in the Track Editor.

First, you'll need to move the last region a little closer in the Timeline.

1 Click-drag the last region in the top track toward the left until it starts around the 32nd measure.

2 Move the scroller in the Track Editor until you can see the end of the looped region and the beginning of the last region.

3 Move your pointer over the last region in the Track Editor above the waveform to see a pointer with arrows pointing left and right.

This allows you to click and move the region in the Track Editor.

4   Click-drag and snap the region into position next to the looped region at
    the 4th beat of the 30th measure.

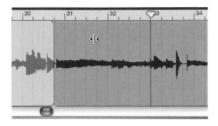

NOTE ▶ If you are editing and moving regions in the Track Editor and
are having difficulty moving things precisely because of snapping, zoom
into the Track Editor with the Track Editor's Zoom slider for more refined
movement. Remember, you should try to keep snapping on while editing
and moving regions so you don't accidentally move them off beat.

Duplicating a Loop to Extend the Recording

You'll finish the second track a little differently than the first. Instead of extending the middle region as a loop, you'll duplicate the loop. By duplicating the
loop, you'll be able to extend the region to reveal the rest of the recording. You
cannot extend a looped region beyond the length of the original loop segment.

1   Click the last region in the second track to select that region.

2   Press Delete to delete the last half of the song in the second track.

3   Click-drag the lower-right corner of the second region in the second track
    to resize the region so that it matches the end of the region in the first track.

    Notice that you can only extend the looped region to the same size or
    smaller than the starting region. You can't resize the region to reveal any of
    the original recording that is not included in the current region.

    Remember, to extend a region as a loop, you grab the upper-right corner,
    and to resize a region to make it longer or shorter, you drag the lower-
    right corner. Once a region has been extended as a loop, you will no
    longer be able to resize the region in the lower-right corner.

4 Press Cmd-Z to undo the loop extension.

Let's duplicate the region instead.

5 Option-drag the region to the right and release the duplicate in the empty
track space to the right of the original region (around the 25th measure).

6 Double-click the new duplicate region to open it in the Track Editor.

7 Click-drag the duplicate loop to the left in the Track Editor until it snaps
into position at the end of the other region (4th beat of the 21st measure).

8 Click-drag the lower-right corner of the new duplicate region toward the
right to resize the region and reveal the rest of the original recording.

You may need to zoom out of the Timeline to extend the full region.

It's olay if the two guitar parts end at slightly different times. Since the
original recorded regions were different lengths, they will still be different
after they are edited.

9 Press Cmd-E to close the Track Editor.

10 Unsolo the top two tracks (the lower two tracks should be muted).

11 Change the Time Display to actual time.

12 Listen to the new extended version of the song and notice that it ends
right around 2 minutes.

13 Press Cmd-S to save the project.

This type of musical surgery in the Track Editor takes a little practice and
patience, but it's an extremely useful skill to master when you need to extend
or loop portions of a Real Instrument region.

Joining Noncontiguous Real Instrument Regions

Now that you know how to edit a Real Instrument region, let's look at an
advanced technique for joining noncontiguous Real Instrument regions.

Why would you want to join noncontiguous Real Instrument regions? Sometimes you edit a recording, as you did in the previous exercise, and you want to keep the edited track as one region to make it easier to move to another project and archive. Also, if you plan to duplicate a region on another track, it's much easier to do so if you have to move only one longer region instead of many shorter edited regions.

When you join regions to create a new file, the original recordings and the new merged file will be stored together in the project's Media folder.

Let's use this technique to select and join the edited tracks from the previous exercise.

1   Click the track header for the top track to select all the regions in that track.

2   Choose Edit > Join Selected or press Cmd-J to join all of the regions into one merged file.

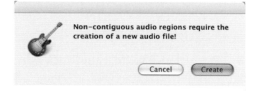

Non-contiguous audio regions require the creation of a new audio file!

Cancel   Create

A dialog box appears to warn that a new file will be created.

3   Click the Create button to create a new file in the project Media folder.

The new file consists of the newly joined regions.

Barre Rhythm Track.3 merged

All of the separate regions in the track have been merged into one new region. Notice the word "merged" after the track name.

The new merged file will be added to the recording files in the project's Package Contents. Let's take a look.

4   Press Cmd-S to save the new version of the project.

5   Open the Finder from the Dock and locate the project file **9-3 Track Editor**.

6   Ctrl-click the project file **9-3 Track Editor** in the Finder and choose Show Package Contents from the contextual menu.

7   Open the Media folder to reveal the new merged file within the folder.

This technique can be very useful for archiving an edited Real Instrument recording, or for doubling a track that consists of numerous shorter edited regions.

Exploring Editing Controller Information in a Software Instrument Region

Many keyboards include controls for pitch bend and modulation as well as a port to connect a sustain pedal. The Pitch Bend and Modulation controls are usually wheels that are placed on the far left of the keyboard controls. These controls are used to add expression and character to your music, and you can view and edit the movements of these controls in the Track Editor.

The editing controller information in the Track Editor looks like a series of lines with control points. You can click-drag control points up or down to change their value, or move them left and right to change when they occur. To add a new control point, click the line, or Cmd-click an empty area to draw a new line. To delete a point, click the control point to select it, and then press the Delete key.

In the next two exercises, you'll look at the advanced editing controller information for sustain and pitch bend in the Track Editor.

Viewing Sustain in the Track Editor

A sustain pedal has only two options: it's either on (pressed) or off (not pressed). When you play a note and press the pedal, the note will sustain after you stop pressing the note. If you press a note when the sustain pedal is not pressed, the note will end when you release the note on the keyboard. You can play more than one note while holding the sustain pedal.

Let's take a look at the sustain that was recorded with the strings track in the song Highway Bound.

1   Choose File > Open and select **9-4 Sustain** from the Lesson_09 folder.

The song **9-4 Sustain** is a variation of the song Highway Bound.

2   Double-click the Hollywood Strings region in the top track to open that region in the Track Editor.

3   Locate the Display pop-up menu in the Advanced section of the Track Editor.

4   Click the Display pop-up menu and choose Sustain to view the Sustain controller movement in the Track Editor.

5   Click-drag the Track Editor's Zoom slider to the far left to zoom all the way out in the Track Editor.

6   Press S to solo the selected track.

7   Play the track and watch the playhead move in the Track Editor across the Sustain controls.

The Sustain controls in the Track Editor look like a series of dots and lines. These dots and lines form blocks that represent the sustain used as the song was recorded.

Sustain pedal pressed (on)   Sustain pedal released (off)

If you look at the Sustain controller information, you will see a line near the bottom that is marked 0 and another line near the top that is marked 1. The lower line (0) represents the pedal in the off position, and the upper line (1) represents the pedal in the on position. If the pedal is held down for most of the song, as it was in this recording, you will see a series of blocks that represent a note or group of notes that are played and sustain until they end. When a new note or group of notes is played while the pedal is held down (on position), a new block forms. If the pedal is released, you will see a space between the blocks with a straight horizontal line at the off (0) position line.

Editing Sustain Controller Movement

Now that you've seen the Sustain controller movement, you can actually edit it to make a note sustain longer or shorter. Your goal in this exercise is to extend the sustain for the last note in the first half of the song.

1   Move the scroller at the bottom of the Track Editor to view the song from the 16th to the 21st measures.

2   Click the Beat Ruler in the Track Editor at the beginning of the 16th measure.

3   Play the Timeline from the 16th to the 20th measure.

    As you listen, pay close attention the last two notes around the 18th measure. See if you can detect when the sustain ends for those notes.

    The sustain ends at the 19th measure. From the 19th measure to the 2nd beat of the 20th measure, the sustain block in the Track Editor is actually a block without any notes played. Then there's a blank space to show that the sustain pedal was released (not pressed).

    Let's shorten the silent area, where the sustain was released, and extend the section with the notes to sustain their sound a little longer.

4 Click the upper-right control point on the sustain block—the one that ends at the 19th measure—and drag it to the 3rd beat of the 19th measure (halfway between the 19th and 20th measures).

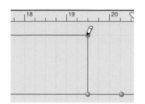

The sustain block to the right of the 19th measure disappears to make room for the extended sustain.

NOTE ▶ The Cmd key changes the pointer to a pencil. However, both the pointer and the pencil do the same thing in this example. You can use either one.

5 Play the section of the song again from the 16th to the 20th measures and listen to the new extended sustain on the last notes.

The notes now sustain until the 3rd beat of the 19th measure, exactly where you set the Sustain controls.

6 Press Cmd-S to save your project.

Viewing Pitch Bend Controls

Now let's take a look at the Pitch Bend controls. The Pitch Bend controller on a keyboard allows you to bend a note up one step or down one step from the original note. You can see an example of the Pitch Bend controls in the project **9-5 Pitch Bend**.

1 Choose File > Open and select **9-5 Pitch Bend** from the Lesson_09 folder.

This project contains two Fretless Bass Software Instrument recordings. Both were recorded from the same keyboard. In the first track, I played each note separately. In the second track, I used the Pitch Bend controller on the keyboard to bend the notes in order to emulate the sound of a fretless bass.

The Track Editor should be open so you can view the Pitch Bend controller movement. If the Track Editor is not open, press Cmd-E to open the Track Editor and choose Pitchbend from the Display pop-up menu.

2   Click the Solo button on the top track (if it is not already soloed) to isolate this track.

3   Play the track to hear the bass recording without pitch bend.

Notice the Track Editor shows no movement or changes for pitch.

4   Press S to unsolo the top track.

5   Press the down arrow to select the lower track.

6   Press S to solo the lower track.

Notice that the lower track shows a series of control points and lines indicating the change in pitch.

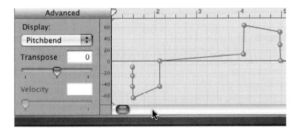

The center line is the actual note that is played. The section above the center line illustrates that the pitch of the original note was bent one step (one note) higher. The section below the center line illustrates that the pitch of the original note was bent one step (one note) lower.

7   Play the entire region on the second track and watch the Pitch Bend display in the Track Editor.

The diagonal lines that move from the center line to the note above or below the line indicate the actual movement of the Pitch Bend control on the keyboard.

You can click-drag the control points in the Pitch Bend display to change the timing of when a pitch change occurs and to change the bend in the pitch. The best way to get a feeling for pitch bending is to actually get in there and try it and hear the results.

8 Click-drag one of the control points around the beginning of the 4th measure downward toward the center line to hear the pitch of the note bend lower.

9 Experiment with bending the sound of the notes either one full note higher or lower.

10 Press Cmd-S to save your project.

The next time you record a Software Instrument region and use Pitch Bend or Sustain controls in your recording, you will know how to use these controls in the Track Editor.

Searching for Loops by Scale

The last advanced technique in this lesson is searching for loops that match the particular scale of your song.

As you know, loops will always change their key and tempo to match the project. Some instruments, like guitars, are usually played and recorded in either a major or minor scale. You don't have to be a music major to understand and recognize the difference. In fact, the important thing for GarageBand is just working with parts that sound good together. Major guitar parts usually sound good together, and minor guitar parts also sound good together. On the other hand, you generally don't want to mix major and minor guitar parts, at least not at the same time.

Let's open the project **9-6 Guitars Key** to hear the different guitar scales.

1 Choose File > Open and select **9-6 Guitars Key** from the Lesson_09 folder.

The first four tracks contain regions that match the scale in the track name. Let's start with the first track that uses loops recorded in the minor scale.

2   Click the Minor Guitar track to select the track.

3   Click Play to play the Minor Guitar track and listen to the loops.

Music played in the minor scale has a serious feel that is often used to evoke tension or drama.

4   Press S to unsolo the Minor Guitar track.

5   Press the down arrow to select the Major Guitar track, and then press S to solo the track.

6   Play the Major Guitar track to hear guitar loops that were recorded in the major scale.

Music played in the major scale has a happier, more positive feel and is often used for more upbeat, feel-good songs.

Changing the Scale Pop-Up in the Loop Browser

To limit your search for loops to a particular scale, you can change the Scale pop-up in the Loop Browser.

1   Press Cmd-L to open the Loop Browser.

2   Locate the Scale pop-up at the bottom left of the Loop Browser.

3   Click the Scale pop-up to view the different scale choices.

There are five different choices in the Scale pop-up: Any, Minor, Major, Neither, and Good For Both.

The default setting is Any scale, which you have been using on all of the songs you've created in this book.

4 Click the Guitars button in the Loop Browser and notice how many guitar choices there are in the results list.

There are 71 guitar loops included with GarageBand.

NOTE ▶ The GarageBand Jam Pack expansion adds over 100 new guitar loops to your collection. You'll learn more about Jam Pack in Appendix A.

5 Change the Scale pop-up to Minor and notice how many guitar loops match the minor scale.

There are 18 guitar loops included with GarageBand.

The major scale is more commonly used than the minor scale.

6 Change the Scale pop-up to Neither.

There are only five GarageBand guitar loops that fit neither scale. Let's take a moment to preview these loops to see what they sound like.

7 Click the first guitar loop in the results to listen to the loop.

8 Press the down arrow to listen to the next guitar loop. Repeat this process to hear all of the loops that fit neither scale.

How would you describe these loops? They aren't really upbeat, or serious. Perhaps you could call them extreme or unique.

9 Change the Scale pop-up again to Good For Both.

There are also five loops that fit the Good For Both scale selection.

10 Preview the different Good For Both loops in the results list.

How would you describe these loops? These really do sound good for both. They could go with a happy song, or a serious song.

If you're building a serious song using the minor scale, and you want the song to transition to the major scale, using a loop that is good for both would make a nice transition from one scale to the other.

Let's listen to a combination of different loops from different scales.

11 Unsolo the Major Guitar track.

12 Solo each of the lower four tracks.

Each of the lower four tracks contains one or more guitar loops that fit the scale in the track title.

13 Play all four tracks together.

As the tracks play, listen to the change in scale and the use of a loop that is good for both scales to transition from a major scale to a minor scale.

Project Tasks

Now it's your turn to combine guitar loops from different scale types. Delete the regions in the lower four tracks and build your own guitar song using mixed scale loops.

1 Change the Scale pop-up to change the scale of the guitar loops in the results list.

2 Combine several Major scale guitar loops on the Major tracks.

3 Combine several Minor scale guitar loops on the Minor track.

4 Use a Good For Both guitar loop as a transition between a Major and a Minor scale loop.

You've come to the end of the Advanced Techniques lesson. Now you should be ready for the most challenging composition or recording project.

Remember, the more you work with GarageBand, the easier it gets. So have fun, keep the music flowing, and don't forget to let your songs breathe.

What You've Learned

- You can monitor your computer processor by looking at the color of the playhead. The playhead changes from white to red to indicate the load on the CPU. White indicates the lowest demand on the processor, and red indicates the highest demand. If the playhead is red, you may be overloading the processor.

- If you are working with a slower processor, you can change the Audio/MIDI settings in GarageBand Preferences to optimize for better performance. You can also mute tracks, turn off effects, or delete unnecessary tracks. Another strategy is to lower the number of tracks and Real Instrument voices in the Advanced Preferences settings.

- You can mix down your tracks by exporting your project to iTunes and then dragging the mixed song from iTunes to a new project. Then you can add additional loops or tracks to the mixed-down version of the song from iTunes. This technique is useful if you are working with a slower computer. It's also useful for consolidating multiple tracks of the same type—drums and percussion, for example—into one Real Instrument track for easier mixing.

- You can drag AIFF, WAV, or MP3 format files to the Timeline from the Finder. If you add an MP3 file to the Timeline, GarageBand will convert it to AIFF. Files added to the project from the Finder are saved with the project as Real Instrument regions.

- Real Instrument recordings are stored in the Media folder for each project. The Media folder for a GarageBand project is located in the Package Contents of the project. You can drag a recording from a project's Media file to the Timeline to reuse the recording in another project. This technique will copy a Media file from one project's Package Contents to the Package Contents of another project.

- You can add additional loops to GarageBand by dragging the loops or folder of loops to the Loop Browser and releasing the mouse. When you add loops through the Loop Browser, they will automatically be indexed so you will be able to search for them in the Loop Browser. Loops that are added to GarageBand are placed in the GarageBand Apple Loops folder in the Application Support section of your Macintosh Library.

- You can select multiple consecutive control points by click-dragging across them in the Volume curve. To select multiple points that aren't next to each other, Shift-click each point you wish to select. Click the Volume curve's header to select all of the control points in an entire track.

- You can split a Real Instrument region in the Track Editor by click-dragging the region with the crosshair and then clicking the selected section of the region.

- You can join noncontiguous Real Instrument regions into one merged file by selecting the regions that you wish to join and choosing Edit > Join. This process will create a new merged file that will be stored in the project's Media folder.

- You can view and edit Sustain, Modulation, and Pitch Bend controls for Software Instrument regions in the Track Editor.

- You can change the Scale pop-up in the Loop Browser to find only loops that fit a particular scale set—Major, Minor, Neither, or Good for Both. The default setting for the Scale pop-up is Any, which means the browser will show all loops, regardless of the scale.

A

Lesson Files	Lesson > Lesson_09 > 9-3 Track Editor
Time	This lesson takes approximately 25 minutes to complete.
Goals	Work with some of the new Software Instruments
	Test some of the new guitar amp simulators
	Apply some of the new effects to a guitar track
	Test some of the new Apple Loops

Appendix **A**

Exploring the GarageBand Jam Pack Expansion

Now that you know how to create music with GarageBand, it's time to expand your musical horizons with Jam Pack. This expansion pack for GarageBand gives you thousands of new ways to enhance your music projects. Literally! Jam Pack is loaded with over 2,000 Apple Loops in a variety of instruments and genres, plus 100 additional GarageBand Software Instruments, 100 additional audio effects presets, and a whopping 15 new guitar amp settings.

Do you remember the first time you ever got to color with the "big box" of crayons? Not the little 8- or 10-pack, but the *big* box that had 14 different blues and colors like sienna, periwinkle, and tangerine. Well, this is the musical equivalent of the big box. In fact, the Jam Pack makes the big crayon box look like a colorful appetizer. So let's dive in and unpack the Jam Pack.

This appendix is designed more as show and tell, with suggested exercises for those of you who already own Jam Pack, and lots of temptation for those of you who don't.

Installing Jam Pack

To install Jam Pack, you simply insert the Install DVD, double-click the install DVD icon on your Desktop, then double-click the **GarageBand_Jam_Pack.pkg** icon and follow the onscreen instructions.

Before you install, remember that you need 3 GB of free disk space to install the GarageBand Jam Pack.

> **NOTE** ▶ If you are installing the GarageBand Jam Pack for the first time, allow plenty of time to play and explore. There are so many exciting new sounds, loops, and instruments that you could easily lose track of time. If you don't believe me, just wait until you try it.

Exploring the New Software Instruments

With this many new Software Instruments, it's hard to decide where to start. Since I'm leading the tour and my favorite instrument is the piano, let's start there.

If you have Jam Pack installed on your computer, go ahead and open a new GarageBand project now and call it *JamPack Test*.

The new project opens with an empty Grand Piano track, just as all new projects do in GarageBand.

1   Double-click the Grand Piano track header to view the other piano Software Instrument choices.

2 Click-drag the lower-right edge of the Track Info window to resize it so you can see all of the piano and keyboard instruments.

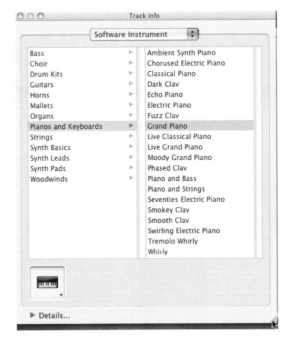

As you can see, there are quite a few new piano and keyboard sounds. If you have a MIDI keyboard, take a moment and play some of the new instruments. Remember, you can also use the onscreen keyboard to test-drive the new Software Instruments.

3 Click the Piano and Strings choice, and play a few notes on your keyboard.

The Piano and Strings Software Instrument essentially doubles the piano track with strings, just as you did in the song **Ivory Groove**.

My favorites are the Live Classical Piano and Live Grand Piano instruments.

4   Click the Live Grand Piano instrument and play a few notes or chords.

These are professionally sampled piano sounds, and they are some of the best I've heard or worked with.

These Software Instruments sound better than some of the live piano recordings I've performed in a recording studio. For those of you who don't work a lot with piano, you may not realize that the piano is an incredibly difficult instrument to record. The size, range, and distribution of the sound makes recording a live piano with microphones a very challenging endeavor. Simulated piano usually sounds like a simulation, and the best digitally sampled piano sounds can be very expensive. Of course, that was before the GarageBand Jam Pack.

NOTE ▶ Feel free to play as long as you want, then continue reading when you're ready to move on to another instrument. I mention this because I just got caught up in playing the Live Piano sounds and an hour later remembered that I'm supposed to be writing this book.

Now that we've all had our piano fix, let's check out some of the other Software Instruments.

5   Click Bass in the instrument column to see the bass choices.

Bass	▶	Ballad Electric Bass
Choir	▶	Chain Saw Bass
Drum Kits	▶	Chirp Synth Bass
Guitars	▶	Deep & Hard Bass
Horns	▶	Deep Round Synth Bass
Mallets	▶	Driving Synth Bass
Organs	▶	Eighties Pop Synth Bass
Pianos and Keyboards	▶	Electric Upright Jazz
Strings	▶	Filter Wah Synth Bass
Synth Basics	▶	Fingerstyle Electric Bass
Synth Leads	▶	Fretless Electric Bass
Synth Pads	▶	Fretless Solo Bass
Woodwinds	▶	Funky Filter Bass
		Hammer Synth Bass
		Muted Electric Bass
		Nasty Synth Bass
		Picked Electric Bass
		Pulse Synth Bass
		Slapped Electric Bass
		Square Wave Synth Bass
		Sub Synth Bass
		Tight Synth Bass

Get a load of all those bass Software Instruments! Fortunately, they all have really descriptive names to help you figure out what they might sound like.

6   Click any of the new bass sounds and play a few notes on your keyboard.

7   Use the up and down arrow keys to select different bass effects presets and continue playing the keyboard to hear how they sound.

8   Try using the Pitch Bend controls on your keyboard as you play the bass part.

If your keyboard has a Pitch Bend wheel, it should be located on the left side of the keyboard. Remember, you can use pitch bend when you record a Software Instrument part and then edit the track using the Pitch Bend controls in the Track Editor.

The next time you need to record a really cool MIDI bass part, you have plenty of choices.

9   Click Drum Kits in the instrument column to see the drum choices.

Have you ever wondered what an Android drum kit sounded like? Well, today's your lucky day because not only does the Jam Pack include drum kits for all of the popular types of music, but also specialty kits like Tribal, Twang, Laser, and—you guessed it—Android.

10 Click the Android Kit and press a few notes on your keyboard to hear how it sounds.

I could have used this in the **SciFiShow** theme song.

11 Use the down arrow key to move to some of the other choices and try them out.

12 Click Guitars in the instrument column to see the guitar instrument choices.

There are many more sampled guitar sounds than the ones shown here. One of my favorites is the 12 String Chords.

Software Instrument ⬍		
Bass	▸	12 String Acoustic
Choir	▸	12 String Chords
Drum Kits	▸	Auditorium Acoustic
Guitars	▸	Ballad Acoustic
Horns	▸	Big Electric Lead
Mallets	▸	Chorus Roundback
Organs	▸	Classical Acoustic
Pianos and Keyboards	▸	Clean Electric
Strings	▸	Delicate Echoes
Synth Basics	▸	Edgy Muted
Synth Leads	▸	Electric Tremolo
Synth Pads	▸	Funky Wah
Woodwinds	▸	Muted Electric
		Roundback Acoustic
		Steel String Acoustic
		Textural Electric

13 Click 12 String Chords to select that Software Instrument sound and play a few notes.

Amazing! I sure could have used this on the song **Highway Bound**.

Each note you play on the keyboard plays an entire guitar chord. If you combine different notes, you create a more complex chord.

This is great if you are looking to add a few guitar chords to your song but you don't play guitar, or perhaps you are still learning the guitar and have a little trouble stretching your fingers to play certain chords.

Project Tasks

Take a few minutes and explore some of the other new Software Instrument sounds. There are a total of 100 new Software Instrument sounds to choose from, including more strings and some really cool synth sounds.

Exploring the New Real Instrument Presets

There are over 100 new Real Instrument effects presets, which means all new sounds for your real instruments, including vocals. Whether you play bass, guitar, drums, or horns, or sing vocals, you'll find plenty of cool new effects presets. For example, the Vocals presets now include RnB, Gospel, Megaphone, and Radio effects.

If you have a microphone handy, hook it up to the computer now, create a Real Instrument vocal track, and test out some of the new presets as you belt out your favorite tune. (I'd sing a few bars as a demo, but since vocals are definitely not my strong suit, it's better to go it alone on this one.)

Previewing the New Guitar Amp Simulators

One of the most exciting features of Jam Pack is the 15 new guitar amp simulators. For this exercise you can either record your own guitar region in an empty track, or open the project from the last lesson that had the recorded guitar parts for "House of the Rising Sun."

1   Choose File > Open and select **9-3 Track Editor** from the Lesson_09 folder.

2   Solo the first track in the Timeline to isolate the guitar sound in that track.

3   Double-click the track header for the top track to open the Track Info window.

4   Move the Track Info window so it is just below the top track.

5   Click Guitars from the Instrument column on the left to see the guitar amp choices.

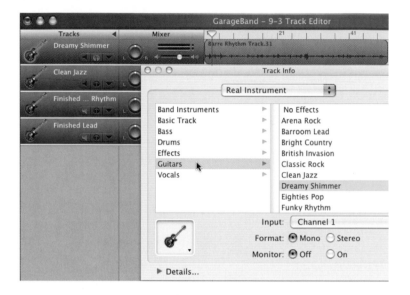

Notice the descriptive names of the new guitar sounds, like Surf, Texas Blues, and Liverpool Clean.

6   Scroll down through the guitar sounds until you locate the Texas Blues choice.

7   Click Texas Blues to select that guitar amp sound.

8   Play the Barre Rhythm Track region (top track) to hear how it sounds using the Texas Blues choice.

This edgy southern guitar sound fits pretty well with this song. In fact, when I originally recorded it, I used the Texas Blues sound.

9   Play the same track again, but this time use the up and down arrow keys to change the guitar sound as the track plays. Choose a sound that you think fits well with this guitar part.

Project Tasks

Now that you've selected a guitar sound for the Barre Rhythm Track region, let's find a good guitar amp for the second track. Repeat the steps from the previous exercise, only this time solo the second track.

When you finish, click the Solo button on the first track and listen to both parts together with the new guitar amp sounds.

Working with the New Effects

The GarageBand Jam Pack comes with over 100 new effects. Let's take a look at some of these new presets and test them out with the guitar amp simulators.

1   Solo the top track in the Timeline and create a cycle region over the entire region.

2   Select the top track in the Timeline and press Cmd-I to open the Track Info window (if it is not already open).

3   Click the Details triangle on the Track Info window to view the effects for the track.

Notice the Effects pop-up, which shows that you are using Amp Simulation on the simulated track.

4   Click the pop-up menu to the right of Amp Simulation—the one that currently shows Manual as the default selection.

These are presets that allow you to further adjust the Amp Simulation sound to match a particular guitar style.

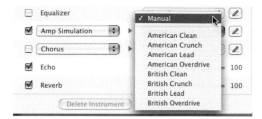

GarageBand comes with five presets for the Amp Simulation sound: American Clean, American Crunch, American Overdrive, British Crunch, and British Lead. Jam Pack adds three new presets: American Lead, British Clean, and British Overdrive.

Let's test these out on the top track to further enhance the Texas Blues guitar sound.

5   Play the cycle region in the Timeline.

6   Choose British Clean from the pop-up menu and listen to the change in the sound of the guitar.

7   Choose American Clean from the same pop-up menu and listen to the change in the sound of the guitar.

Can you hear the difference between the British Clean and American Clean guitar presets?

8   Pick whichever sound you like best and close the Track Info window.

Of course, all the presets are editable, so you can always click the Edit button (pencil) next to any of the presets to make your own adjustments and save the changes as an entirely new effect.

Project Tasks

Now that you have a feel for the new guitar amp simulators, why not record a new region using the new sounds? If you are a prolific guitar player with an extensive repertoire, I challenge you to play a different riff with each simulated amplifier sound. Know any surf tunes? Then try playing a surf tune with the Surf amplifier sound. Do you prefer country? Then pick along with the Bright Country sound. How about Liverpool Clean? If you know any songs that originated in Liverpool, this might be the sound you're looking for.

Exploring the New Apple Loops

If you enjoyed working with the original 1,000 prerecorded Apple Loops that come with GarageBand, you're really going to love the 2,000 additional loops you get with the Jam Pack. You'll now have almost 800 Drum loops, over 650 Rock/Blues loops, 50 additional sound effects (FX) including Birds, Breaking Glass, Sirens, and lots of Swirly filters, Sci Fi textures, and Abstract Atmosphere loops.

Let's preview a few of the new Apple Loops just to get your creative juices flowing. Then I'll leave you to your music composing.

1   Press Cmd-L to open the Loop Browser.

2   Click-drag the gray area to the left of the Record button upward to view the full Loop Browser with all of the keyword buttons.

3   Locate the FX button and click it to select the Sound Effects.

4   Click any of the loops in the results list to listen to the different choices.

5   Use the up and down arrows to preview different sound effects.

    Now let's try some of the new melodic loops (loops with melody).

6   Click the Melodic button to list the different melodic loop choices.

Name				
Single	Ensemble		12 String Dream 01	140
Clean	Distorted		12 String Dream 02	140
Acoustic	Electric		12 String Dream 03	140
Relaxed	Intense		12 String Dream 04	140
Cheerful	Dark		12 String Dream 05	140
Dry	Processed		12 String Dream 06	140
Grooving	Arrhythmic		12 String Dream 07	140
Melodic	Dissonant		12 String Dream 08	140
FX	Fill		12 String Dream 09	140
1086 items			70s Ballad Piano 01	80
			70s Ballad Piano 02	80
			70s Ballad Piano 03	80

Notice that you now have over 1,000 Melodic Apple Loops. GarageBand comes with around 390 Melodic Apple Loops, so Jam Pack has significantly increased your Melodic loop stock.

7   Click any of the Melodic loops in the results list to preview the loops.

8   Use the up and down arrows to browse through your extended melodic loop library.

Notice some of the colorful loop names like Cop Show Clav, Burning Rock Organ, Groovy Electric Bass, Hip Hop Piano, and Island Reggae Organ. You're sure to find loops to accompany any type of music you wish to create. You might even find inspiration for songs you never would have dreamed of.

Project Tasks

Browse through the different loops (not just the melodic loops) and mark your favorites in the Favorites column for easy access as you build your future projects.

That's the end of this appendix and also the end of this book, but hopefully just the beginning for you and your GarageBand experience.

> **NOTE ▶** I strongly recommend that you try out the GarageBand Jam Pack for yourself, if you weren't able to play along with this section of the book. Perhaps you could take your book over to the local Apple store and follow along with this appendix on one of the GarageBand workstations with Jam Pack installed. Tell them I sent you. Or just tell them you're interested in trying out the Jam Pack. Just be prepared to stand in line.

Appendix **B**

Apple's Digital Production Platform: An Integrated Workflow

Apple has developed a line of professional film, video, and audio production applications that, taken together, give professionals an affordable high-performance, integrated digital production platform. Each product is recognized as an industry standard in its respective field. When used together, they form a complete pipeline from content creation to delivery.

Here's a brief overview of how the four keystone applications—Final Cut Pro, Shake, Logic, and DVD Studio Pro—work together in a variety of standard production workflows.

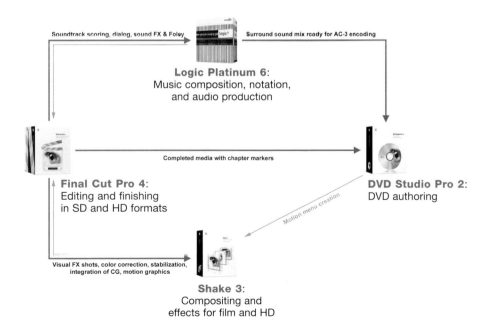

Soundtrack scoring, dialog, sound FX & Foley

Surround sound mix ready for AC-3 encoding

Logic Platinum 6:
Music composition, notation, and audio production

Completed media with chapter markers

Final Cut Pro 4:
Editing and finishing in SD and HD formats

DVD Studio Pro 2:
DVD authoring

Motion menu creation

Visual FX shots, color correction, stabilization, integration of CG, motion graphics

Shake 3:
Compositing and effects for film and HD

Final Cut Pro

Final Cut Pro is a fully scalable nonlinear editing system designed to work with all standard video formats from DV to High Definition. More than just an editing application, Final Cut Pro lets you easily add filters and transitions to clips and play them in real time using an effects engine known as RT Extreme. Real-time color correction, customizable keyboard commands, dynamic and asymmetric trimming, broadcast video scopes, and support for multichannel audio editing, mixing, and output are a few of the features that make Final Cut Pro a great tool for serious editors.

Four integrated applications are also included with Final Cut Pro: LiveType, a powerful title generation tool; Soundtrack, an audio creation application that lets you build original, high-quality musical scores for your video; Cinema Tools, a sophisticated relational database that lets you shoot and finish on film and 24P (HD) while using Final Cut Pro for your editing; and Compressor, a high-speed encoding application that offers a variety of distribution formats including MPEG-4 and MPEG-2.

In the Pipeline

For more robust compositing, special-effects plates can be exported from Final Cut Pro and layered and manipulated in Shake. Audio elements in need of additional processing and mixing can be exported to Logic Audio for sweetening, and rough scores created in Soundtrack can be enhanced by professional composers in Logic. When completed, all treated media can be imported to DVD Studio Pro for professional DVD authoring.

Shake

Shake is a high-end compositing system used to create visual effects for award-winning broadcast commercials and feature films such as *The Lord of the Rings* and *The Matrix*. Shake is typically used for combining elements from multiple sources into a single image, creating the illusion that everything was filmed "in camera." These elements include 3D animation, particles, procedural painting, and live-action plates.

Unlike the timeline-based compositing in Final Cut Pro, Shake uses a node-based architecture. Each operator is a discrete unit that can be plugged into other operators in an incredibly flexible, nonlinear fashion, creating a detailed process tree that leads to the final composited shot. Shake also includes two industry-standard keyers for greenscreen and bluescreen work—Photron's Primatte and Framestore/CFC's Keylight— along with numerous precise color correction tools.

In the Pipeline

Any shot that requires multilayered visual effects is a job for Shake. One of the most common shots to be sent to Shake is a bluescreen or greenscreen. While Final Cut Pro has built-in keyers, Shake includes far more sophisticated keying techniques based on color difference and 3D color space technology.

Another common use for Shake is footage stabilization and match moving. Shake can stabilize position, scale, rotation, and perspective, salvaging shaky footage that would otherwise be unusable. Using the same technology, Shake can match the motion in a camera shot so that composited elements seem to "belong" in the scene.

Logic

Logic Platinum is a complete virtual recording studio used to create and edit music sound tracks, dialogue, and sound effects as well as to mix and master final audio files (including surround sound). Logic contains a fully scalable mixing console, dozens of effects processors, and the option to add Emagic's world-class software-based synthesizers as virtual instruments. In addition, it is designed with advanced MIDI handling to access external synthesizers, keyboards, and other MIDI-enabled instruments. The software contained in Logic rivals some of the most sophisticated hardware-based recording studios in the world in both audio quality and creative control.

In the Pipeline

Logic works simultaneously with SMPTE timecode, meaning that sounds can be positioned based on events in time, rather than on musical beats and bars. This makes it ideal for work on film and video sound tracks.

Video can be previewed in a floating window or viewed as a thumbnail track in order to make precise matches to cuts and significant events in the narrative.

The most obvious use for Logic is in the creation of a musical score. Logic is also indispensable for working with nonmusical elements in a project, cleaning up inaudible dialogue or restoring room ambiance in scenes where overdubbed dialogue had replaced the original audio.

In addition, Surround sound mixing is directly incorporated into Logic. DVD Studio Pro includes a Dolby AC3 surround sound encoding system, which can take Logic output tracks and encode them for DVD distribution.

DVD Studio Pro

DVD Studio Pro is a complete DVD authoring platform. It takes video, audio, and image content and combines them into an interactive menu-driven DVD. This can include motion menus, chapter and title access, special features, and slide shows. Basically, anything you've seen in a commercial DVD product can be created using DVD Studio Pro. The application also includes Compressor, a powerful software-based MPEG2 encoding tool, as well as the AC3 encoder mentioned in the Logic section above.

In the Pipeline

DVD Studio Pro is obviously the last step in a production workflow, where media content is assembled for delivery. The DVD authoring may be one of several delivery streams coming from the Final Cut Pro media; others may include video mastering, Web streaming, or even external film edits. One handy feature of Final Cut Pro is its ability to create and export chapter markers for use in DVD Studio Pro.

Other ways DVD Studio Pro and Final Cut Pro can work together include the creation of 4:3 pan-and-scan versions of a 16:9 piece, preparation of multiple-angle clips, and development of complex motion menus. Shake can be used for motion menus, its nonlinear workflow making it ideal for quickly generating alternate motion selection and rollover button states.

Index

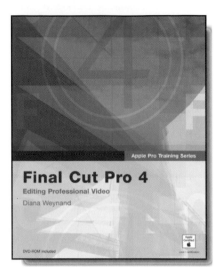